UNIVERSITIES AND THEIR LEADERSHIP

UNIVERSITIES AND THEIR LEADERSHIP

Edited by
William G. Bowen
Harold T. Shapiro

PRINCETON UNIVERSITY PRESS   PRINCETON, NEW JERSEY

Library of Congress Cataloging-in-Publication Data

Universities and their leadership / edited by William G. Bowen and Harold T.
Shapiro.
    p.   cm.
Essays initially presented at the Princeton Conference on Higher Education, held
at Princeton University in Mar. 1996.
Includes bibliographical references and index.
ISBN 0-691-05921-7 (cloth : alk. paper)
1. Universities and colleges—United States—Administration—Congresses.   2.
College presidents—United States—Congresses.   3. Universities and colleges—
United States—Faculty—Congresses.   4. Science—Study and teaching (Higher)—
United States—Congresses.   I. Bowen, William G.   II. Shapiro, Harold T., 1935–   .
III. Princeton Conference on Higher Education (1996 : Princeton University)
LB2341.U567   1998
371.2'00973—dc21   97-41085

This book has been composed in Palatino

http://pup.princeton.edu

Printed in the United States of America

10 9 8 7 6 5 4 3 2 1

Contents

Preface

THE ESSAYS brought together in this volume were initially presented at the Princeton Conference on Higher Education, held on the Princeton University campus in March 1996. Though the essays cover a considerable range of subjects, they are clustered around the topics of accountability and the nature of the relationships that exist, or should exist, either between the contemporary university and the society it serves or among different elements of the academic community.

The University Overall

Frank Rhodes's essay, "The University and Its Critics," confronts a number of the contemporary criticisms—informed and uninformed—of the American university (e.g., fragmentation, trivialized scholarship, political correctness), considers how the American university has changed over recent decades, and suggests a number of principles that in part respond to the criticisms but in any case would enhance the vitality and social usefulness of these institutions. Rhodes underlines the importance of viewing scholarship as a public trust, taking seriously the university's obligation for service, and the characterization of teaching as a moral vocation. The essay concludes with a more tactical view: a kind of action plan designed to restore public confidence by reasserting control over an increasingly fragmented curriculum, rekindling the bonds of community within the university, and giving greater evidence of the university's ability to articulate and implement its priorities.

Martin Trow's essay, "On the Accountability of Higher Education in the United States," begins with a careful articulation of what is meant by accountability and responsibility to others and then proceeds to deal in detail with current forms of academic accountability, both internal and external, and a set of alternatives (e.g., trust versus market mechanisms) or supplements to current practice. One of the most powerful parts of the essay deals with what universities ought to consider regarding their own programs of internal accountability or quality control.

The Presidency

Harold Shapiro's essay, "University Presidents—Then and Now," is (in the opinion of the other author of this preface) a fine blend of the personal insights of a man who has served with distinction as president of both a public and a private university and an historical account of changes over time in the day-to-day lives of university presidents. Based on study of the archival records of four university presidents—Wayland (of Brown), Eliot (of Harvard), Angell (of Michigan), and Wilson (of Princeton)—the essay points out the obvious and less obvious ways in which the functions of the office have changed in direct response to far broader changes in society and in society's assumptions about the role of universities. Shapiro is particularly interested in the ethical aspects of the role of president and argues persuasively that "in the more complex modern university, this ethical dimension of presidential leadership has evolved from a more strictly delimited and almost rule-governed activity into a more diffuse but no less significant role of helping to set the moral tone for the academic community—and beyond—via one's choices, policies, actions, and words." In Shapiro's view, there has been a tendency for modern presidents to neglect the task of providing this more subtle yet all-embracing kind of moral leadership—a loss that he believes we must begin to repair.

In her companion essay to Shapiro's, Hanna Gray combines her skills as an historian, her experiences as president at Yale and Chicago, and her sage and witty observations of the human condition. The result is an arresting contribution that is both great fun to read and highly instructive. She recounts, with particular effect, speeches of two of her predecessors at Chicago, Harper and Hutchins, to demonstrate that modern-day notions of the limitations on the power of the president and the need for consultation are in fact far from new. The alleged "giants" of yesteryear certainly knew the meaning of the word *constrained*. Gray is particularly eloquent in discussing the reasons why it would be "inappropriate for presidents to see the function of moral guidance as their rightful role" and why those who "deride" the presidents' "pusillanimous caution" would be infuriated if the president did, in fact, do what they ask. In her view, the president's major role is as an "enabler," and the virtue to be defended above all others is intellectual integrity.

The Faculty

Henry Rosovsky and Inge-Lise Ameer's essay, "Professional Conduct of College and University Teachers," focuses on the important but much neglected issue of the need for a shared code of conduct for college and university professors. The authors' concern is the apparent lack of agreement among college and university teachers about appropriate standards of professional conduct toward students, colleagues, and others. The authors speculate about the source of this deficiency and the lack of any formal or informal instruction in these matters and then move on to suggest how the professoriate might in fact remedy this situation. The essay concludes with some appropriately provocative and interesting case studies that provide useful illustrations of the issues at hand.

Amy Gutmann's essay titled "How Can Universities Teach Professional Ethics?" focuses on the difficult practical issue of how a college or university might, in fact, structure instruction in professional ethics for professors. Gutmann's thoughtful and challenging essay provides an excellent articulation of the difficult issues—conceptual as well as practical—that one would encounter in actually implementing the Rosovsky-Ameer program. She then proceeds to offer her own action agenda, which consists of three items: first, the serious efforts that must be made to articulate and then incorporate the ethics of higher education in our institutional rules and procedures; second, the development of rigorous but broad-based courses in practical ethics in the undergraduate curriculum; and third, the provision of equally rigorous but more specialized courses in professional ethics to future members of the professoriate (i.e., graduate students).

Oliver Fulton's essay, "Unity or Fragmentation, Convergence or Diversity," discusses the change in internal conditions, understandings, and aspirations at universities—particularly among the university and college faculty—that resulted as higher education in Europe entered the "mass higher education era." The data underlying this analysis, which focuses on the United Kingdom, western Germany, the Netherlands, and Sweden, are drawn from the 1992 Carnegie survey of the academic professions. The Carnegie survey covered fourteen countries, including the United States. The author is particularly interested in the differences, if any, that these changes in circumstances may have generated by country, by academic discipline, by institutional type and sector, or by national system. The essay therefore focuses primarily on the changes in the internal life of the university that may have been caused by the great expansion of this sector. The specific issues addressed concern the value orientation of the faculty, faculty involvement in teaching and research, faculty involvement in governance, and the overall levels of satisfaction of university faculty. The results are mixed in the sense that while differences in response are clearly visible in the various countries, further analysis may be required to understand the full nature and causes of these discrepancies. Clearly, however, the null hypothesis of "no difference" seems an inadequate explanation of the data.

The Planning and Oversight of Science

Daniel Kevles's essay, "A Time for Audacity," is much more than a call for the community of scientists, particularly university-based researchers, to put forward a new vision of the role of research and development as America faces the post–Cold War era. The essay begins by providing a fascinating historical perspective on the research partnership between the American government and the community of research performers—particularly the university sector—which has been so crucial to both America's continued leadership in science and technology and the shape and growth of American higher education in the post–World War II era. The author then provides a detailed analysis of developments in more recent years that serve as a necessary prelude or set of initial conditions for consideration of the feasible options in the years ahead, both for the scientific community and the government. Kevles concludes by pointing to the crucial role the scientific community has played in helping shape U.S. public policies in previous times of change and calling for similar efforts today.

Frank Press's essay focuses on the shifts that have taken place in the past few years, giving special attention to how the two major political parties have shifted—almost interchanged—their perspectives on federal responsibility for the vitality of the nation's research and development base. Press concludes with a set of well-thought-out and provocative suggestions regarding a mechanism for obtaining an optimal allocation of federal research resources in a time of budget austerity.

Maxine Singer's essay addresses two particular implications of the current situation: the extraordinary set of opportunities that has been created by the scientific advances of recent years and the increasing internationalization of the scientific enterprise. Singer also worries about the capacity of the different scientific disciplines to set internal priorities and also participate in effective and responsive communication with the general public. Taken together, the Kevles, Press, and Singer essays provide a valuable range of insights that can stimulate and guide the current national discourse on the planning and oversight of science from the perspective of public policy.

We wish to thank the authors of this volume for their thoughtful contributions to the Princeton Conference on Higher Education, and to our better understanding of the evolution of higher education.

William G. Bowen
Harold T. Shapiro

Contributors

Inge-Lise Ameer is a doctoral candidate at the Harvard Graduate School of Education.

William G. Bowen is president of the Andrew W. Mellon Foundation and president emeritus of Princeton University.

Oliver Fulton is professor of higher education at Lancaster University in Great Britain.

Hanna H. Gray is professor of history at and president emeritus of the University of Chicago.

Amy Gutmann is Laurance S. Rockefeller University Professor of Politics at Princeton University.

Daniel J. Kevles is J. O. and Juliette Koepfli Professor of the Humanities and Director of the Program in Science, Ethics, and Public Policy at the California Institute of Technology.

Frank Press is principal of the Washington Advisory Group, trustee, and the Cecil and Ida Green Senior Fellow at the Carnegie Institution of Washington.

Frank H. T. Rhodes is president emeritus of and professor of geological sciences at Cornell University.

Henry Rosovsky is Geyser University Professor Emeritus at Harvard University.

Harold T. Shapiro is president of and professor of economics and public affairs at Princeton University.

Maxine Singer is president of the Carnegie Institution of Washington.

Martin Trow is professor of public policy at the Richard and Rhoda Goldman School of Public Policy at the University of California, Berkeley.

THE UNIVERSITY OVERALL

The University and Its Critics

FRANK H. T. RHODES

IT IS MOST FITTING that we address the subject of the university and its critics here at Princeton University, which remains a pearl among America's research universities, shining true when so many others are accused of being made of paste. And it is fitting that we gather for this purpose during the celebration of Princeton's 250th anniversary. For here on this campus, and at this moment, we can look back over two and a half centuries and clearly see the processes that shaped today's university, the modern world in which it has come to exist, and the criticisms it must answer if it is to continue to flourish.

Princeton was, as Don Oberdorfer has noted in his beautiful book on Princeton's first 250 years, "a national institution before there was a nation," drawing its first students from at least twelve of the thirteen colonies. And from the first, it viewed its mission broadly. Mr. Oberdorfer refers us to an unidentified New Light Presbyterian founder who declared, "Though our great intention was to erect a seminary for educating ministers of the Gospel, yet we hope it will be useful in other learned professions. . . . Therefore we propose to make the plan of education as extensive as our circumstances will permit."[1]

Princeton has done that superbly, and after 250 years of leadership in higher education, the university is, in many ways, stronger than ever before. Its large endowment is a source of pride for Princetonians and a source of envy for other institutions. It has added new programs in recent years—in molecular biology, in materials science, in the environment and other fields—to keep it at the forefront of research and scholarship. It educated two U.S. presidents, James Madison and Woodrow Wilson, as well as more contemporary statesmen from Adlai Stevenson to James Baker III and George Shultz. Among its alumni are a dozen Nobel laureates, including John Bardeen, the only person to win two Nobel Prizes in the same field (physics). Many more Nobel laureates have served on the faculty, including Toni Morrison, who won the Nobel Prize for Literature in 1993. Other Princeton alumni include writers F. Scott Fitzgerald and

Eugene O'Neill, consumer advocate Ralph Nader, and Wendy Kopp of the class of 1989, who founded the Teach for America program as an outgrowth of her senior thesis project. Princeton alumni continue to be energetic, generous, and involved.

If Princeton has fewer critics than most research universities today, perhaps it is because Princeton has dealt with the issues that critics complain about better than most. Although indisputably among the nation's very best research universities, it has never stopped putting undergraduate education first. Its reputation as a great place for undergraduate learning is reflected in the fact that it routinely fills almost half of its freshman class through early decision applicants.

But even Princeton, which has done so much so well during its first 250 years, must be aware of and responsive to the criticisms now affecting higher education as a whole. There is no doubt that America's universities are caught in a paradox: public expectations have rarely been higher, public confidence and support rarely lower. The complaints against universities during the last five years or so are as serious as they are comprehensive:

Unreasonably high tuition
Neglect of undergraduate teaching in favor of inconsequential research
Fragmented fields of study
Garbled educational purposes
Trivialized scholarship
Improper accounting techniques, particularly with respect to federal research funds
Falsification of experimental results
Conflicts of interest
Preaching politics
The imposition of political correctness

Perhaps most damning, in an era when the American people are being asked to "sacrifice" for the sake of the nation's long-term strength, universities are perceived as self-indulgent, arrogant, and resistant to change.

In his remarkably popular book, *The Closing of the American Mind*, Allan Bloom described the problem this way: "The university now offers no distinctive visage to the young person. He finds a democracy of the disciplines. . . . This democracy is really an anarchy, because there are no recognized rules for citizenship and no legitimate titles to rule. In short there is no vision, nor is there a set of competing visions, of what an educated human being is."[2]

Charles Sykes, the author of *ProfScam*, lays the blame for the loss of vision at the feet of the faculty: "Almost singlehandedly, the professors—working steadily and systematically—have destroyed the university as a center of learning and have desolated higher education, which no longer is higher or much of an education."[3]

Nor do critics view university research more kindly. Page Smith, in *Killing the Spirit*, contends, "The vast majority of the so-called research turned out in the modern university is essentially worthless. . . . It does not result in any measurable benefit to anything or anybody."[4]

And Thomas Sowell, in his book *Inside American Education*, frames his discussion of political correctness this way: "Educators . . . have proclaimed their dedication to freedom of ideas . . . while turning educational institutions into bastions of dogma."[5]

These critics are, by and large, insiders who have had a greater degree of involvement with universities than most Americans, and that makes their criticisms all the more troubling.

Yet as unhappy as many Americans seem to be about aspects of their universities, most also acknowledge the institutions' great value to the nation. Having conquered polio and other devastating diseases with vaccines and antibiotics developed in their labs, surely they have something valuable to offer in the fight against drug-resistant tuberculosis and AIDS. Having given us the laser, the transistor, and the high-speed computer chip, surely they can give us more of the high technology the nation needs to compete in the markets of the world. Having conferred substantial earnings advantages on their graduates, surely they can continue to provide economic opportunity to future generations of young people, especially those from groups not formerly well-represented in higher education. Having applied research to make American agriculture preeminent, surely they can apply social science to redeem America's cities. And although it is much harder to document the contributions of the liberal arts or humanities, whose teaching has itself become a target of criticism, surely these disciplines still have much to teach about what it means to be human.

But why have the expectations for universities grown at the very time confidence in them has declined? What is often unrecognized in the current debate is the extent to which the universities have already changed from the ivory towers of earlier years. Woodrow Wilson, in his sesquicentennial address of 1896, "Princeton in the Nation's Service," proclaimed a commitment that had characterized Princeton from its earliest days. Since then, Princeton and other research universities have become, both by demand and by choice, far more actively involved in the large issues of public life. They are now citizens, partners in a social compact that places great responsibility and high expectations upon them. They provide not only the products of their research but also experts who can advise government and business, and graduates with the talent and energy to engage the issues of tomorrow.

In their greater social engagement, universities have themselves undergone significant changes, some of them controversial and confusing. I believe that these changes reflect deeper changes rooted in America's character. The most critical deeper changes are inclusiveness, professionalization, and the ascendancy of science. I want to talk about each of those in turn and then suggest how we might deal effectively and productively with the evolving interface between universities and the society in which they are embedded.

First, universities have deliberately become more inclusive in their membership and in their programs of study and research. In aggregate, they have made a deliberate and far-reaching commitment to equal access and social mobility. The origin of this commitment can be traced back to the founding of the land-grant colleges in the nineteenth century, but the pace of the process has accelerated in the past fifty years, and it has come to embrace all institutions, private as well as public. In the 1920s and 1930s, Princeton had no black students enrolled and very few Jews. President Robert Goheen turned the tide in the 1960s, convincing the university and its board of trustees to actively recruit black students. Black enrollment climbed from 7 in 1962 to 318 in 1970. The university's "Official Statement of Commitment to Diversity," issued in 1994, indicates that Princeton's commitment continues: "We actively seek students, faculty and staff of exceptional ability and promise who share in our commitment to excellence in teaching and scholarship and who will bring a diversity of viewpoints and cultures." In fall 1994, minority and foreign students comprised nearly a third of the incoming class of 1998.

Even more progress has been made on the status of women at Princeton. The graduate school was the first to admit female students, beginning in 1961 under rules that granted entrance to women qualified for studies that were unavailable elsewhere. It became fully coeducational, along with the rest of the university, in the late 1960s.

When President Goheen brought the idea of coeducation to the trustees on June 12, 1967, he said, "In my judgment, the time has now come when it can no longer be reckoned to Princeton's advantage to postpone entry into the education of women on a significant scale. . . . A university with so profound a sense of obligation to the world can no longer, I believe, ignore the educational needs of one half of the human race." After careful study, coeducation was approved on January 11, 1969, by a 24–8 vote of the trustees.

Universities have also become more inclusive in their curricula.

They have responded to public needs by offering new fields of study, from environmental health, safety, and policy issues to urban and regional planning, from gerontology to real estate management. These inclusive changes in membership and in programs, and the growth in size they have brought with them, have effectively ended the isolation of the campus and transformed the nature of the university. Ivory towers they are no longer; they are, more than ever, embedded in the society that surrounds them and reflective of its membership.

Second, over the past fifty years, university studies have become far more professional in the scope of their curricula and far more practical in their orientation. It is not the presence of professional and practical studies that is new but rather their dominance. Most of the new additions are professional, while longer-established schools—of medicine, dentistry, public health, law, engineering, architecture, agriculture, management, public communication, and other professional disciplines—loom larger than ever before, both in enrollment and in influence. Premedical education, for example, has had a major influence—distorting and stifling in some ways—on the general pattern of undergraduate education. Even the humanities and social sciences, disciplines that were once coherent fields of study, have now been splintered and subdivided into a host of subspecialties in an attempt to link them more directly to training for a specific career.

Princeton has resisted these temptations more successfully than many institutions, maintaining a single faculty that conducts research and instructs graduate students as well as undergraduates and avoiding the temptation to establish separate professional schools in fields such as law, medicine, and business administration. It does now have a school of architecture, but between 1948 and 1995, the number of academic departments at Princeton increased from twenty-six to thirty-two while the number of interdisciplinary programs increased from three to more than thirty. That shows commendable restraint and a willingness to think broadly about knowledge.

Third, the ascendancy of science, both as a professional study and as a dominating influence, has noticeably changed the culture of the university. Unlike most other countries, the United States concentrates much of its basic research in universities rather than in government laboratories and institutes. Along with the desirable results of this arrangement—the closer linkage of the basic sciences to medicine and engineering, the practical benefits of the association of education and research—there have been results of more debatable value. The model of scientific knowledge—abstract, quantifiable, impersonal, "value-neutral"—has been adopted uncritically by other fields, and the style of teaching—factual, sequential, undebatable, and unengaging—has often had a baleful effect, not only within science but also far beyond it.

It is the cumulative effect of these changes, which began to build around the turn of the century and accelerated rapidly after World War II, that underlies virtually all the charges that are leveled against America's universities.

America's research universities may attract half the world's graduate students, but they also attract controversy as they try to resolve the political, social, and cultural conflicts of the larger society. Like it or not, the moral influence of the great universities has diminished as they have assumed new responsibilities and new priorities and established new partnerships with business and government. Moral pronouncements tend to flow more freely from those in ivory towers than from those with rolled-up sleeves and grimy hands laboring in the trenches. And as Alexander Astin's annual surveys of freshman attitudes have shown, far more freshmen today believe it is more important to prepare for a well-paying career in college than it is to find a meaningful philosophy of life.

But on the whole, the new university's benefits to society have been immense, and the changes wrought by increased inclusiveness, professionalism, and the ascendancy of science are very much American. Though their effects on our universities seem compressed into several decades, they sum up the journey America itself has made since its founding. But inclusiveness, professionalism, and science, without a moral foundation, lead to empty success. Universities, as much as nations, need their moral moorings. More people knowing more facts about more fields has nothing to do with how wisely or happily they live. However dazzling may be the material implications of palm-held supercomputers, they will not in themselves elevate the quality of our national life any more than television did fifty years ago. I would not presume to reform society at large, but I do have some ideas for our universities.

As Princetonian Adlai Stevenson wrote in *What I Think*, "Criticism, in its fairest and most honest form, is the attempt to test whether what is might not be better."[6]

In that spirit, I believe there are three simple affirmations we need to make to the public if they are to understand that research universities are unique and vital and serve a role that no other institutions in our society can fill.

The first affirmation is this: scholarship is a public trust. Our scholarship is supported by the public, and that puts two obligations on us that I see rarely fulfilled across the country. First, as creators of knowledge, we must also engage in explanation and application where appropriate. We need to become advocates for scholarship because our voice is not being raised in response to the Allan Blooms, Page Smiths, Charles Sykeses, and all the rest of our critics. Most of us regard our scholarship as completed when it is published, exhibited, or performed. But we need to move beyond mere publication to explanation and advocacy for research as such. We hear again and again that useful research is the only kind worthy of support by the state or federal government. We must become champions of the scholarship we represent.

Within this affirmation of scholarship as a public trust, we must also begin to build bridges internally so that we link research to the undergraduate experience in increasingly effective ways. And we need to build bridges to the community and linkages between our colleges. We talk a lot in universities about interdisciplinary efforts, but in practice most universities are still divided into departmental cells. For educational and economic reasons, we must work to build bridges, not walls, between researchers and scholars with complementary interests no matter where in our administrative structure they may be found.

The second affirmation I believe universities must make is that service is a social obligation. Our greatest service is providing educated men and women and highly trained professionals for society at large. But we should also reexamine other ways in which universities are of service. Not every research program will yield marketable results, and I would be the first to argue for a strong program of federally funded basic research. But if service is truly a social obligation, then we must do far better than we have in ensuring that the fruits of our research are developed for the public good.

I mentioned earlier that Woodrow Wilson, in his sesquicentennial address "Princeton in the Nation's Service," proclaimed a commitment that had characterized Princeton from its earliest days. In his 1994 commencement address, President Harold Shapiro asked whether the time had come to broaden Wilson's phrase to encompass service to other nations. "In the world that lies ahead of us," President Shapiro said, "serving our nation and serving the world must—in some respects—be one and the same." And so it must be for all research universities worthy of the name, for our community is now the world.

The third affirmation is that teaching is a moral vocation. I believe teaching has a moral dimension because of its impact not just on the mind but on the character and the will. I believe, as most of you probably do, that it is a "calling" and not just a means of earning a living that allows us to do research. Woodrow Wilson realized the centrality of teaching when he introduced the preceptorial system in 1905. Modeled on the English tutorial system, the preceptorial system made students active participants in their own education. He called for replacing lectures and textbooks in the upperclass years with small group meetings and independent study led by young but accomplished scholars who would be "companions and coaches and guides." If teaching is the core business of faculty members, as I believe it should be, both the content and the method of teaching should attract our attention and our concern.

But verbal affirmation in the absence of consistent behavior and improved performance is unlikely to be persuasive. We must "walk the talk" if we are to restore public trust and serve the public's needs.

Let me suggest three urgent imperatives for our campuses that could move us in that direction:

> We must recapture the curriculum.
> We must rekindle community.
> We must reinforce our priorities.

First, recapturing the curriculum. Woodrow Wilson once noted that it is easier to move a graveyard than to change the curriculum, and those of us who have served on curriculum committees—those black holes of academic life that absorb an enormous amount of matter and energy without anything ever coming back out—will agree. Yet Wilson was able to reform the Princeton curriculum in such a way that juniors and seniors were permitted to specialize in the department of their choice, while underclass students took a more structured and inclusive program of required courses.

An earlier Princeton president, James McCosh, in his famous debate on the curriculum with Harvard's president, Charles Eliot, advocated an elective system grounded in an established framework so that student choice, which he recognized as valuable, would not become a way to avoid difficult courses or to focus so narrowly on a subject of specialization that large gaps would be left in the students' educational framework.

President Harold Dodds, with support of the faculty, again revised the Princeton curriculum so that each department was encouraged to develop a general introductory course for underclassmen. Students were required to satisfy "distribution requirements" by taking at least one course from each of four broad areas: mathematics and the natural sciences, the social sciences, the humanities, and the group consisting of history, religion, and philosophy. In 1995, the Princeton faculty adopted a revised and somewhat broadened set of requirements, which became effective with the class of 2000.

That is commendable progress, and it is notable for its contrast to what is going on elsewhere. I believe that in many institutions, the curriculum has escaped from the faculty at large and has fallen into the hands of individuals. We pile on course after course after course. We need to ask ourselves the point behind the courses. Do undergraduates really need the four thousand choices offered at many research universities? Can't we do a better job of bringing some coherence to the undergraduate experience so that a baccalaureate degree stands for something more than having sat through some number of courses whose cumulative credit hours add up to some magical but meaningless number like 120 or 125? Wouldn't our students be better served by fewer choices but a clearer idea of what, as new graduates, they should be expected to know and be able to do?

Again, Princeton may have shown us a way. In 1993, a strategic planning committee under the leadership of College Dean Nancy Weiss Malkiel, with representation of undergraduate students and faculty members, formulated goals for a Princeton undergraduate education:

The ability to think, speak, and write clearly
The ability to reason critically and systematically
The ability to conceptualize and solve problems
The ability to think independently
The ability to take initiative and work independently
The ability to work in cooperation with others and learn collaboratively
The ability to judge what it means to understand something thoroughly
The ability to distinguish the important from the trivial, the enduring from
    the ephemeral
Familiarity with different modes of thought (including quantitative, histori-
    cal, scientific, moral, and aesthetic)
Depth of knowledge in a particular field
The ability to see connections among disciplines, ideas, and cultures
The ability to pursue lifelong learning

Let me be clear, however, that dedicated teaching and advising are not to be done in place of research and scholarship. John Slaughter, president of Occidental College, had it right when he said, "Research is to teaching as sin is to confession. If you don't participate in the former, you have very little to say in the latter."[7]

We need our best scholars to be our teachers, and we need them to give the same creative energy to teaching as they give to scholarship. We need to identify, support, and reward those who teach superbly. There is no antithesis between teaching and research. Great teaching can, in fact, be a form of synthesis and scholarship. In fact, Princeton's adoption of a senior thesis as the capstone of independent research seems to be exactly what students ought to be getting from study at a research university. Some years ago, forty percent of the alumni polled said the thesis was "the single most valuable academic experience at Princeton."

The second thing we must do is to rekindle community and restore dialogue. That is easier said than done. In 1963, Clark Kerr wrote an insightful book on the uses of the university. He commented then that the original community of the university had become fragmented, and instead of a single community, there were many communities: a community of sciences, a community of arts and letters, a community of social scientists, a community of undergraduates, a community of graduate students.[8] Over the thirty-plus years since Kerr wrote his book, fragmentation has increased so that now we sometimes do not even have a community of a single department. You remember John Donne's lament on the new Copernican universe: "'Tis all in pieces, all coherence gone."[9]

If universities are to be effective, they need to reestablish a sense of community, and without discounting the special role that athletics has in bonding the members of any university in a strong and passionate way, our community must be held together by more than the fortunes of the football team on a Saturday afternoon.

Universities were invented because medieval monks believed that scholarship could flourish better in community than in the isolation of monastic cells. Although we cannot return to the early days of Princeton, when all students roomed, ate, recited their lessons, and attended prayers and other assemblies in Nassau Hall, we can perhaps hope for something more like what Professor Charles Osgood described of life at Princeton circa 1905:

> The town is small, the college large. It is properly secluded, but not remote; and it gives a chance for the rearing of ideals upon equal support of the active and contemplative life. Friendliness between colleagues and by the help of preceptorial teaching in small groups, between student and teacher . . . does much to effect in students just what a university ought—to teach them the art of living a good life.[10]

I applaud Princeton's system of "residential colleges" for all freshmen and sophomores, a modified version of the Quad Plan that Woodrow Wilson advocated in the early 1900s that was implemented in the 1980s under Bill Bowen's leadership. Each college has a senior faculty member who serves as college master, a director of studies who is responsible for academic advising and disciplinary matters, and several dozen other faculty members, administrators, and other members of the Princeton academic community as fellows. There are one-semester freshman seminars in the residential colleges on subjects of the faculty members' own choosing, including one of the history of higher education taught by Princeton's eighteenth president, Harold Shapiro. In addition, each college sponsors a variety of social, sports, and recreational activities for members. This seems to be a way of reinforcing the ideal of community and bringing together social and academic life.

Harold Shapiro has commented, in thinking ahead to the Princeton of the future, that the residential community of students and scholars will persist at Princeton. Its special collegiality cannot be replaced by virtual communities of Princetonians meeting on the Internet. We need the stimulus of face-to-face communication and shoulder-to-shoulder cooperation on our own campuses, not just the temporary, often anonymous, and usually disengaged communities of cyberspace. It is in the rough and tumble of day-to-day living and daily, direct conversation that faculty members and students can best carry out the work that research universities were invented to do.

Princeton's residential colleges are an important step toward creating that kind of community where living and learning enrich each other. But we must ask if there is more we can do. Would more joint appointments help not only provide a more balanced perspective to students but also enable faculty members to take a broader view of the community of which they are a part? Perhaps more joint courses might be useful, as well as more campuswide activities, such as focusing on a particular theme that the campus as a whole might address for a semester with visiting speakers, faculty colloquia, panel discussions, and the like. The goal of these efforts would be to create a community of scholars where living and learning are intertwined and where all are committed to the life of the mind.

The third imperative for research universities is to reinforce institutional priorities. We must decide what our priorities are. How do we establish them? How do we build consensus about them? How is performance evaluated? Can we benchmark our own success against the industry leaders in particular areas? Can and should tenure be preserved? How do we recognize, reward, and reinforce the changes we see as needing to be made?

Princeton's strategic plan, released in October 1993, is a promising start. It envisions Princeton as an institution that will remain roughly the same size; expand and improve its commitment to teaching; sustain its capacity for excellence, leadership, and new initiatives in scholarship and research; maintain its strong commitment to financial aid for undergraduate and graduate students; and improve the quality of campus life.

None of this will be easy. It will at times be controversial, time-consuming, and divisive. But ultimately it will be collegial, timesaving, and unifying. And its benefits will be felt not just in education but in research, scholarship, and outreach as well.

It has been said that "no one should tamper with a university who does not know and love it well." Those here to celebrate with Princeton on the occasion of its 250th anniversary know well the American research university—this one and others that have used it as a model of what they can hope to achieve. As we celebrate Princeton's dramatic success over two and a half centuries, we can aspire to make Princeton and all of higher education more vibrant, more stimulating, and more in tune with the needs and aspirations of our current age.

Woodrow Wilson, in his sesquicentennial address, said, "When all is said and done, it is not learning but the spirit of service that will give a college place in the public annals of the nation. . . . We dare not keep aloof and closet ourselves while a nation comes to its maturity."

So, too, it is with us. And on the occasion of Princeton's 250th anniversary, there can be no more worthy goal.

Notes

1. Don Oberdorfer, *Princeton University: The First 250 Years* (Princeton, N.J.: Trustees of Princeton University, 1995), p. 12.

2. Allan Bloom, *The Closing of the American Mind: How Higher Education Has Failed Democracy and Impoverished the Souls of Today's Students* (New York: Simon & Schuster, 1987), p. 337.

3. Charles Sykes, *ProfScam: Professors and the Demise of Higher Education* (Washington, D.C.: Regnery Gateway, 1988), p. 4.

4. Page Smith, *Killing the Spirit: Higher Education in America* (New York: Viking, 1990), p. 7.

5. Thomas Sowell, *Inside American Education* (New York: Free Press, 1993), p. 296.

6. Adlai Stevenson, *What I Think* (New York: Harper, 1956), p. xii.

7. John Slaughter, speech delivered at Engineering Deans Institute, Salt Lake City, Utah, March 29, 1982.

8. Clark Kerr, *The Uses of the University* (Cambridge, Mass.: Harvard University Press, 1963), p. 18-19.

9. John Donne, "The Progress of the Soul: The Second Anniversary of the Death of Mistress Elizabeth Drury," 1641, l. 244.

10. Charles Osgood, quoted in Oberdorfer, *Princeton University*, p. 104.

On the Accountability of Higher Education in the United States

MARTIN TROW

How do American colleges and universities meet the demands of accountability placed on them by society and other institutions, and can current practices in this area be improved? These are the modest questions that Patricia Graham, Richard Lyman, and I addressed in our essay "Accountability of Colleges and Universities,"[1] which emerged from a study directed by Greg Fusco at Columbia University during the summer of 1995. We were responding to a number of developments in the area of accreditation that had troubled many observers and leaders of higher education.[2] Yet we were asked by various sponsors[3] to take a fresh look at the matter, not focused primarily on the issues in the newspapers or the politically divisive concerns of the day (which already seem somewhat dated), but rather with a broader perspective. And that is the perspective of accountability, a perspective in which the contentious issues of accreditation are merely one way, and perhaps not the most important way, in which American colleges and universities discharge their obligations to report to the society that supports them and to justify their activities and the use of resources to those who have a stake in what we do and how we spend their money.

That report made a number of recommendations about accreditation in higher education of a fairly concrete and practical kind. But before turning to the questions of accreditation, which in a way initiated our concern with accountability, let us consider some other aspects of accountability of higher education in this society and in others.

In its broadest terms, accountability in higher education refers, first, to the relations of colleges and universities to the people, groups, and institutions in the society that support them and, second, to the relations of the members of a particular college or university to one another.

What does it mean to be accountable, or to be held accountable? I think in ordinary discourse the essence of accountability is the obligation—legal, financial, or moral/intellectual—to report to others about the activities of an institution, its parts and members, to explain, to justify, and to answer questions. The first question we might ask about accountability is what is it for, why are there these obligations to report, what are their functions? The next and related questions are, who is to be held accountable, to whom, for what, and through what forms are those obligations to be discharged?

With respect to its basic functions, first, accountability is a constraint on arbitrary power and on the corruptions of power—fraud, manipulation, malfeasance, and the like. In serving these functions, accountability strengthens the legitimacy of institutions, including colleges and universities, which meet their obligations to report on their activities to the appropriate groups or authorities. In addition, it is claimed that accountability sustains or raises the quality of performance of institutions by forcing them to examine their own operations critically and by subjecting them to critical review from outside. And beyond those functions of constraining power and raising standards, accountability can be (and is) used as a regulatory device, through the kinds of reports it requires and the explicit or implicit criteria it requires the reporting institutions to meet. Although, in principle, accountability operates through reports on past actions, the anticipation of having to be accountable throws its shadow forward over future action. It thus is a force for external influence on institutional behavior, an influence that can vary from a broad steer, leaving to the institution a measure of autonomy over the implementation of policy, to the direct commands of an external regulatory agency, which uses accountability to ensure compliance with specific policies and directives and designs its system of reports to ensure that conformity.[4]

But that note reminds us that accountability is a double-edged sword. Though it generally gets a good press in a populist society, we have to keep in mind that accountability is exercised at a price to the institutions under its obligations, and not least to our colleges and universities. For one thing, accountability is an alternative to trust, and efforts to strengthen it usually involve parallel efforts to weaken trust. Accountability and cynicism about human behavior go hand in hand. Trust has much to recommend it in the relation of institutions to their supporting societies, and not least for colleges and universities, even though it is sometimes violated and exploited.[5]

Related to this, and of special interest to educators: accountability to outsiders weakens the autonomy of institutions. Obligations to report are usually disguised obligations to conform to external expectations. And there is, or at least has been, a special case to be made for a high measure of autonomy of institutions of higher education. (Indeed, in a sense, Princeton's 250th anniversary, which we celebrate here, is also a celebration of the extraordinary autonomy of a great private university in the United States and the concomitant relative weakness historically of its accountability to outside authorities—a balance that may be changing as we speak.)

Accountability to outsiders, depending on the nature of the obligation, can also be at odds with the confidentiality of sensitive issues within colleges and universities, of which personnel decisions and preliminary discussions about the treatment of departments and units at times of financial stringency are only the most obvious. It can thus be the enemy of effective governance and also of plain truth-telling within the institution as aspects of accountability to outsiders tend toward the character of public relations. External accountability can also be a threat to the freedom of professionals to manage their own time and define their own work. And external accountability, when it applies common standards and criteria to many institutions, can work against diversity among them.

But whatever our ambivalence, the obligations inherent in accountability are central to democratic societies and have become increasingly so over the long secular trend toward the fundamental democratization of life that Max Weber spoke of. As traditional authority is weakened and trust in traditional elites undermined, more formal and open accounts and justifications have to be made to the variety of bodies that claim the right to judge the performance of institutions. Accountability, as I have noted, is a major constraint on the exercise of power; the constraint lies in what people and institutions to whom reports are owed might do if they do not like what they hear. The opposite of accountability is the exercise of arbitrary power or of power exercised through manipulation, exercised in secret precisely to avoid having to report actions that would be condemned, obstructed, or punished if known.

This idea was invoked recently in the long-awaited report by Sir Richard Scott on Britain's sale of arms to Iraq in the years leading to the Gulf War. There he pointed out that in the official "Questions of Procedure for Ministers," "ministers are obliged to give 'as full information as possible . . . and not . . . deceive or mislead Parliament.'" Sir Richard concluded that in 1989, British ministers had in fact deceived Parliament; *The Economist* observed that Sir Richard "rightly concluded that such behavior undermines the democratic process." And they continue, "Under Britain's unwritten constitution, Parliament has an often-tricky dual responsibility. On the one hand, it chooses the executive and sustains it in office through the votes of the majority party. On the other, it holds the executive to account, preventing it from abusing its power, and acting as the forum and source for informed public debate."[6] Here we see accountability invoked when it is violated; when actions, taken in this case by ministers, should have been reported to another body, in this case Parliament, but were not.

Issues of accountability are also raised not only when it is violated but also when trust in an actor or institution has been weakened or withdrawn, when traditional forms of academic authority fail and the legitimacy of behavior is called into question. A historian reflecting on what he sees as the chaos of relativistic and deconstructionist history recently observed that "for better or worse, we no longer live in a world in which our authority alone can legitimate the work that we do. We have to be able to give a persuasive account of it. We have to be able to reflect more deeply on the proper uses of the work we do, and if we find that we are able to explain those uses clearly and forcefully to our students, then accountability to the larger public will not be a problem. If we can succeed in even so small an endeavor, the result will go a long way toward preserving the preconditions for vital and reorganized historical writing."[7] So accountability to students and indirectly "the larger public" through explanation and persuasion is to give academic work legitimacy when academic authority can no longer do so. I wonder.

Issues of accountability are raised when the obligations are violated, when authority is called into question, or when accountability is discharged in other countries in ways that we find strange or unusual. Comparative perspectives allow us to see lines of accountability that in our own country and institutions are often obscured by custom and are even wholly invisible if not keyed to a formal structure of reporting. This accounts for why in American higher education there is so much discussion of accreditation and so little of accountability: in a way, accreditation is the bit of the accountability iceberg that shows above water, the bit that involves formal institutions and lines of communication and decisions. And indeed, discussions of accreditation in the United States have sometimes proceeded as if it were the only way colleges and universities were held accountable for their behavior by the larger society.

If the American discussion of accountability centers on accreditation, which is where problems have arisen, in Europe accountability issues take the form of discussions of assessment and evaluation of quality, performance and achievement, how those judgments should be made, and whether or how to link them to funding. And that is because higher education in Europe is funded almost completely by governments that, in recent years, have been stressed by the costs of their move toward mass higher education to try to achieve greater "efficiencies" in the operation of their costly systems. Toward this end they have tried to link measures of "outputs" more closely to funding, and this linkage seems to require assessments of the amount and quality of the work accomplished by their universities. And that points in the direction of greater direct management by agencies of central government. But these efforts are attended by many difficulties, not least of which is the recognition by most European governments that the growth of their systems, both in size and complexity, points toward the advantages, almost the necessity, of granting greater autonomy to their universities, and we see that happening in countries as different as Sweden, the Netherlands, and France.[8] With the exception of the United Kingdom, where management by central government has steadily grown, developments in Western European higher education over the past decade have largely pivoted around the tension between more accountability to government and more autonomy for the universities. Government policies in Europe have recently tried to achieve both, with varying success.[9]

Aspects of Accountability

Most broadly, colleges and universities (sometimes systems of universities) are accountable to the institutions, groups, and people inside and outside the institution who in some way support its activities.[10] Of course, the nature of that obligation and the ways in which it is honored or discharged vary quite a lot among the various claimants. Princeton University can be held accountable to its alumni or to the parents of its students in a quite different degree from the accountability to the alumni or parents of community college students just down the road, and both are accountable to the federal government for their disposal of hazardous wastes in ways that are quite different from their accountability to parents or alumni. So there are difficulties in discussing a set of legal, financial, and moral or normative obligations that are so various in themselves. It may therefore be helpful to point to two dimensions or aspects of accountability in higher education immediately, the first being the distinction between external and internal accountability, and the second the distinction between legal and financial accountability, on one side, and academic (moral and scholarly) accountability on the other.[11]

On the first distinction, *external accountability* is the obligation of colleges and universities to their supporters, and ultimately to society at large, to provide assurance that they are pursuing their missions faithfully, using their resources honestly and responsibly, and meeting legitimate expectations. *Internal accountability* is the accountability of those within a college or university to one another for how its several parts are carrying out their missions, how well they are performing, whether they are trying to learn where improvement is needed, and what they are doing to make those improvements. External account- ability is something like an audit, giving grounds for confidence and continued support, while internal accountability is a kind of research: inquiry and analysis by the institution into its own operations, aimed primarily at improvement through investigation and action. And our published essay was particularly concerned with how the forms and practices of external accountability can be made to reinforce rather than undermine good internal accountability.[12]

The second distinction, between legal and financial accountability and academic accountability, cuts across the first. *Legal and financial accountability* is the obligation to report how resources are used: Is the institution doing what it is supposed to be doing by law? Are its resources being used for the purposes for which they were given? Accountability for the use of resources has its own traditions and norms, and the financial audit by both internal and external indepen- dent bodies is a well-developed mechanism for discharging it. *Aca- demic accountability* is the obligation to tell others, both inside and outside the institution, what has been done with those resources to further teaching, learning, and public service, and to what effect. There is usually a good deal more controversy over academic accoun- tability than about legal and financial accountability—the rules gov- erning inputs are generally clearer than our ability to assess and eval- uate the outcomes of teaching and research. We can see the contrast also in the forms by which these two kinds of obligations are dis- charged or enforced: in one case, through financial reports, audits, and lawsuits; in the other, by the myriad of ways that academics and academic administrators talk to one another and to outsiders about what they are doing.

Efforts through accreditation to provide accountability to outsiders for the academic quality of whole institutions are currently the most contentious of these various forms of accountability. To a considerable extent, external academic accountability in the United States, mainly in the form of accreditation, has been irrelevant to the improvement of higher education; in some cases, it has acted more to shield institu- tions from effective monitoring of their own educational performance than to provide it; in still other cases, it distinctly hampers the efforts of institutions to improve themselves. It encourages institutions to report their strengths rather than their weaknesses, their successes rather than their failures—and even to conceal their weaknesses and failures from view. As long as accreditation is seen as *the* means by which higher education polices itself, alternative and better means will be ignored. This is where much dispute has occurred and where the committee made one of its central recommendations: that we transform accreditation from external reviews of institutional quality into searching audits of each institution's own scheme for critical self-examination, its own internal quality control procedures.

The Peculiar Problems of Accountability in Higher Education

Accountability of some sort is an obligation of all social institutions, and we can find considerable discussion of the issue in connection with private business and industry. And a good deal of political philosophy can be seen to turn around questions of accountability: to whom do power holders answer. But the accountability of colleges and universities poses special problems.

Colleges and universities are peculiar combinations of academic guilds and administrative and bureaucratic structures. Authority is diffused throughout the institution, depending on the activity. And for many activities, authority is exercised through the joint operation of several actors, blurring the locus of responsibility and thus of accountability obligations.

Moreover, a great deal of authority over the actual teaching and learning—what I have called the private life of higher education, in contrast to the public life of institutional governance, administration, and finance—is held and exercised at what one might think of as the bottom of the structure of the institution. Higher education is almost unique in this respect: doctors, lawyers, and engineers are now mostly all salaried, and their activities are (increasingly) closely monitored—they all have "products" that can be enumerated, and behavior, particularly their outputs in important respects, that can be managed. I do not need to point to the pain felt and expressed by doctors as they lose control over their own time to big, bureaucratized health providers whose managers are concerned with a bottom line. Of course, the academic's control over his or her time varies a good deal in different kinds of institutions. But teaching and learning, especially at the postsecondary level, continually escape efforts to rationalize and standardize them. The control by the academics over what goes on in the classroom and laboratory is to some degree required, or at least justified, by the monopoly claimed by academics over the specialized (in some cases arcane) bodies of knowledge that they possess and that make up the college curriculum. Moreover, this control is sanctified by traditions of academic freedom—traditions that have other sources than the specialization of knowledge.

Of course, all this varies between institutions and disciplines. For example, big science and team research impose their own disciplines and constraints on their practitioners—constraints tied to the expenditure of large sums of money, which becomes the chief vehicle for oversight and accountability. But where the resource employed by academics is chiefly time and not money (beyond salaries), and where there is no very good "bottom line" linking "outputs" with money inputs, the problems of forcing meaningful "accountability" for what they do is enormously frustrating to managers and administrators in public colleges and universities (often under pressure from businesspeople concerned with "efficiency" and lawyers who bill by the hour) who may want to develop tidy systems of accountability that mirror those employed in private business. Indeed, we all know of abortive efforts to require academics to report the actual time spent on various activities. But what is a poor administrator to do with reports that come back itemizing "fifteen hours reading" or "ten hours walking dog and thinking"? And the institution of assured tenure further weakens efforts to require the kind of detailed reporting that these conceptions of academic accountability require. It is, as rationalizing administrators complain, something like trying to herd cats. We find further empirical support in these encounters for the well-documented linkage of frustration and aggression.

I mentioned earlier that the essence of accountability is the obligation to report, to tell interested or concerned others about an individual's or institution's activities and use of resources. But inherent in obligations are sanctions: what do the people to whom reports are made do if they don't like what they hear?[13] So accountability embodies a bundle of normative expectations, held in principle by both sides—those doing the reporting and those to whom reports are made. And these expectations encompass the issues of who is reporting what, to whom, about what, and with what consequences on both sides, and importantly, a question whose answer can no longer be assumed: Is there agreement between the parties on these questions? Clearly the process of accountability will go awry if the parties are not agreed on what is to be reported to whom about what.[14]

Trust as an Alternative to Formal Accountability

I have been talking so far chiefly about formal accountability, the procedures by which individuals and institutions fulfill the obligation to tell certain others what they are doing, to explain, justify, and answer questions. But there are two important alternatives—legitimate, acceptable alternatives—to formal accountability in the relations between an institution and its support community, its stakeholders. One of these is trust; the other is the market. Indeed, the processes of accountability, the reporting to others of what one is doing, can be seen as a substitute for trust in a situation where market processes are weak. And the weaker the levels of trust, the more elaborate and formal the procedures for demanding and gaining accountability, and the bigger the regulatory bureaucracy. This is clearest where trust was strong and is now weak, where it has been replaced by procedures rather than never having existed. Conversely, the stronger the trust, the weaker and less developed the systems of formal accountability.

Trust by adults in people and their institutions is not ordinarily blind but assumes the operation of different kinds of accountability, kinds that formal accountability procedures do not recognize. One is the accountability demanded of their members by the academic guilds—the departments and the disciplines. Again, we hear about this kind of accountability when professional and scholarly norms are violated, as in recurrent scandals about academic plagiarism or the falsification of research findings. The fact that they *are* scandals attests to the power of the norms that are violated and the structure of sanctions still in place to enforce the norms.

There is, in addition, the personal accountability to which one is held by one's conscience—accountability to values that are internalized. Some people in academic life still think in terms of what they conceive to be their duty, who do it without external constraint or coercion but see it as meeting the dictates of honor or loyalty or what is required to be a good citizen of the university. All of these forms of inner direction, as David Riesman called them many years ago, stand apart from, and indeed are opposed by, the formal requirements of accountability. That is because formal requirements for accountability are inherently suspicious of claims to professional and personal responsibility, claims that were in fact the basis on which academics in elite colleges and universities escaped most formal accountability for their work as teachers and scholars.

We can see all this most clearly in the relation of British universities to central government, whose trust in those universities has been largely withdrawn over the past decade and a half. Before about 1980, the relatively small elite university system in the U.K., buffered from government by the University Grants Committee which distributed the block grant from the state, largely managed its own affairs within the overall limits of its grant. Over the past decade, and especially with the demise of the University Grants Committee in 1985 and its replacement by a funding council that is an administrative arm of government, the high levels of trust that gave to British universities their freedom and autonomy have been replaced by a large bureaucratic staff employed by central government, which manages the life of the universities in great detail through complex and frequently changing funding formulas, quality assessments linked directly to funding, and firm rules prescribing the numbers of students that can be admitted and the funds that will attach to those numbers. The Department of Education and Employment, through the Higher Education Funding Councils, uses a combination of funding formulas and directives to determine not just the broad size and shape of the system but also the size of each institution, its balance of research and teaching, the mix of the subjects it offers, the number of students permitted to enroll in each, and the character and direction of research. And the mountains of reports required by the central funding agency from each university and each academic department on every aspect of their programs and activities are tangible evidence of an elaborate and counterproductive structure of formal accountability where trust has been replaced by hostility and suspicion.[15]

So in Britain, we are currently seeing the loss by academics of the persuasive power of their claims to personal and professional responsibility—claims that, when honored, underlay the extraordinary trust that British and American society have placed in their leading colleges and universities.[16] Academics in elite British universities were assumed to be "gentlemen," men and women who governed their own behavior according to the dictates of conscience, considerations of honor, or professional norms, depending on their social origins.[17] And that is why, in transforming that elite system of higher education into a system of mass higher education, the British government in the past decade has gone to such lengths to deny the relevance of such claims to trust and to subject the whole of the system and its members to what can only be seen as a kind of mass degradation ceremony involving the transformation of academic staff—scholars and scientists, lecturers and professors alike—into employees, mere organizational personnel. And like other employees, they are expected to respond to penalties and incentives devised by the funding agency, required like any other employee of the state to account for them-selves and their behavior to a bureaucracy that knows little of honor, conscience, or trust.

In such a world, claims to personal responsibility in academic life are met with derision or cynicism, as a transparent device to justify the old privileges of university life and incompatible with state poli-cies for higher education (which, of course, they mostly are). Refer-ences by academics to their personal responsibilities for their work or to professional standards and obligations are often totally incom-prehensible to people to whom the very vocabulary of personal re-sponsibility is foreign except as they have heard it in historical films. Unfortunately, when these claims to personal responsibility or profes-sional status have to be made explicit, they are already weak. Trust cannot be demanded but must be freely given. In Trollope's novels, a gentleman who claims to be a gentleman is almost certainly no gen-tleman.

But the decline in trust as one of the three basic forces in the sup-port of higher education is not wholly the result of policies aimed at reshaping higher education in the image of private enterprise while increasing the regulatory power of central government, though the British case might lead us to believe so. In European countries, the decline in trust is inherent in the growth of mass higher education since World War II; in the tremendous increase in its costs, especially to the public purse; and in the increasing diversity of forms that higher education takes, many of which cannot claim the academic authority of elite forms of higher education.[18] In Europe more than in this country, the enormous growth of enrollments over the past three decades has not only made higher education into a competitor for support with other elements of the welfare state but has also raised questions about the quality and standards of those institutions. That anxiety about "quality" has been exacerbated by tendencies in all Eu-ropean countries to cut the budgets for higher education, at least on a per capita basis. And that, in turn, has generated what can only be called an evaluation industry engaged in writing and consulting about problems in the assessment of teaching and research in postse-condary education and the possible linkage of assessment to state funding. The same forces have also led to a growing interest in the role of market forces in maintaining both the funding and the quality of European universities. We find this, surprisingly, even in countries that have long mistrusted the role of the market in cultural affairs as increasing the influence of incompetent forces, which tend, so it is believed, toward the democratization and vulgarization of high cul-ture and the decline of "standards." In all this, the U.K. is exceptional

chiefly in its greater anxiety about "economic decline" and political
weakness of its universities in the face of a government that, under
both Margaret Thatcher and John Major, showed mistrust of all the
old institutions of the establishment, and most particularly the universities, as agents of decline.

There is less anxiety about the "quality" of higher education in the
United States both because our system is so variable in that regard
and because we never made (or could make) any commitment as a
nation to the maintenance of common standards across our thousands
of colleges and universities. We are also less embarrassed by the role
of the market in cultural affairs. As Louis Hartz reminded us, in
America by contrast with Europe, the market preceded the society.[19]
But that has not relieved our colleges and institutions from the problem of defining and defending a distinctive character or mission not
wholly defined by market forces.

Market Mechanisms as an Alternative
to Formal Accountability

To some degree, market mechanisms, and the involvement of colleges
and universities in those markets, mute the demands for formal accountability by serving as an alternative source of evidence to its support community of the quality and relevance of what the institution is
doing. The market, as we say, sends signals, at least about things that
the markets are interested in, such as the employability of graduates
and the usefulness of research findings. And that is certainly a supplement to other forms of accountability. For proprietary schools,
which do not offer degrees but teach skills for specific labor markets,
accountability may come down to nothing more than the information
needed to provide consumer protection against fraud and close monitoring of student loan defaults.

Markets learn about institutions and act on what they learn. But
there are limits to the effectiveness of markets as substitutes for trust
and accountability, limits arising largely out of the arcane nature of
the specialized subjects taught and learned in colleges and universities and the difficulty laymen have to judge their quality or value. A
good deal of what is studied in college, by students or by scholars
and scientists, may not have immediate market value—though what
is learned there may have substantial value over the course of a lifetime. But the effects of higher education that is not narrowly vocational are difficult, if not impossible, to measure; those effects may be
long delayed in showing themselves and then emerge intertwined be-

yond disentangling with many other kinds of knowledge and experience. So in practice, neither laymen nor specialists can make a definitive judgment of the worth or long-term value of the education offered in a particular institution at a particular time.

Colleges and universities compete for students, staff, gifts and contributions, public support, research support, and academic status. Participation in the various markets in which colleges and universities compete has been a powerful force in American higher education almost since their beginnings. This is unlike the situation in most other systems in advanced societies, at least until recently,[20] and arises out of the absence of assured and full state support in this country. Competition can be imagined to affect quality negatively or positively: we could imagine the competition for students, for example, driving entry and completion standards down; we can also imagine the competition for resources and prestige working to maintain higher academic standards. My own judgment is that on the whole, competition in various markets has worked to sustain academic quality, perhaps most clearly among institutions that are competing for the highest ranks and status in their respective academic niches.

But competition in academic life, as we all know, is not wholly confined to competition in markets. In good colleges and universities of every kind, and not just in the leading research universities and liberal arts colleges, what fuels internal efforts at self-improvement is a desire shared by many within the institution that it excel, that it fulfill its own potential to be all that it can be. And those motivations reflect the socialization of most academics during their graduate studies, their personal pride and ambition, and their quest for a good reputation, among other sources. Often that spirit takes the form of a brisk competition with other academics in the same field or between departments or institutions. This striving for excellence is often reflected in a striving for academic reputation and status, and if that striving remains within the bounds of academic life and faithful to its norms, it is a valuable spring of motivation. Where that spirit is weak, external agencies may try to provide the motivation for improvement by a mixture of rewards and punishments. But as most of us know from our own lives, that is a poor substitute for the motivations that we find within ourselves and in our own intellectual and normative communities.

But competition in markets by itself is not an adequate force for the maintenance of academic quality for a variety of reasons reflecting the usual sources of market failure: some institutions and parts of many are insulated from most market processes; the market may not have adequate information; the market may not have the sophistication to use what information is available and so on. And although the market may provide signals about an institution's relative success, it usually does not give much of a clue about what to do to improve its performance. Market forces and competition of various kinds are major elements in the strength of American higher education, but they are not themselves adequate to sustain and improve the quality of our institutions. That depends also, and in very large part, on a large measure of trust by the outside stakeholders, together with strong and effective processes of internal accountability that are audited by outside "accrediting" agencies.

What we see in higher education are complex and variable combinations of formal measures of accountability, trust and market mechanisms. And the combinations of these ways of linking institutions of higher education to their support communities vary enormously among different kinds of institutions, different departments, different activities, and different stakeholders.

External Accountability

There is no lack of accountability by American colleges and universities to the larger community: it takes many different forms and is addressed to many different audiences. The question is whether these are the right forms and what their effects are on the quality of work done in those institutions. Currently, American colleges and universities account for some or all of their activities in the following ways:

• Every institution that offers credit toward first degrees is accredited by one of six regional accrediting agencies. These are now supplemented by an additional accrediting body for a small number of liberal arts colleges, which establishes the principle of "alternative" accrediting bodies and reestablishes the principle of voluntary adherence to the six existing regionals.
• Many but not all professional schools are accredited by specialized accrediting bodies "representing" professional schools across the country.
• The federal government issues many rules and regulations governing the activities of nongovernmental bodies, including colleges and universities. These cover many areas of life, including the use of federal funds, the conditions associated with the appointment of staff, the admission of students, the use of animals for research, the treat-

ment of toxic wastes, and many others. The often elaborate and lengthy reports detailing compliance with these laws and regulations constitute a major form of accountability to central government. It has been estimated that colleges and universities are required to comply with some 7,500 federal regulations of one kind or another, with compliance reports associated with almost all of them.[21]

• Similar reports are made by colleges and universities, both public and private, to state and local authorities, varying with institution and locality.

• Every college or university (or system) is linked to the larger society through a governing board of trustees or regents. This board, unique to this country in its powers and characteristics, has broad responsibility for the activities of the institution it governs. It is ordinarily made up of laypeople, in public institutions named by the governor or state legislature or elected by the people. In private institutions, the board is self-coopting, but its members are almost always drawn from the groups and institutions that provide the institution its support. Boards vary greatly in their operation, but all of them name the institution's president and define its central mission; most keep close watch over its finances and capital budget but play a much smaller role in monitoring the "private life" of the institution or its academic quality.

• Every state has some kind of higher education coordinating council as a condition of receiving federal funds for higher education. These councils vary enormously in their power and activities, but at the very least they collect and publish information about the public (and usually also the private) colleges and universities in the state. They may also serve as an additional governing board alongside or in place of the traditional board of trustees. Every state will also have some legislative committee or subcommittee charged with responsibility for the state's support and oversight of its public institutions of higher education.

• The nonacademic employees of most public institutions and many private ones belong to trade unions that bargain over salaries and the conditions of work. This commonly requires colleges and universities to give the unions details of their finances and operations, another form of accountability. Apart from those in the leading research universities and four-year liberal arts colleges, most academics also belong to unions. Both unions and academic senates in many institutions have access to their institution's budget and finances, about which they are able to comment and perhaps even influence.

• Every college and university publishes a variety of reports on its activities, starting with the catalog of courses and including annual reports, newsletters, alumni magazines, varying greatly in number and content.

• A number of organizations currently provide a kind of "consumer's guide" to colleges and universities, providing a purported quality ranking using information provided either by the institution or by expert assessors in other institutions. Among these are the now recurring rankings of graduate departments in research universities carried out every five years by the National Academy of Sciences and the annual rankings of undergraduate programs in a wider range of institutions conducted and published by the magazine *U.S. News and World Report*.

• For more sophisticated readers, the financial conditions of institutions are reported by professional bodies that exist to protect the interests of organizations and individuals who loan money to colleges and universities.

While all these forms of accountability individually and collectively link colleges and universities to the larger society and make their activities known more widely to various audiences, they each and all together have shortcomings as adequate forms of accountability. I am not suggesting that yet another layer of accountability needs to be laid down to supplement those in place, but it is worth noting the limitations of those I have mentioned.

REGIONAL ACCREDITING BODIES

Over the past fifty to one hundred years, in the minds of many, the six regional accrediting bodies have carried the burden of accountability of American higher education to the larger society. They began as threshold agencies, to attest that an institution was a college rather than a secondary school. As that function evaporated, they gradually assumed the fairly innocuous role of appointing committees to visit institutions from time to time to encourage them to raise their standards in some way—more books in the library, better labs, and the like. Some institutions have welcomed the self-studies that such reviews require; others bemoaned the costs involved. The reviews also provided an opportunity for special interests in a college to lobby a visiting committee and use a review to strengthen their cause in internal debates, thus playing a role in the internal political life of colleges that was not part of their original mission. But perhaps the greatest weakness of the regional agencies is that they apply common standards to institutions that differ profoundly in character and mission. The strongest argument in favor of the regional agencies is that they are not governmental agencies (though they acquired their power somewhat unexpectedly in the mid-1970s by being linked to the federal government's student grant and loan programs). The loudest outcry against them has come in recent years as some regional agencies, notably Middle States and the Western Association of Schools and Colleges, began to intervene directly in sensitive elements of collegiate life by issuing directives to colleges bearing on such matters as the racial and ethnic ratios of students, faculty, and governing boards and the role of multiculturalism in the curriculum.

In recent years, and especially since the demise of the Council for Postsecondary Education (COPA), various national organizations have proposed the creation of a national coordinating body that would link the regional agencies together, perhaps through the development of national standards of accreditation, among other things. The writers of the "Accountability " report did not believe that was a good direction in which to move. For the moment, it will be enough to suggest that we wanted to find and recommend a form of external accreditation that would help institutions monitor and improve their own practice. And that, we believed, will best take the form of an external audit of the procedures that each institution has developed for policing and improving its own practices.

SPECIALIZED AND PROFESSIONAL ACCREDITATION

Here fundamental questions arise about the value and function of these institutions. In the course of our interviews, we heard widespread criticism of these bodies—from deans of professional schools in law, education, engineering, and social welfare, to name a few. Designed to monitor and support "quality," these professional accrediting bodies have in too many cases assumed the authority to dictate to professional schools about admissions, hiring, curriculum, and physical plant, with real risks to the autonomy of those professional schools. Professional schools tend to be found in research universities that have a strong interest in the maintenance of the quality and reputation of their professional schools. Moreover, in contrast to undergraduate education, the "consumers" of professional education—mostly graduate students on one hand and employers on the other—are more sophisticated than beginning undergraduates and less in need of "consumer protection." Moreover, in many professions, the state introduces its own requirements for licensing, which further serve to maintain the quality of professional practice. We believe that the combination of these factors—strong quality control and assurance procedures by the university, a knowledgeable market for students and employers, and state licensing—makes the kind of external "accreditation" embodied in the professional accrediting agencies unnecessary. As our committee report said, "The unit of analysis for accreditation should be the institution itself, not some separately designated program, school, or department. The responsibility for the institution lies with its faculty, administration, and board. They must consider the overall well-being of the institution, not just some part or unit of it." In addition, we suggested that "if specialized accreditation is to continue, it should shift its activities to strengthened internal reviews focused on learning. These reviews could be audited by external peers, including scholars, practitioners, and clients."[22] Consistent with that view, our report suggested that the quality control procedures of the university with respect to its professional schools should also come under the review of the external auditing bodies that we were recommending.

FEDERAL, STATE, AND LOCAL REGULATORY BODIES

No simple judgment can be made of the thousands of rules and regulations that affect teaching and learning in colleges and universities and require the kinds of reporting that we have identified as a form of accountability. In many cases, these rules would strike most people as reasonable and defensible. Institutions must be able to account for their expenditure of public monies; no one can object to their being required to comply with the ordinary laws and regulations governing health and safety. But our committee was not wholly satisfied with the present bearing of governmental regulations on higher education, for three reasons.

First, the sheer number of regulations that apply to colleges and universities—it has been estimated that 7,500 federal regulations so apply—place a very heavy and in many cases unnecessary burden on colleges and especially on research universities. The costs of complying with these directives and administering them directly compete for resources with the research and teaching that these institutions exist to pursue. Again, different judgments would have to be made about each rule and regulation, but many knowledgeable observers are concerned with the increase in the number of these regulations and the growth of their administrative and compliance costs and are not persuaded that they are all necessary or desirable. President Gerhard Casper of Stanford University has noted that his institution is required to handle and account for its ounces of toxic waste in the same way that Dow Chemical handles its tons of the same wastes.[23] Governmental regulations have a tendency to be sweeping and standardized across widely different institutions, often at the expense of the universities and colleges.

Second, government agencies are sometimes guilty of a tendency to provide limited resources for specific purposes and then to use that support to require the receiving institution to account for a much wider range of its expenditures and activities. This practice imposes significant additional administrative burdens on the institutions.

Finally, the reporting obligations associated with compliance with governmental rules and regulations do not address the core functions of colleges and universities, the teaching and learning that comprise the private life of these institutions. They address financial accounting and compliance with law, but they have little to do with the quality of the work of these institutions. The power to apply penalties that lie with these government agencies may be necessary for compliance, but they certainly do not encourage institutions to explore their own difficulties and failings beyond what is narrowly required for compliance. In short, however necessary and appropriate these regulations may be, they are mostly irrelevant to the quality of academic work and to its improvement.

GOVERNING BOARDS

These are important bodies both in the governance of colleges and universities and in their accountability to the larger society. They are responsible for the fiscal soundness of the institutions and for compliance with all the federal, state, and local laws and regulations to which their institutions are subject. They play a crucial role in linking their institutions to the groups and individuals that support them—governmental authorities, businesses, alumni groups, foundations, and the like. These boards also choose the institutions' presidents and have the power to fire them and have a direct effect on the internal life of the institutions through such appointments. Beyond that, boards vary greatly in their involvement in the inner or private life of their institutions. Here they walk a fine line: how to take an active interest in the academic life of their institutions without undermining the authority of the president or invading the jealously defended areas of academic freedom. Boards in the past have crossed that line, to severe criticism by observers both inside and outside their institutions, while running the grave risk of a vote of censure by the American Association of University Professors. Many boards are naturally and properly cautious about intervening directly into the intellectual life of their institutions. But that appropriate caution reduces their effectiveness as monitors of the academic quality of their institutions and of its efforts to improve that quality.

STATE COORDINATING COUNCILS AND LEGISLATIVE COMMITTEES

These bodies are fundamentally concerned with broad public policy regarding higher education: the size and shape of state systems and especially of its public institutions, the nature and breadth of access to these institutions, the budgets of the institutions and the systems as a whole, the costs of student support, and similar matters. These are all of vital importance to the institutions, but they are at one remove from the questions of academic quality and excellence. State coordinating councils and legislative committees require and use a variety of reports from the institutions over which they exercise varying degrees of authority and in turn produce reports of their own. But these are mainly quantitative reports about income and expenditures, enrollments, persistence and graduation rates, faculty-student ratios, teaching loads, and the like. These reports by state agencies are important to the life of institutions of higher education since they are necessary for state funding, student aid, and the like. They may also provide indications of what is going on in the institutions; for example, changes in the length of time to degree or in graduation rates can point to issues of quality. But my impression is that on the whole, these state offices, however important they may be in shaping broad issues of educational policy, are too far removed from the institutions to play much of a role in identifying their academic problems or in helping institutions deal with them. On the contrary, the intervention of these agencies into the private life of higher education is as likely to harm as to help. An example of this has been the effort in some states to mandate teaching loads, without regard to variations among institutions and departments or to the division of labor among members of individual departments.

TRADE UNIONS

These groups ordinarily represent and bargain for their members' wages, benefits, and working conditions; they do not ordinarily enter into purely academic debates. Sometimes these overlap: issues of academic tenure, faculty-student ratios, and the like do in fact bear on the quality of academic work. But the effects of union involvement on the academic programs are a by-product of their defense of their members' material interests; they may have adverse as well as positive effects on the quality and standards of the institution.

INSTITUTIONAL PUBLICATIONS

Publications such as alumni magazines and institutional newsletters help bind a community of participants and supporters together. They play a role in redefining and reaffirming the character and mission of an institution and in sustaining the support and interest of students, staff, and alumni in the institution. But they naturally tend to report good news about the institution and the achievements of its departments and members. They do not ordinarily dwell on the institution's problems or failures or on contentious issues regarding appointments, the allocation of resources, or other sensitive issues. They are instruments of accountability for information and reassurance rather than for institutional self-criticism and improvement.

QUALITY RANKINGS BY EXTERNAL BODIES

These vary in what institutions and units they rank, their criteria of quality, and the kind of evidence they use. These rankings gain intense attention from the members of the units they rank, for whatever the validity of the rankings, they have large consequences for student and staff recruitment and more generally for the status and prestige of the unit. These rankings may also stimulate change and reform in the institutions so ranked; the rankings of graduate departments by the National Academy of Sciences have been known to have had such effects. They also stimulate efforts by institutions to improve their rankings through changes in what and how they report information without changing the quality of education. This has been the response of some institutions to the national rankings of colleges and universities by *U.S. News and World Report,* institutions that also complain that those rankings heavily weight measures of input rather than academic quality and are vulnerable to distortions and exaggerations in the information supplied by the institutions being rated.

CREDIT RATING BODIES

These serve the financial community, which may be providing credit to colleges and universities. Their importance is that they work with relatively hard data—the financial condition of an institution—and their professional interest is to inform rather than to persuade or justify. They may also provide a benchmark against which to assess the quality of an institution's own public relations and the information they provide to external assessing bodies. They are thus a supplement to other forms of external accountability by colleges and universities.

Internal Accountability

The United States is home to some 3,700 colleges and universities, which vary enormously in their character and mission and also in how vigorously they pursue their mission. Put differently, they vary in what they conceive of as "academic excellence" and also in how seriously and successfully they pursue their own conceptions of excellence. My own view, put briefly, is (1) that the quality of work in a college or university ultimately lies with the faculty and administrators of that institution, (2) that the maintenance and improvement of that quality rests on the procedures in place in that institution for discovering and correcting weaknesses and failures in the institution and its component parts, and (3) that the efforts of colleges and universities to improve themselves will be strengthened by a system of regional audits of the procedures put in place by the institutions themselves. Let us look briefly at what some of these procedures are. Among the procedures that can be found in some but not all institutions are those that focus on the following factors.

THE QUALITY OF UNIVERSITY TEACHERS

• The single most important force for the maintenance of high quality in academic work lies in the close scrutiny and competitive review of candidates for appointment. This competitive review before appointment may be carried out by a department, a dean, a president, an academic senate, or some combination of those actors. It may involve ad hoc committees composed of qualified academics from within the university or committees that include members from other institutions. The quality of an academic community is almost wholly determined by two factors: the attractiveness of the institution to the ablest teachers and scientists, and the care and rigor with which it recruits and appoints people. And this principle applies to community colleges as well as to research universities—the difference lies only in the nature of the abilities they seek.

• Many institutions appoint new teachers to a probationary period before the review leading to a permanent appointment. This review can be a significant element in the maintenance of the quality of a department or university only if it is not pro forma and can lead to the dismissal of a candidate. This period may include interim reviews, like the "progress review" of a candidate's performance in the department after three years in some institutions.

• Promotions and other rewards in some colleges and universities are based on meritocratic assessments of an academic's achievement: among these are permanent appointment; promotion in rank, especially to the higher ranks; salary linked to rank or achievement; and the various honors awarded by the academic community. These are all motivations for high academic performance.

THE QUALITY OF STUDENTS

• No more than two hundred colleges and universities in America can be truly selective among the students who apply for admission. Selective admissions and academic requirements for admission of all kinds maintain the academic quality of students and directly affect the nature and level of instruction. This selectivity in admissions is also an important element in the attractiveness of the institution to teachers and scientists and thus affects the quality of its overall academic performance indirectly.

• Examinations and grades serve to motivate students and to monitor their performance. They may also give teachers evidence of how successful their teaching is. But the United States, unlike most other countries, does not attempt to maintain common standards throughout the higher education system and therefore does not have the same high concern for the quality and objectivity of examinations and their comparability across teachers and institutions. This reduces the value of grades as elements of a system of accountability externally.

The value of examinations as monitoring instruments is sustained in some institutions and systems by the recurrent analysis of patterns of grades awarded, with special concern for variations in the awarding of grades between departments and universities and of patterns of grade inflation over time. Though in the United States grades are not a particularly useful form of external accountability, efforts to study patterns of grades and grade inflation increase their value for internal monitoring and quality control.

• The awarding of fellowships, scholarships, and other honors on the basis of academic performance rewards student performance and sustains motivation for work of high quality.

THE QUALITY OF RESEARCH AND SCHOLARSHIP

• Research grants are commonly made on the basis of competitive excellence by peer review.

• Reference is commonly made to citation indexes as indicators of the quality and significance of published research, of the academics who publish it, and of their departments and institutions. These indexes can serve as symptoms of a decline in performance as well as of distinction.

• Publication in refereed journals and by legitimate publishers of academic and scholarly books is also an indicator of scholarly quality.

• Reviews of books in respected academic journals are also used as indicators of their scholarly quality.

• A powerful indicator of the scholarly reputation of a department, closely watched by many leading American research universities, is the "take rate"—the acceptance of first offers to candidates for appointment, both as academic staff and as students. A decline in these acceptances is taken as an indicator of declining quality, calling for remedial measures.

• The quality of departments in research universities is monitored through the use of periodic external competitive assessments by other academics. The best example is still the periodic assessments of the quality of a wide range of graduate departments in leading research universities by the National Academy of Sciences. These assessments, carried out every ten years, are diagnostic rather than budgeting tools and are not keyed to funding. Even more important than the level of quality of a department is its direction of movement, which can be seen by looking at the trends in its ratings from one assessment to the next. It is interesting that these assessments are both part of the way in which universities are held accountable to the larger society and also part of their internal accountability and quality control systems.

• Many colleges and universities have developed systems of internal reviews of departments, clusters of departments, or whole institutions. Some of these reviews are regular and periodic; others are ad hoc. These are ordinarily designed to help the units they review, to be supportive and not directly determine their funding, though they may influence administrative decisions. These are crucial to quality maintenance; we will have more to say about them later.

THE QUALITY OF CURRICULUM, COURSES, AND INSTRUCTION

• Almost everywhere, what is required to earn a degree in a given institution is periodically reviewed by academic departments, faculties, and collegewide bodies. Sometimes external bodies, coordinating committees, or state officials have a say in this; universities in different states differ in these respects. But regardless of where formal authority for such changes lies, the academics who have the special knowledge in given areas and who actually teach to the degree play a major role in the determination of its requirements. The key point here is that the nature and variety of work required of students (and, indirectly, of their teachers) is in some institutions subject to periodic critical review and discussion within the academic community.

• Specific courses within a curriculum ordinarily fall within the discretion of smaller units than the curriculum as a whole—they can be designed and approved by a college, a department, or a single instructor. Courses are added to or subtracted from a curriculum in response to changes in the map of knowledge, student demand, or the interests of teachers. But ordinarily, the decision to create a course will be made by some body that represents the department or a faculty or the college or university, not solely on the initiative of an instructor. And the discussions and criteria entering such a decision are among the ways through which an institution seeks to maintain or enhance the quality of its work. Any given decision may not contribute to the quality of education offered by the institution, any more than may any specific new appointment to the staff. But the internal discussions and decision about a course are ordinarily rooted, at least in part, in a wish to maintain or improve the quality of the education offered by the institution, however "quality" may be defined in a given case.

• Student assessments of teaching are now almost universally used as a way of monitoring or assessing the quality of instruction in universities. It is debatable how well students can judge the quality of the teaching to which they are currently being exposed. But there can be little doubt that student assessments can identify egregious ineptitude or the violation or evasion of the norms of academic life: that instructors be competent in their subjects, meet their classes on time, treat their students fairly and with respect, and not exploit their vulnerability through political or ideological indoctrination. If students cannot assess the quality of teaching or know its long-term effects on them, they can certainly identify the phenomena of "nonteaching" by teachers and bring those incidents to the attention of others who may be able to take action. And that is certainly part of an institution's own process of quality control and maintenance.

• Most universities now have units and programs of faculty development. Under various names, these units employ groups of specialists whose primary skill and task is to help teachers improve the quality of their work in the classroom and to help them organize their coursework.

COORDINATION AND MONITORING OF THE MECHANISMS
OF QUALITY CONTROL

Many of the activities described so far are largely in the hands of the
academic staff, whether in their departments or in broader faculty or
universitywide committees. Senior academic administrators have a
wide variety of functions, but among them is the task of monitoring
and overseeing the various quality control activities. Unlike deans
and heads of department, presidents, academic vice presidents, and
provosts have responsibility for the quality of the whole institution,
not just a part of it. And if they have an interest in its quality and
reputation, their efforts toward strengthening and monitoring the
quality control mechanisms already in place do much to keep those
mechanisms alive and functioning. Indeed, to exercise academic leadership is in large part to ensure that these mechanisms are functioning as they ought and are not captured by the communities that they
nominally regulate.

However many and however effective these mechanisms of quality
maintenance in universities, they require a large measure of trust on
the part of the supporting society. These arrangements and mechanisms are largely invisible to outsiders. Even when the rules and procedures are public knowledge, the operation of those procedures often rests on professional or expert judgments that by their nature are
arcane or obscure. For example, no matter how clear the procedures
for the appointment and promotion of academic staff may be, the
decisions finally rest on judgments of scholarly or scientific achievement and potential, which can only be made by the professional community and are always subject to doubts about the intervention of
"particularistic" criteria arising out of biases of the electors—scholarly, personal, ideological—or even of racial and gender prejudice. A
good deal of time and energy is spent in the best institutions trying to
insulate the crucial acts of judgment, with respect both to staff and
students, from these biases, which cumulatively must affect the academic quality of teaching and research. But not all universities, not all
departments, not all academics maintain the highest standards in
their performance or in the way they operate the mechanisms of quality control. And that fact partly accounts for the number and variety
of these mechanisms.

Pathologies of Academic Life

In recent years, many books and articles have made charges of widespread corruption in higher education, particularly against an aca-

demic guild that has in their view little interest in teaching and an inappropriate concern for their own perks and privileges. The "Accountability" report did not accept those sweeping attacks as accurate; we know too many academics, and indeed whole institutions, that maintain high standards of scholarly commitment and academic performance. But the basic failure of these sweeping charges is that they do not take into account the enormous variety of institutions that make up American higher education and the equally great variation in their missions and character—a variety that defies assessment by any simple set of criteria.

Nevertheless, it is not necessary to share the apocalyptic views of such critics to acknowledge that there are persistent pathologies in academic life, violations of its own norms and the reasonable expectations of the society and institutions that support our colleges and universities. For example, Derek Bok has observed that "there is no justification for letting graduate students instruct undergraduates with no prior training of any sort, no excuse for allowing foreign teaching fellows with limited English to inflict themselves on students, no reason to appoint professors with only the scantiest evidence of their teaching abilities and then give them little or no feedback about the quality of their instruction. Most of all, there is no justification for continuing to do so little to discover how to make the process of learning more effective."[24]

We know that these failings occur, and it is not necessary to know how common they are to acknowledge the importance of meeting and correcting them. Let's look at some further examples.

• The relatively light teaching obligations of teachers in research universities are meant to give research scholars and scientists the time they need for the active pursuit of knowledge. And for academics actively engaged in research, there is never enough time; the time free from teaching is well and fully engaged. Indeed, research academics ordinarily spend more than sixty hours a week on their combination of teaching, research, and the many forms of service that academic distinction brings with it. But even in the best research universities, at any given time, a substantial number of faculty are not doing research or pursuing serious scholarship. And the practice of most universities gives people who are not doing much research the same light teaching obligations that are accorded active researchers. Academics in such universities do not accept—are not asked to accept—a balance of teaching and research that reflects what they are actually doing. Universities need to develop a more differentiated distribution of labor that reflects the actual work of its academic staff—and one that can vary over time as the interests and energies of the academic staff members change.

• Much has been said about the incompatibility of research and teaching or the neglect of teaching by a research-oriented faculty. I do not accept that research and teaching are inherently at odds; on the contrary, the close connection between teaching and research has been a source of the preeminence of American research universities in the world. Nevertheless, in many colleges and universities—and not just research universities—undergraduate education is weaker than it should be, not necessarily because of the competition of research, but because of the lack of status and attention given to teaching by the academic community. Despite the existence in most institutions of staff development offices and a substantial body of knowledge about how teaching can be improved, few academics use those resources— they are left to graduate students and new appointees. Many colleges and universities need to attack the improvement of undergraduate teaching and learning by finding ways to employ their staff more sensibly, by encouraging or requiring them to improve their teaching skills, and by linking their rewards more closely to their perfor- mance—as teachers as well as researchers.

• The quantity and quality of research based in our universities is the envy of the world. But in recent years, claims of fraud and falsi- fication in science have grown, perhaps resulting from the fierce com- petition for the status attaching to scientific discovery, perhaps arising out of the increasingly close link between science and its commercial applications. Whatever the sources, science and the institutions in which it is pursued need to find better ways to police research; the leaders of research teams need to take fuller responsibility (and not just credit) for the work of their junior colleagues and graduate stu- dents and for the products of their laboratories and research teams.

• A perennial complaint against American higher education has been the charge of the incoherence of the undergraduate curriculum. In fact, this is closely associated with the unit credit and elective sys- tem that makes American higher education so flexible, so responsive to different interests, so accommodating to student migration and to students' growing tendency to drop in and out of different colleges and universities over time in pursuit of a qualification. But whatever the structural and historical explanations of the lack of coherence of undergraduate education, especially in the first two years in Ameri- can colleges and universities, it is perhaps even less coherent than is necessary. Reforms of the undergraduate curriculum may be in order, but they must be made by each institution in light of its own charac- ter and mission. Efforts to force changes in the curriculum of colleges by visiting committees is one of the most serious criticisms we heard of by the regional accrediting agencies. Nevertheless, it is not unreasonable for an outside agency to inquire whether an institution is reviewing its own patterns of teaching, its own curricula, on an ongoing basis. That is the form that an external audit would take in this area.

This is no inventory of problems faced by our institutions; it merely illustrates them. But all of them require that colleges and universities be able to learn where these problems occur and have the will and structures that allow them to respond appropriately. Let us look a little more closely at the nature of internal accountability and its dependence on candor and truth, confidentiality, and the development of an internal culture of self-scrutiny and self-criticism.

Accountability through Internal Reviews and Assessment

As I have suggested, assessments and evaluations by colleges and universities of their own operations fall into two categories: one is concerned with learning, the other with explaining and justifying. The first of these addresses the question, Is the work in the institution up to its own standards, and how can it be improved? In the United States, those standards vary—and are intended to vary—quite substantially among different kinds of institutions and even within the same class or category of institution. That variability is the essence of the diversity of form, mission, and character among American colleges and universities.

Nevertheless, each institution projects an idea of what its goals and missions are, how it will pursue them, and what standard of performance it will try to achieve or surpass. *Internal* reviews and evaluations, where present, are a central instrument in an institution's efforts to sustain that standard by subjecting its own processes to critical examination.

A second function of reviews by a college or university of its own operations is to demonstrate to outsiders that what is going on inside the institution is worthy of their support. It often embodies efforts to demonstrate that the institution is using its funds, especially public funds, effectively for purposes that outside sources approve of. If the essence of evaluation of the first kind is learning—what is going on and how it can be improved—then the essence of self-evaluation of the second kind, for outside consumption, is persuasion: How can outsiders be shown or persuaded that what is going on inside is worthy of support?

The dissociation between these two kinds of assessment—the fact that they are conducted in different ways, answer to different criteria, and produce different kinds of evidence and arguments—marks a lack of trust by outside authorities regarding the university and what it is doing. Where trust is high, assessments based on what the institution learns about its own operations can also serve for legitimation and persuasion, with the persuasion embedded in the trust. By contrast, where trust is low, the necessity for persuasion is high, since the internal evidence that embodies what the institution learns about itself is not accepted outside as an adequate description of its realities.

Why is it so important to keep these two kinds of assessments distinct and not to confuse them? Because there is a danger that the criteria an institution uses in making its self-assessment for external authorities over time become the criteria by which it judges itself. And those criteria are for the most part the wrong criteria to use—simplified and often inaccurate statements about institutional outcomes and products that cannot be verified, claims of efficacy and efficiency that, if taken seriously and internalized, would distort an institution's character and function and divert it from the business of improvement. Moreover, the evidence and arguments developed by institutions for justification to external bodies are at odds with the quite different kinds of evidence they need to determine where their problems lie and how to address them.

Effective assessments of departments and schools that have as their aim improvement rather than justification must be chiefly internal and carried out by academics and administrators who are close to the department in question. They can be supplemented on occasion by visiting academics and committees who are also committed to the welfare of the institution rather than in the service of some external regulatory agency or budget. In light of the diversity of our institutions and the dangers of a policy of "one size fits all" for any aspect of accountability in higher education, there is no one way in which an institution can monitor itself. Nevertheless, our study and experience suggest a number of elements common to most effective systems of internal review aimed at the improvement of educational practice.

Elements of Internal Accountability Systems

• The crucial factor in a system of academic quality control, monitoring, and improvement lies in efforts to create an institutional culture marked by self-criticism, openness to criticism by others, and a commitment to improvement of practice. This, above all, is the responsibility of institutional leadership.

• The institution must have in place a system of regular reviews of every teaching and research unit to be carried out in a routine way every five or seven years. The routinization of reviews removes any suspicion or stigma from attaching to units "under review."

• The committees conducting such reviews should be appointed by an academic administrator (normally a dean) or collegewide academic senate, and be composed chiefly of members of other units in the same institution who are competent to assess the quality of the work of the unit under review. Such reviews may involve people from outside to provide additional disciplinary or technical competence when needed.

• The reviews should begin with a self-study by the subject department. Review committees should insist that these self-studies center on exploring the unit's weaknesses and plans for improvement, rather than on providing a persuasive justification for its existence, practice, and budget. They need to start (though not necessarily end) with the unit's own sense of its mission and standards of excellence. The unit may also supply other relevant information, such as rankings by external agencies or records of employment of graduates, where appropriate.

• Reviews should be oriented toward help and support for the subject unit; they should be primarily diagnostic rather than judgmental, though of course judgments of success and failure and of the overall quality of performance of the unit will be made. The reports of the review committees should not be directly linked to budget, though again they will provide central administration with information helpful in making budgetary decisions.

• Review committees will initiate discussions with the members of the unit meeting together but should also meet separately with its chair or director, its senior and junior staff, its students, and alumni. The members of the unit should have a chance to discuss the work of their unit and its future at length with members of the review committee. They should also have a chance to respond to a draft of the committee's report, and their response should be attached to the report.

• It is of prime importance that the report of the review be held in strict confidence by the review committee and the administrators or senate committee to which it is submitted. The value of such reviews depends heavily on the candor and truthfulness with which the subject unit explores its own work and identifies areas in need of improvement. The readiness to tell the truth about themselves—indeed, the creation of a climate of candor and self-criticism—depends on units not being punished for identifying their areas of weakness. The report of the review committee, but perhaps even more the discussions and conversations that go into its writing, can give the unit and the responsible administrators a sense of what the unit is about, where it is going, how it is making its decisions, and how it defines success and quality.

Administrative officers in extreme cases can take a weak or paralyzed department into receivership by bringing in a chairman from outside the department and giving him or her extraordinary powers. But that is rare; most of the time these recurrent departmental reviews, where they are done, are effective both in motivating departments to review their own operations and in giving them useful advice and criticism, at the same time providing administrative officers with the kind of detailed knowledge necessary for them to make budgetary or personnel decisions. No external agency, no accrediting body or coordinating council, can assess academic units with the accuracy and in the detail necessary to make good judgments and decisions. Nor can their assessments have the legitimacy for the institution and its units that internal reviews carry with them when they are done properly.

Federal Regulations

The federal regulations applying to colleges and universities are a very heavy and often unnecessary burden on higher education. They are a quiet tax: they do not engender the kind of public discussion that arises around affirmative action or the organization of accreditation, but they are a central concern for every university administrator facing stable or declining budgets and growing enrollments and research costs. The regulations most worrying are not even designed with higher education in mind; they are the casual swipe of the dinosaur's tail as it wheels around to face larger and more powerful adversaries, in most cases big business and industry. But even though the conditions in colleges and universities are very different from those in commercial enterprises, most regulations ignore those differences and the administrative and financial problems that flow from them.

Among the most onerous of these regulations are those bearing on the management and disposal of toxic wastes, the provision of access and services for physically handicapped and disabled people, and the accounting requirements for federal research grants. In all these cases—indeed, in most areas covered by government regulations—academics object not to the underlying purposes of the legislation or regulation but rather to the weighty and inappropriate burdens of compliance and reporting. At a time when governmental regulations of all kinds are under critical review, it may be appropriate to review those that bear on colleges and universities.[25]

If one great problem posed for higher education by federal government oversight and accountability is the number and cost of often inappropriate regulations applied to colleges and universities, another arises out of its understandable and laudable efforts to reduce the burden on the taxpayer of defaults on federal student loans. Happily, default rates have fallen substantially in the past few years, apparently due largely to more effective pursuit by the Department of Education of defaulters and of the institutions whose students show the highest rates.[26] But we know that most of the loan defaults are committed by students in proprietary vocational schools (some of which are simply engaged in fraud) and in some four-year and community colleges with large numbers of "at risk" students. A major step toward freeing reputable four-year colleges and universities, where default rates are very low, from unnecessary levels of review and accountability focused around loan defaults would be to distinguish in federal regulations between proprietary and nonprofit institutions and then direct the federal agencies to focus their attentions on institutions in both categories with records of high student defaults. Insofar as they do that and bring down default rates, we might anticipate that the federal government will have less incentive to take a larger or more direct role in the assessment and accreditation of colleges and universities.

Audits Rather than Assessments

I have earlier summarized the great number and variety of ways in which higher education is currently held accountable to the groups and institutions that are able to demand such accountability, either by law or by the resources they supply. These vary from the thousands of governmental regulations that apply to colleges and universities to the magazines and other publications that each institution sends out to its supporters to tell them what it is doing. Most of these forms of accountability will persist, though I would also hope and urge that the myriad regulations, so enormously expensive to administer, would be trimmed in number and reviewed for their applicability to institutions quite different in nature from those for whom they were written.

But it is to the bodies that currently "accredit" institutions of higher education that I wish to speak most directly. I have already pointed

out some of the shortcomings of the regional accrediting agencies—
their costs, their intrusiveness, the threat they pose to institutional
autonomy, their inherent tendency to apply common criteria to diverse institutions. Yet in principle they stand between government
and the institutions of higher education and so serve to certify to
government the basic legitimacy of the institutions they accredit. If
we are to recommend any radical departure from their current character and functions, we must offer an alternative that will perform
similar functions for discharging the accountability of colleges and
universities to the larger society.

The basic shortcoming of existing accrediting bodies, from which
all others flow, is their policy of developing broad criteria or standards to which all the institutions they accredit must conform,
whether or not those are acceptable or appropriate to the institution.
Moreover, armed with these general statements or standards, the visiting committees come to the institutions to "review" their practices
and to judge whether they should be accredited or not. In the course
of these reviews, these committees are not at all reticent about giving
what they call "advice" on a whole range of issues, reinforcing the
advice with firm warnings about what might happen to the institution if it is not accepted and acted on. The chief sanction they possess
is to recommend withdrawal of accreditation, but short of that, they
can postpone accreditation until evidence is forthcoming that the advice has been accepted. The withdrawal of accreditation effectively
precludes the awarding of grants or loans to the institution's students;
the postponement of accreditation alone can be devastating to the
reputation of the institution and prove a powerful reinforcement for
groups and interests inside the institution that would profit from the
proffered advice.

So there is clear evidence that some of the regional accrediting
bodies have gone very far toward playing a role—in my view an
illegitimate role—in the mission and governance of colleges and universities. This interference is greater in smaller and less well known
colleges and universities; the famous ones can defend their own autonomy more successfully. But even for institutions that are beyond
the threat of a loss of accreditation or even its delay, the accrediting
reviews are often a ritual to be endured, costing many hours of administrative time to prepare a "self-study" that is largely a document
of public relations devoted to showing just how strong and successful
the institution is and has been since its last review. And the visits
themselves are also largely ritualistic; the work of colleges and universities, even the smaller ones, is so varied and complex that no
group of academics could hope to make useful observations about

them on the basis of self-serving "self-studies" and carefully scheduled visits over a two-to-three-day period. The observations that are made in the reports of the committees are almost always either banal or irrelevant to the life of the institution.

If the current accreditations of colleges and universities are an odd combination of arrogant intervention and irrelevant ritualism, what could external accrediting bodies do that would strengthen rather than undercut the institution's own efforts at monitoring and improving its own practice? One answer is to urge that the regional and other accrediting bodies transform themselves or be transformed from organizations that purport to accredit the "quality" of the institution—its teaching and learning—into bodies that have the responsibility for determining whether the institution has in place procedures and practices that enable it to learn about itself, its weaknesses as well as its strengths, and is able to use that knowledge to address those weaknesses and overcome them. They would be changed from bodies that review and advise institutions to bodies that audit the institutions' own quality control policies and procedures. The analogy with financial auditing is clear: external financial auditing bodies chiefly serve to advise other external interested parties about the soundness of an institution's financial procedures; it ordinarily doesn't tell the institution what business it should be in, what its range of products should be, or whether its marketing division is effective. It describes how well the institution is looking after its own financial condition—and, among other things, how much it knows about its own financial processes and how well protected it is against theft and fraud.

The analogy is only an analogy; the intellectual life of a college or university may rest on its financial probity, but it is much more complex than its finances. The forms of an academic audit by an accrediting agency, as distinct from a "review," have still to be worked out. But at the least it would differ in focusing chiefly on the institution's own procedures for learning about and addressing its academic weaknesses. That, I believe, lies within the competence of external committees. They would still start with an institutional self-study, which now would present in detail what the institution does about quality control and improvement and what procedures are in place to subject those procedures to critical scrutiny from time to time. What the institution would be asked to report every five or ten years is evidence (largely embodied in formal procedures) that it has developed or is developing a culture of self-scrutiny and self-improvement. What institutions do along these lines may be as various as their character and missions, though I have already suggested some of the elements of internal review procedures that have been and might be adopted, with variations, by institutions of many different kinds.

On the whole, I believe with most other students of the subject, here and abroad, that American higher education as a system is the best in the world. But I also believe that many, perhaps most, colleges and universities do not attend adequately to the quality of their own work. They leave it to the academics that they hire to maintain that quality, as a product of their own norms and values, their competitive situation (which applies more to research than to teaching), and the sheer ability and talent of the teaching staff. These are not trivial forces and may even be the ultimate sources of the quality of the institution and the work it does. But in many institutions, there are tendencies toward mediocrity and other pathologies that these personal qualities do not adequately preclude. Teaching is not given the attention it deserves, is not done as effectively as it might be, or is not linked to research and scholarship as fully as it should be; the division of labor within the institution may reflect the strength of the guild of teachers or the traditions of a department more than the needs of the subject and its students; some graduate departments are producing far more Ph.D.'s than their markets can absorb; and so on. I believe that many institutions can and should be encouraged to improve their capacity to learn about and act on their own weaknesses and shortcomings. And the audits of accrediting bodies can be that encouragement. Moreover, I believe that these audits can be as tough and searching in their way as good external financial audits are in theirs. And an institution can be less worried about encroachments on its autonomy if the accrediting agency is not asking about its mission and governance but about its capacity to study itself and improve itself on the basis of what it learns. Egregious and persistent failures to meet those tests should face the ultimate sanction of the threat to withdraw accreditation, though I doubt that such sanctions will have to be applied any more frequently than they are currently by the regional accrediting agencies.

The issue is not what might lead to the withdrawal of accreditation from institutions, the overwhelming majority of which would meet any reasonable threshold criteria as institutions of higher education. The issue is what the relationship between a college and an accrediting agency should be. Should that relationship center around periodic conversations about whether and how the college has been trying to improve itself, as I believe, or should it center around the preparation of a report by a visiting committee in which it tells the host institution how it believes the institution should be functioning and governing itself, as now? Audits, in my view, are greatly superior to accreditation reviews in that while they focus on the institution's own efforts at improvement and strengthen those efforts, they can also serve the external accountability function, attesting to outside agencies and the federal government that the college or university in question is worthy to enroll students who get federal financial aid. In academic audits as recommended here, the two distinct functions—of supporting institutions while also judging them and reporting those judgments to outsiders—are not, as currently, at odds with each other; they are compatible. And that is a strong recommendation for the replacement of the current accreditation reviews with audits of the institution's own quality control procedures and activities.

If the regional (and similar) accrediting bodies come to have as their central function the administration of audits of the quality control procedures in place in their member colleges and universities, they can also develop the ancillary but important function of becoming clearinghouses for information about quality assurance, control, and improvement. This would put them squarely in the business of education, with their member institutions as colleagues and students. The accrediting bodies will in the course of their audits gather a large amount of information about how various institutions go about improving their work and improving their monitoring procedures as well. These bodies can disseminate this information through seminars and conferences, journals, and other means, at the same time building a body of knowledge that nowhere now exists on the effectiveness of various approaches to the improvement of quality.

There are problems with replacing reviews and advisories with academic audits as the main function of accrediting bodies of the kind I have described. The chief, in my view, is the tendency for what Aant Elzinga has called "epistemic drift," the tendency of institutions of all kinds to modify their character in response to social rewards and temptations. The academic community would have to be alert and guard against the tendency of agencies and committees charged with conducting audits of quality control procedures to broaden their charge and fall back into the habit of telling institutions how to improve themselves. Academia has its share—maybe more than its share—of people who do not feel the need to pursue the truth because they already have it. And such true believers, whatever the substance of their beliefs, have difficulty restraining their impulse to impose those beliefs on others. Armed with even the modest powers of accrediting agencies, such people on their boards, their staffs, or their review committees may not be content with the clear if modest function I have been describing for such agencies but will try to return them to their current much broader charge. A new constitution for these agencies must be clear enough to discourage that drift of function.

Assessment of Academic Performance

One objection to the recommendation for accreditation through audits of quality control procedures may be that such audits would not reveal the actual effectiveness of the colleges, their academic performance. Colleges and universities are increasingly the object of demands, often by state governments, for more and more evidence, preferably quantitative, bearing on their efficiency or effectiveness. This approach to the assessment of the quality of an education is to try to measure the effects of that education on individual students by testing their performance on various tasks and then aggregating individual student performance on these tests into "performance indicators." But such measures of academic "outputs" capture only a fraction—a small fraction—of the contributions of higher education to the life of students and the life of the society.

But why confine the assessment of the outcomes of higher education to what can be captured on objective tests of student performance? There are other ways to assess the impact of higher education, not just on students but on institutions and society as a whole. What large effects do we hope our systems of higher education will have on society? How do we weigh the effects of higher education on reducing levels of racial and ethnic prejudice, or enabling people to change their jobs, skills, and professions as the economy changes, or motivating people to enroll in continuing education throughout life, or enabling people to raise children who seek more schooling than their parents?

Do we use the school achievement rates of children twenty-five years after the graduation of their parents as performance indicators of the colleges and universities of 1970? How do we weigh the value to the society of the organizations created to protect the environment, defend battered wives, reform the criminal justice system, or help new immigrants or the emotionally disturbed—all the voluntary institutions outside of government that make life more civilized and compassionate, and all of them disproportionately led and staffed by college and university graduates? Are leadership or participation rates in those institutions to be used as performance indicators as well?

Education is a process pretending to be an outcome. That is what makes all measures of educational outcomes spurious. Our impact on our students can never be fully known; it emerges over their whole lifetimes and takes various forms at different points in their lives. Those effects are mixed up with many other forces and factors over which we in higher education have no control—and among these are the student's character and life circumstances. Moreover, our influence on their lives takes many different forms, the most important of which are unmeasurable. One of the major functions of higher education, which evades all measurement, is our ability to raise the horizons of our students, to encourage them to set their ambitions higher than if they had not come under our influence. Colleges and universities at their best teach students that they can actually have new ideas, ideas of their own rather than merely collections of ideas produced by others. That is not a conception of self very often gained in secondary school, and yet it lies at the heart of most of what people who gain a postsecondary education achieve in their lives. No formal assessment measures this increased self-confidence and belief in one's capacity to think originally and effectively, yet can we doubt that it is one of the great goods that attaches to a university education? And it is wrong and snobbish of us to think that it is only people like ourselves, professional academics and intellectuals, who possess this capacity. More and more we see the importance of initiative, originality, and the capacity to think in bold and fresh ways as a central element in success in the professions and in business enterprise. We do, at our best, teach people how to think and how to think more effectively, but whether they do so is a function of how well we communicate the novel idea that they can have novel ideas. How successfully they can put an idea into effect is a function not only of how they think but also of character, mind, habit, and life circumstances. The real and substantial effects of the experience of higher education extend over the whole lifetime of graduates and are inextricably entwined with other forces and experiences beyond our reach.

We can see the process of education and get a sense of the intelligence and energy that goes into it, but we cannot see very clearly what contributions universities are making to the life of our society, any more than we can measure the enduring influences of particular teachers on their students. But our inability to measure the outcomes of teaching does not preclude our learning about what the institution is doing well and what it is doing badly. And that is the work of internal accountability through the kinds of reviews and other procedures discussed here.

But if internal reviews and assessments are to be more accurate and fruitful than those done by outsiders, it is necessary that the institution subject itself and its units to serious and recurrent internal review, with real teeth and real consequences. The loss of institutional autonomy is both cause and consequence of the abdication of responsibility by colleges and universities for managing their own affairs. And preeminent among those affairs is the maintenance of the quality of their teaching and research.

Some Recommendations Regarding Institutional Accreditation

The "recognition" of the American Academy of Liberal Education by the Secretary of Education's National Advisory Committee on Accreditation as the accrediting agency for a group of (mostly) small liberal arts colleges is the first break with the monopoly that the six big regional agencies have held on the accreditation of credit-awarding and degree-granting colleges and universities. The American Academy challenged the regional agencies at a particularly vulnerable point: on the effectiveness of a single regional agency to accredit all the institutions in its region, from the biggest comprehensive research university to the smallest religiously linked liberal arts college, and to do that within the framework of rules, guidelines, and standards. However hard the regional agencies tried to accommodate diversity among their members, inevitably the common conceptions of higher education built into the rules and norms of the agency constrained the freedom of at least some of their members, and was a force tending to make the institutions more alike. This tendency was clearest where the accrediting agency was most activist, as in the region governed by the Western Association of Schools and Colleges.

I have already developed the view that accrediting bodies, whether regional or specialized, should shift their reviews away from assessments of the "quality" of the colleges under review toward audits of the procedures the institutions have in place to monitor and improve their own teaching and learning. But in addition, accrediting agencies need not cover all the various higher education institutions in their region; they might better be more specialized to include similar kinds of institutions—for example, comprehensive universities or private liberal arts colleges. Moreover, it is not clear why these agencies need to be regional if they are specialized around a given kind of institution. There is much to be said for an agency concerned with auditing the quality control and maintenance procedures of liberal arts colleges across the country, for any institution that chooses to be a member. Such an agency not only can organize the visits made by audit committees but also, as suggested earlier, might also become a clearing-house for the collection and dissemination of ideas about how such institutions can reinforce their quality control procedures, procedures that probably would not be applicable to research universities twenty times bigger with large graduate and professional schools.

Thus my own recommendations for the reform and redesign of institutional accreditation (which only partly overlap with those of our essay on accountability) has these elements:

1. Accrediting bodies should take as their main task the auditing of the procedures and activities in their members' institutions that are devoted to the maintenance and improvement of academic quality.

2. Accrediting bodies should add to that function service as a clearing-house of information, drawn partly but not exclusively from the experience of their audit committees, on how to improve academic quality. They would thus themselves become educational institutions, giving advice but not orders to their member institutions.

3. Accrediting bodies should no longer attempt to provide advice across the whole spectrum of institutions but should be organized around distinct types of institutions—the Carnegie typology of colleges and universities would be a good place to start.

4. The principle of voluntary membership in an accrediting agency must be maintained. Alternative accrediting bodies should be "recognized" by the Department of Education if they serve a legitimate function and are not devices for escaping serious audits of their quality control procedures.

5. The federal government should accredit nonprofit and proprietary institutions through different mechanisms and should focus its efforts on the minority of institutions in both categories whose students have high default rates on their student loans.

6. Specialized accreditation should be folded into the audits of the institutions of which they are part.

Conclusion

It is an irony of our current discussions in America about accountability of higher education that most of the talk has centered on external accountability—for example, efforts to develop a national coordinating body for the regional accrediting agencies—while there has been much less discussion of internal accountability, the ways institutions monitor their own quality. The irony lies in the fact that we may have more external accountability than we need (though not all of it of the right kind), whereas many institutions do not have adequate internal accountability systems in place and functioning. Therefore, in conclusion, I want to return to the heart of our subject, the quality of education found in our colleges and universities: how to improve it while making those institutions more accountable to their external supporters and internal participants.

Ultimately, it rests on academics, their departments, and their institutions to sustain a high level of academic quality in teaching and research; outsiders can do little more than assure themselves and to insist that creative energies are employed by the institutions toward that end. Quality in teaching is there to see in the engagement of senior learners (teachers) with junior learners (students) in common intellectual pursuits. And that, after all, is what higher education is supposed to be about. Quality control in higher education is a matter of constantly searching for evidence that intelligence, energy, and creativity are being put into teaching or, conversely, to discovering where teaching has degenerated into dreary routines boring to teacher and student alike. Where they find the latter, academic authorities need to intervene, not necessarily to put things right themselves, but to encourage and reward, and even require, improvement by the teacher in question. Every university now has some office for instructional improvement, too often used only by teaching assistants or newly appointed staff. It is no infringement on academic freedom to make use of these resources by teachers more common and, in specific cases, mandatory. And institutions need to be accountable to students, students' parents, and other parts of their support communities for the procedures they have in place to monitor and maintain the quality of their teaching.

Poor teaching is not always the result of ineptitude or boredom. The causes may vary widely: alcoholism, clinical depression, and serious marital problems occur among academics just as they do in the general population—and maybe with greater frequency. And here we are talking not about unimaginative or routinized teaching but about problems of a deeper kind that may interfere with effective teaching. Solutions to some kinds of failures by teachers may be beyond the reach of "instructional improvement" and require personal counseling, a leave of absence, or even separation from the university. And other options may be available to the institution through its health and psychiatric services. These rare events are among the most difficult and most delicate problems that colleges and universities face. But it is no kindness to either teacher or students to turn a blind eye on them. And an external academic audit should want to ask what procedures an institution has in place for dealing with these most difficult cases of faculty failure.

Poor teaching, whatever its sources, needs to be identified if it is to be addressed. Students and colleagues may help in identifying it but are less helpful in doing anything about it. On that score, there is no substitute for strong academic administrators, department chairs, and deans. They have broader responsibility and can act in the name of the institution. Of course, they must work closely with the academic senate to avoid any suggestion that actions in support of teaching are convenient covers for sanctions against troublesome teachers. And all parties must be compassionate, out of regard both for the individual and for the community of which all are part. But they must also have in mind the interests of the students, sometimes generations of them, who find themselves forced to study under teachers who may be doing them little good or even more harm than good.

We know good teaching when we see it; we need to institutionalize arrangements for looking for it and also for learning where it is poor or worse. What happens then will differ in different colleges and universities; institutional cultures differ, and academic authority is differently located in different institutions. But academic authority, wherever it is located, justifies itself in part by finding ways to encourage liveliness, innovation, and creativity in teaching, in taking steps to recreate it where it has declined, and in acting even more decisively in the small number of cases where that is required. And academic audits administered by external accrediting agencies can strengthen academic authority internally by insisting that it show evidence for a culture of inquiry and self-criticism, one that leads to action toward a stronger and more effective institution.

Postscript: The Information Revolution and Its Implications for Accountability

I have been talking about colleges and universities of a kind that have existed in the West for 800 years, in North America for over 350 years, and in the familiar form of research universities in the United States for about 100 years. I have left for last any consideration of the implications of the information revolution currently under-way for colleges and universities and for their accountability. The authors of the essay on accountability reflected on this question and commissioned an informative report by a specialist on the impact to date of new forms of instructional technology on higher education.[27] But we declined to address the issue in our report chiefly because that revolution is in its earliest stages, and the nature of its future impact on higher education is still quite unclear. However unclear its lineaments, I believe that impact will be very large. I believe it will make learning at a distance much more common, and raise questions for many institutions of how they might best teach various parts of their curriculum, or revise their curriculum to accord with the new modes of instruction.

One clear effect of the new forms of instruction made possible by new technologies is that in some subjects they reduce the importance of teachers and students being in the same place at the same time, as increasing amounts of teaching are carried electronically. This could either complicate or facilitate the efforts institutions make to monitor and maintain the quality of teaching and learning. It certainly will make more difficult the tasks of accrediting institutions which provide instruction to students thousands of miles away, many of whom are interested in gaining skills and knowledge rather than grades or additional academic credentials. Accountability in higher education assumes a distinguishable institution with recognizable boundaries, employing an academic staff with identifiable qualifications to instruct a defined population of students enrolled for some kind of credential. But the new technologies threaten many of those assumptions, and begin to blur the distinction between "higher education" and "lifelong learning." The latter, however much to be welcomed, will be more difficult to assess and accredit or hold accountable to anyone.

Notes

1. Patricia Graham, Richard Lyman, and Martin Trow, "Accountability of Colleges and Universities: An Essay," Columbia University, October 1995.

2. Among these had been the collapse of the Council on Postsecondary Education (COPA), the sharp conflict between the Department of Education in the Bush administration and some of the regional accrediting bodies over what appeared to be the politicization of the criteria for accreditation, and somewhat threatening elements of the Education Act of 1992, particularly Part H, which seemed to introduce the federal and state governments too closely into accreditation.

3. We are especially indebted to The Andrew W. Mellon Foundation.

4. The nature and detail of required reports can and often do have effects on institutions quite apart from the policies they are designed to implement. The heavy burden of the many and lengthy reports that marks the current system of central government funding of British universities has effects on them over and above the problems for British universities generated by central government policies and cost cutting.

5. A case can be made that our two most successful federal programs in higher education—the Morrill Land Grant Act of 1863 and the GI Bill after World War II—were both marked by relatively light oversight and little ac-

countability for the large sums expended. Both were attended by a measure of corruption in the administration of the programs. But most people would see the gains to American society from both these programs as far outweighing the costs, both the legitimate costs and those of corruption. I believe that this was true in both cases less as a result of considered policy than of the small size of the federal bureaucracy available for oversight at both times. Nevertheless, the examples do raise questions about the bearing of accountability, of its nature and detail, on the effectiveness of public policy, perhaps especially in higher education.

6. *Economist*, February 24, 1996, p. 20.

7. Wilfred M. McClay, "Clio in 2013: The Writing and Teaching of History in the next Twenty Years," *Academic Questions*, vol. 7, no. 1, Winter 1993–94, p. 28.

8. See for example, Guy Neave, *The Core Functions of Government: Six European Perspectives on a Shifting Educational Landscape* (Amsterdam: National Advisory Council, June 1995); Martin Trow, "Reflections on Higher Education Reform in the 1990s: The Case of Sweden," in Thorsten Nybom, ed., *Studies in Higher Education and Research* (Stockholm: Council for Studies in Higher Education, 1993–94); and the essays in Guy Neave and Frans Van Vught, *Prometheus Bound: The Changing Relationship between Government and Higher Education in Western Europe* (Oxford: Pergamon Press, 1991).

9. See Guy Neave, "The Politics of Quality: Developments in Higher Education in Western Europe, 1992–1994, *European Journal of Education*, vol. 29, no. 2, 1994, pp. 115–134; and Frans Van Vught and Don Westerheuden, "Towards a General Model of Quality Assessment in Higher Education," *Higher Education*, vol. 28, 1994, pp. 355–371.

10. There are at least two other conceptions of accountability and to whom it is owed. One is that accountability is owed to all the people, groups, and institutions that are or will be affected by what the accountable actors are doing; this conception emphasizes accountability for the consequences of action. But since higher education ultimately affects everybody directly or indirectly, that idea dilutes the obligation of accountability beyond enforcement. Still another conception looks at accountability as a set of norms, and it is those notions of what is owed to whom that determine the obligations of accountability. These different conceptions of accountability give rise to controversy and conflict.

11. I include the *moral* aspect of accountability to stress the obligations of higher education to groups and individuals who are part of a support community but who are not in the narrow sense stakeholders. One example might be foreign scholars; another might be secondary school teachers.

12. See note 1.

13. As Robert Merton taught us many years ago, norms have sanctions behind them; otherwise they are just hopes or ideals.

14. In public university systems, this question often raises issues of institutional autonomy; in big research universities and university systems, the question often arises between governing boards and their chief administrative officers.

15. For a fuller discussion of the motivations and consequences of central government policy toward higher education in the U.K., see Martin Trow, "Managerialism and the Academic Profession: The Case of England," *Higher Education Policy*, vol. 7, no. 2, 1994, pp.11–18.

16. On the Continent, academics have had something of the status of civil servants and, with obvious exceptions in dictatorships, were by virtue of their special work accorded a considerable measure of academic freedom in universities that were not as autonomous as in the United States and Britain.

17. Of course, these concerns for personal and group responsibility for behavior were and are not confined to "gentlemen." For a recent discussion of these issues in Victorian England, see Gertrude Himmelfarb, *The De-Moralization of Society* (New York: Vintage Books, 1995), pp. 143–169.

18. I am skeptical about widespread claims of a deep decline of trust in higher education in America since that is a convenient and indeed almost a necessary condition for introducing greater regulation by way of more formal accountability. There is considerable evidence in various measures of tangible confidence and support that trust in American colleges and universities has not declined in recent years as is widely assumed, though there is no doubt that it occupies a different position in the public mind than it did before, say, 1966. Over the decade 1981–1991, total enrollments continued to grow (by 14%) despite the fact that colleges and universities were raising their tuition rates much more rapidly (by 54% in constant dollars) than the consumer price index; during that decade, the differential in income between college and high school graduates grew very sharply, by 88%; private giving to colleges and universities increased by 66% in constant dollars; federal support for academic research increased by 53% in real terms between 1981 and 1991; the number of foreign students in American colleges and universities grew by 31%; and measures of "satisfaction" in surveys of students and recent graduates have not declined in recent years (Ross Gotler, "Indicators of Confidence," report prepared for the Accountability Project, Columbia University, March 2, 1995.) But between 1981 and 1995, the proportion of people who expressed "a great deal of confidence" in "major educational institutions such as colleges and universities" fell from 37% to 27% in a national poll, though it has been rising slightly since then (Harris Poll 1995, no. 17, March 6, 1995). In this poll, higher education ranked third "on the list of institutions in which the public has the most confidence. . . . The public's loss of faith in higher education lags behind its loss of faith in institutions on the whole." There is certainly room for debate on this issue and its implications; see Graham, Lyman, and Trow, "Accountability," pp. 3–5.

19. Louis Hartz, *The Liberal Tradition in America* (New York: Harcourt Brace, 1955).

20. An important exception was the situation in nineteenth-century Germany. There "the condition that counteracted the oligarchic tendencies of university senates was the competition among the great number of universities within the large and expanding academic market of the politically decentralized German-speaking areas of Central Europe. Competition among universities checked the development of oppressive academic authority within the

individual universities. As long as these circumstances lasted, a situation existed where effective use of resources could be combined with great freedom of the scientific community." Joseph Ben-David, *The Scientist's Role in Society* (Chicago: University of Chicago Press, 1971, 1984), p. 123.

21. See Terry W. Hartle, "The Battle over Governmental Regulation of Academe," *College Board Review*, Summer 1994.

22. Graham, Lyman, and Trow, "Accountability," p. 21.

23. Gerhard Casper, "Government and the University" (speech), Stanford University, April 19, 1994.

24. Derek Bok, *The Cost of Talent* (New York: Free Press, 1993), pp. 176–177.

25. Hartle, "Battle over Government Regulation." See also "The Regulatory Environment for University Science," Council on Governmental Relations, National Association of College and University Business Officers, Washington, D.C., April 1992; and Andrea Baird and S. Dawn Robinson, "The Array of Federal Regulations Facing Independent Colleges and Universities," National Institute of Independent Colleges and Universities, Washington, D.C., January 1992.

26. "The rate of borrowers defaulting on student loans dropped to 11.6 percent in the 1993 fiscal year, the latest year for which figures are available. That was the lowest rate since official reporting on the default rate began in 1988. The rate has steadily declined since 1990, when it peaked at 22.4 percent." "Steep Drop in Rate of Student Loan Default," *New York Times*, January 24, 1996, p. A12.

27. Pamela H. Atkinson, "Distance Education in Institutions of Higher Learning in the United States: A Background Paper for the Study on Accountability of Colleges and Universities," Columbia University, October 1995.

THE PRESIDENCY

University Presidents—Then and Now

HAROLD T. SHAPIRO

> The position of a university president has certain prism-like qualities in the sense that a change in one's perspective or position yields somewhat different colors.

THERE IS much misinformation, mystery, and nostalgia abroad regarding the work of contemporary university presidents.[1] Are they giants of intellectual vision, full-time fund-raisers, unprincipled propagandists, or "merely" thoughtful managers of some of society's most important and successful institutions? In this essay, I have attempted an initial characterization of the changing nature of a singular—and some would say odd—occupation, the presidency of an American university.[2] On the one hand, this position involves the nurturance, safeguarding, and sponsorship of a venerable, even sacred, public trust. It is, at least in part, an ethical endeavor in that the president provides leadership to an institution that deals with matters society believes to be important—an enterprise based on the belief that the future is of ethical significance. On the other hand, the position also involves its share of shallow, frivolous, sentimental, and occasionally demeaning activity. Whatever else it may be, the presidency of a university is a very human endeavor and therefore a very humbling and humorous experience. This essay is written, therefore, with an approach to its subject that is both serious and lighthearted. I hope you will recognize which is which! I begin with some background material.

Ostensibly similar institutions—that is, organizations with broadly similar inputs and outputs—are often structured in somewhat different fashions in the sense that authority, responsibility, and leadership expectations, both de jure and de facto, may be distributed in different ways. Thus although contemporary British and European universities exhibit many similarities to their American counterparts, the role, authority, and responsibility of the administrative heads of these institutions often differ. The disparities stem principally from the particular history and social role of higher education in these different localities. In particular, it is worth noting that the distinction and authority of the American university presidents and their capacity for effective leadership, however limited, are considerably greater than those of their European counterparts. This stems, of course, not from any greater passion, vision, courage, determination, intelligence, or commitment but from a set of historical traditions and institutional arrangements that invest the American university presidency with considerably greater authority over both the allocation of resources and the making of senior appointments. Potentially, then, the American university president has a greater opportunity to mold the character and direction of the enterprise than his or her European colleagues.

When I speak of university presidents, I am referring to the administrative heads of these institutions of higher education, who may or may not be faculty members as well. To borrow a convenient phrase from corporate vocabulary—always a dangerous move in academic circles—university presidents are their institutions' CEO, although in contemporary times they often face more constraints on their authority than their corporate counterparts. All modern universities have such a position, but titles vary from place to place. Chancellor, vice chancellor, rector, and other titles can reflect varying expectations and responsibilities, but often they merely signify some local preference or historical accident and have little operational significance.[3] In any case, the particular package of roles that has come to define the American college presidency is, in a comparative context, quite distinct. In other venues, the administrative head of the university may, for example, be a "nonacademic" civil servant or a faculty member elected for an intentionally short time (the responsibilities being too great or too trivial for a longer term of office) and have a different portfolio of rights, responsibilities, and expectations. The focus of this essay, however, is the American university presidency, how it has evolved over the years, and where its challenges and opportunities are found today.

The nature of the American university presidency—its particular bundle of authority and responsibility—grew directly out of the special history of American higher education. American universities began not as student-faculty "communes" or guilds of masters but as community-based efforts to gather together faculty and students for particular civic purposes. Moreover, in the earliest years, the president may have been the only senior faculty member! As a result, ultimate responsibility and authority have always resided in an external board, and the president appointed by this external board became, among other roles, the campus-based representative of this external authority. The U.S. college president, however, has always served not only the needs and objectives of this external authority (often focused on fiscal responsibility, tranquillity, and particular notions of virtue and civic responsibility) but increasingly has represented to this external authority the needs and objectives of faculty, students, and the worlds of education and scholarship (often focused on the growth of programs and the need for academic freedom, autonomy, and independence).

Despite much rhetoric to the contrary, members of the external board generally show little sustained interest in the needs and aspirations of the members of the academic community, and vice versa. Consequently, the role includes representing and promoting external interests to the university community as well as university interests to the board and therefore always encompasses important interpretive, mediative, and integrative facets. In other words, there has always been the necessity for the American university president to champion the interests and aspirations of the academic community to the broader society and to play a role in ensuring that the academic community is in touch with society's interests and needs. Indeed, the president was expected not only to reflect and project (promote) the character and direction of the institution (its values and goals) to both internal and external constituencies but also to resolve any conflicting demands that arose. This particular role took on a new urgency in the immediate post–World War II decades with the increasingly pervasive role of the scientific ethic on the nation's campuses—when it was often thought that a certain isolation from social and political influences and yet a certain level of resource entitlement were *both* required for the university to achieve its fullest flower and thus meet its obligations to society. As the university community has become an ever more complex tapestry of ideas, values, commitments, and educational and scholarly themes, this has become a more complex, more difficult, riskier, and, correspondingly, potentially more rewarding responsibility.

In the American context, therefore, a key leadership challenge for the university president is to ensure that the external governing board, in both public and private universities, comes to view the education and research programs of the university and the internal intellectual culture necessary to support these (which need nurturing as well as autonomy) as providing a very valuable social product—one well worth considerable investment despite many risks. In the context of a modern university, this task is rarely easy as many people wonder why a public or private community should exuberantly support, respect, honor, and treasure a set of activities designed in part to be critical of just those arrangements within which most, if not all, members of the governing board, including the president, have prospered.[4] Yet it is a fundamental responsibility of the university to question society's current structures and to construct, entertain, and test alternative visions—new ways to understand the natural world, to organize society's institutions, and to rethink its fundamental values. Of course, the modern university also has many functions—including education, research, and even entertainment programs of various stripes—that directly serve the existing needs of society. Nevertheless, the issues of balance, control, and direction of the educational and scholarly agenda provide a continual source of potential tension between the campus-based community and both the external governing board and other external patrons of the university such as the government. As a result, an important and ongoing task for the president of an American university—and the allies that he or she must mobilize—is to provide sufficient leadership to ensure that both the patrons and the members of the academic community, each with their own specific preferences, not only continue to understand and to value the social product of the university but also commit themselves to the conditions necessary to generate maximum social dividends: free inquiry, intellectual autonomy, the acceptance of an organized and disciplined skepticism, thoughtful and considered debate, a long-term perspective, cross-subsidization of programs, and on and on. Given the need of the contemporary university to serve society as both faithful servant and thoughtful critic, controversy—both internal and external—is difficult to avoid, and it falls, in part, to the president to prevent such controversy from either distorting the internal intellectual culture or seriously undermining external support.

The leadership required of a university president in these respects is not the mere task of managing to placate the various interests involved until they reach some type of sullen agreement. It is rather the type of moral act that involves not only the assertion of a "vision" of the contemporary academic enterprise and its legitimate social functions but also the energy to pursue this vision and the capacity to inspire others—including faculty—to support this remarkable venture despite the inevitable criticism that arises when an institution's success often includes leaving the familiar for new territory. It is difficult to say how many contemporary presidents meet this challenge successfully. We would do well to understand, however, that the scope, size, and complexity of the American university often make it difficult to mobilize enough energy to lift one's vision beyond the demanding tasks of management to the essential task of leadership: shaping the character and direction of the enterprise. This is especially true in an environment where neither the academic nor the non-academic community expects or desires such leadership from the president. But as Nannerl O. Keohane pointed out over a decade ago, exciting and effective presidential leadership usually involves a creative collaboration between the president and other key members of the academic community, including faculty, trustees, and students.[5] The process of articulating problems, proposing solutions, making decisions, and generally ensuring that appropriate new arrangements replace existing ones is therefore a shared rather than a solitary activity. It is shared by those members of the academic community who have a passionate commitment to the ultimate purposes of the enterprise.

At times all this goes quite well: internal and external interests are sufficiently overlapping, and the president and others have the necessary "vision," courage, and commitment and also successfully mediate between and among internal and external constituencies in a manner that sustains the intellectual environment. At other times, of course, various groups, either internal or external, are dissatisfied and expect the president to do something—anything—to establish a more satisfactory state of affairs. On one issue, however, all sides nearly always agree: it is the president's responsibility somehow to mobilize the resources (from students, alumni, government, or whomever) necessary to accomplish the work of the institution.

A quite different expectation is rooted in the close association of the early American colleges with the aims and aspirations of the various religious denominations. The university president was "endowed" with the expectation that he, like some of the early Oxford tutors, would see to the appropriate moral development of the student. Moreover, he would be expected to ensure that members of the faculty had the "right" moral commitments. Indeed, in colonial and nineteenth-century America, the college president was often specifically identified with the capstone course in moral philosophy, which was frequently his responsibility to offer to graduating seniors in order that they leave the college with an adequate dose of "right thinking." As a result, presidents of this earlier era seem enshrined, "reigning" from above in our collective memory not only as Renaissance figures at "home" in many disciplines (as opposed to simply playing the intellectual gadfly!) but as ethical leaders on their campuses as well as on the broader civic stage.

In contrast, today's American university president in our contemporary public imagination does not choose or cannot afford to be the philosopher king (or queen) of his (or her) institution, let alone society at large. The new scale and scope of these institutions require, for good or ill, the careful balancing and blending of a wide range of "interests" rather than the striking of a particular moral or prophetic pose. In fact, the moral imagination of the American public has always been very skeptical of the words of the "explaining classes" (priests, professors, and the like) or indeed of authorities of almost any sort. Moreover, in recent years, the reverence for authority, for good or ill, has decreased even further, and if contemporary college presidents do capture the public imagination at all, it is often the result of perceived moral, social, or political failure. In this latter respect, however, many of my less well-remembered nineteenth-century colleagues and many other contemporary "authorities" have received the same reception. Finally, there are simply many more university presidents (and other "voices") about these days, and their individual influence may have become somewhat more diffuse for this reason alone.

Memory, no matter how inaccurate, is a wonderful thing, making it much easier for us to imagine some long-departed university president as engulfed in the flowing robes and farsighted vision of the prophets who warned us of the error of our ways or mobilized entire institutions (however peripheral to society's concerns) to a new level of understanding and a new or renewed set of commitments. As a result, even a judicious and thoughtful combination of understanding, values, courage, and fairness in balancing the many obligations and "interests" of today's institutions of higher education—a significant accomplishment for any contemporary university leader—may be no match for the more prophetic figures that reside in our imaginations and had a clear notion of what was right for almost everyone. Nevertheless, some of my earlier predecessors were genuinely heroic figures who did mobilize or transform entire institutions. I will return to the moral responsibilities of the contemporary college or university president as I see them, but first let me take a moment to examine how others, in previous eras, have seen the job.[6]

Seeking usually to *prescribe* rather than to *describe* a president's duties, several students of the office have been quite clear, if rather limited, in their views. "A university president is supposed to go down town and get the money. He is not supposed to have ideas on public affairs; that is what the trustees are for. He is not supposed to have ideas on education; that is what the faculty is for. He is supposed to go down town and get the money." So, at least, opined one author in *Harper's* in 1939.[7]

The legendary William Rainey Harper of Chicago expressed himself in somewhat more edifying terms: "How does the president of a university spend his time?" he asked. And answered, "Largely in seeking ways and means to enable this or that professor to carry out some plan which he has deeply at heart—a plan, it may be, for research and investigation, or for improving the work of instruction." In Harper's view, "the office of the college president is an office of service." And he rightly recognized the consequence that "everything good or bad which connects itself with service is associated with this office."[8]

Certainly, alongside the high ideal of service, we find such pronouncements on the college president as "For one purpose is he really selected and coached: he must develop proper skill and tact in securing large legacies, gifts, or legislative appropriations" (this, rather poignantly, from the President of Adelphi College in 1906).[9] And Harper himself notes (in a paper written in 1904 but published posthumously) that "a superficial observer will find much to substantiate the very common accusation that the college president is professionally a prevaricator."[10] In this latter respect, Harper may have had in mind the differences that can arise between the private beliefs and sentiments of a particular university president and the opinions that he or she may feel comfortable expressing in public. For many presidents, public expression may be "constrained" to cases where the perceived benefits exceed both the expected costs of being misunderstood and the anticipated penalties imposed for expressing unpopular opinions. Among the highly conflicting characterizations of the presidency, Princeton's Harold Dodds's measured view strikes a welcome note: "The only course is to accept it for what it is, a queer vocation, infested with worries but rich in satisfactions and opportunities."[11]

University presidents have also been described in various "academic novels," many of them written by faculty members. Once in a great while in these venues we read of presidents who are modest, self-effacing, and dedicated to their university. More commonly we encounter presidents with serious failings of one kind or another. We meet presidents filled with vanity and ambition, whose behavior is arrogant, aloof, and haughty, presidents who sponsor deeply flawed academic programs, presidents who oppose all new ideas, presidents who are unable to deal with student protesters, and even presidents who lead sexually unconventional lives. On the fictional front, even "good" presidents—those protecting faculty interests—are often dismissed for their efforts by various heathens pursuing other agendas!

Then and Now

Whether today's chief executives of universities do their jobs better or worse than their predecessors may be a moot point. First, the answer probably does not matter. The important issue is whether university presidents today could do a better job. Second, this question of comparing past to present is probably unanswerable, since the nature of the institutions themselves, the environment within which they are operating, the resource base available, and the civic objectives they pursue have changed in such significant ways. Specifically, in the past century, the scale and scope of the institutions have been transformed almost beyond recognition, as has the secondary school system that supplies the students. It is helpful to recall that even by 1850, the average American college had an enrollment well under one hundred students, and scarcely 1% of white males aged 15 to 20 attended college. Moreover, the nation's secondary school system had yet to be fully established.

Compared to the nineteenth-century American college or university, contemporary higher education features, among other characteristics, increased size, scope, and responsibility; new curricula in engineering, science, social science, applied science, and the humanities; more serious preparation for advanced (graduate) education; a much greater commitment to graduate and professional programs; a discipline-based (and professionalized) organization of the faculty and curriculum; a new focus on innovation and critical thinking; and a novel concept of the structure and aims of liberal education. Finally, over the past century, American colleges and universities have evolved from a trustees-plus-president "imperium" to a more faculty-based hegemony to a somewhat more broadly based sovereignty that includes government (state and federal) and students.

The most important of these changes has been the rising influence of the scientific ethic and the related and dramatic shift in our expectations regarding the nature of undergraduate education. This has changed the role of universities in a manner that has had a direct impact on the roles and responsibilities of American college and university presidents. With respect to undergraduate education, the focus has shifted from the promotion and nourishment of a particular set of values and traditions to the development of cognitive and technical skills and from a rather narrow Renaissance and humanist curriculum to one that is much more open and speculative. As a result, the aim of a university education, especially undergraduate education, has moved to the production of one particular character type, quite different than the one previously sought. New values and commitments have displaced older ones, and in the process, sharp changes have occurred in attitudes toward the relative importance of such issues as the role of authority of all types (including that of university presidents), access to higher education, the role of traditional values, the uses of reason, the social function of innovation and new ways of thinking, and the appropriate overall relationship among liberal, vocational, and professional education. In short, the balance has shifted perceptibly from tradition and conviction, on the one hand, to innovation, skepticism, and tolerance, on the other.

In this respect, it is important to recollect once again that the curriculum of universities in nineteenth-century America, although slowly broadening to include science, history, and vernacular literature, still reflected the basic notions of the Renaissance and humanist curriculum that had been imported into colonial America. This tradition, we should remember, placed very little emphasis on speculative and critical philosophy, preferred rhetoric over logic, and focused on the aesthetic qualities of the text, a very particular sense of virtue, and a moral philosophy that emphasized self-control, obedience, and deference to authority. It was a humanist education that focused on the Bible and classical literature with a passing exposure to Renaissance art and literature. What is also striking about this approach was that the same curriculum was considered optimal both for "liberal arts students" and for the professional training of public servants and clergy. In any case, innovation and critical thinking were devalued or ignored. How different this is from the free, open, and thoughtful debate now expected or the prevalence of noncoercive deliberative and critical practices that we now find—to say nothing of the novel idea that the university must be a center of the development of new knowledge of all kinds. For many nineteenth-century American university presidents, this new environment and transformed academic culture would have represented both a difficult challenge and an unfamiliar moral space.

All this, together with the changing demographics of the student body and the changing relative importance of various revenue streams, has also led in recent decades to the increasing importance of a continuously enlarging central bureaucracy. This qualitatively new dependence on the central administration was, for most members of the university community, an unwelcome but apparently unavoidable or even genuinely tragic evolutionary step. The lack of alternative proposals has not prevented what is often a kind of sullen hostility to this development as well as to the members of the academic community or outsiders who accept appointments as administrators. The most common response of faculty to the news that a colleague has moved to an administrative post is that they must, until that very moment, have overestimated the person's IQ! Because of such attitudes, you may see many a former faculty member who is now a university president looking back with nostalgia at his or her previous work. In many cases, a somewhat grateful but rather reserved (suspicious?) relationship develops between the faculty and the administration. On the one hand, the faculty—quite understandably—are grateful that they do not have to trouble themselves with this kind of work and yet still may be the recipients of financial and other support such as protection of their academic freedom. On the other hand, they resent the fact that resources of any kind have to be devoted to such tasks and fear that sooner or later the faculty's aspirations may not be adequately understood or supported by the central resource allocators—chair, dean, provost, or president.

It is important to recall, however, that this new relationship of faculty with the central administration—which exists, as the modern university does, both to serve and to lead—is qualitatively much different from the "moral dependence" that reigned in the nineteenth century. This new dependence is designed to relieve faculty of administrative chores (new and old)—remember that nineteenth-century faculty meetings were devoted primarily to student discipline—and to focus responsibility for relationships with trustees and other external patrons as well as for resource mobilization in the hands of others. In most cases, it is no longer even imagined that this dependence encompasses guidance from the president or trustees on moral issues. Yet it is important to note that on certain moral issues (for example, South African divestment, defense of the values supporting the university's intellectual culture, affirmative action), leadership may still fall from time to time to the president and the trustees, who may themselves be responding to external pressures of one kind or another. This newfangled codependence between the faculty and the administration, in which a wide variety of necessary administrative chores are delegated to a cadre of functionaries, has been abetted by the increasingly specialized and professionalized faculty (self-regulating by discipline), which has in many cases left effective faculty governance and many other communitywide issues in shambles. What remains in many cases, as others have pointed out, is active competition among the various specialized departments. This only serves to increase the influence of the central administration, whose members look more and more like taskmasters.

It is now difficult to recall that in its early years, the administration of a U.S. college was a model of simplicity, as was the college itself. There were few administrative tasks and no separate cadre of administrators. The simplicity was in good part the result of very small scale, sparse budgets, and narrow curricula. These characteristics also permitted every detail of the administration to remain under the direct scrutiny of the president, who also had time to maintain a significant academic role. Among the earliest purely administrative functions were those of the librarian, who might also serve as bursar, treasurer, and business manager. At the turn of the twentieth century, the entire administration of many colleges consisted of the president, the registrar, a bursar, a librarian, and a part-time secretary. Growth in size, scope, and complexity put an end to this!

Why look back, then, at an enterprise of such different scope? For one thing, I am curious, but before I make broad generalizations about changes in the "character" of the American college presidency, a review of the archival record might help articulate more carefully just what, in fact, *was* the job of a college or university president. Let us try, first, to answer the question of what specific tasks filled the working days of a nineteenth-century college or university president. Have those tasks changed significantly for the contemporary incumbents of these positions?

Then

The initial research I have undertaken has been an attempt to characterize the nature of some of the distinctive issues and activities that occupied the professional lives of earlier college presidents. I have focused on a handful of mostly nineteenth-century figures who loom large in the mythology of the college presidency—names that come to mind when the claim is made that "there were giants on the earth in those days." More specifically, I have tried, through the use of archival material, to get a more accurate understanding of what university-related issues occupied the minds and time schedules of some of my distinguished predecessors. In particular, I have begun by studying some of the available material on Presidents Wayland (of Brown), Eliot (of Harvard), Angell (of Michigan), and Wilson (of Princeton). There were, of course, other nineteenth-century "giants" —White (at Cornell), Gilman (at Johns Hopkins), Tappan (at Michigan), and others—but I have not yet had the opportunity to review the archival material on these leaders, distinguished and otherwise. This essay must therefore be considered work in process. One final comment before presenting some of the outcomes of the archival research: the quantity and quality of the actual surviving archival material varies a great deal, and the overall power of the inferences I am able to offer, therefore, is not as high as I would like. Nevertheless, there is some real information here that has at the very least improved my understanding and perspective on the work of my predecessors. With respect to the current situation of American university presidents, I have relied on my own characterization of their contemporary role.

For the purposes of this essay, then, I have focused my attention on four past presidents: Francis Wayland, president of Brown University from 1827 to 1855; James Angell, president of the University of Michigan from 1871 to 1909; Charles Eliot, president of Harvard University from 1869 to 1909; and Woodrow Wilson, president of Princeton University from 1902 to 1910. Each of these men made a distinguished mark on his institution, often reforming the curriculum dramatically and in the process substantially transforming the institution's educational mission or self-image. Moreover, in each case, the perceived leadership of these educators extended beyond the campus to the community, the state, and even the nation. With the help of research colleagues using archival materials at the four institutions, I have sought to gain some understanding of the day-to-day lives of these giants of the past—not necessarily the grand educational philosophies they promulgated and more occasionally implemented, but the tasks and concerns that occupied their daily working lives.[12]

Before beginning to detail these, however, it is extremely important to consider rather more specifically a contextual factor noted earlier, the size of the institutions these leaders led. When Francis Wayland became president of Brown in 1827, the school employed three faculty members; at his retirement almost thirty years later, Brown boasted a faculty of eight. At the University of Michigan, thirty-three faculty members taught 1,100 students when Angell arrived in 1871. By 1909, when he retired, there were four hundred faculty and 5,400 undergraduate students at the university. Harvard at the time of Charles Eliot's inauguration in 1869 was a university of 23 faculty members and 529 students. On his retirement forty years later, there were 160 faculty and 2,200 students. One of Woodrow Wilson's extraordinary actions at Princeton was to double the size of the faculty within six years of assuming office in 1902; his hiring of forty-seven young "preceptors" (each of whom he personally interviewed and selected) created a vastly expanded faculty of 113 who taught a student body of 1,400.[13] There is no question in my mind that the sheer factor of size—to say nothing of a vastly expanded scope—must constantly come into play as we consider the activities of the college president and how they evolved.

What Did They Do?

One major distinction in the schedules of the earlier and the contemporary college president is the time allocated by the former to teaching and other interactions with undergraduates (there were, of course, few graduate students). Wayland, in the second quarter of the nine-

teenth century, spent a good deal of time each day reading and preparing for his classes. Further, when he found the texts in the broad
range of subjects he himself was teaching inadequate, he wrote new
ones! In 1835, he published *The Elements of Moral Science*; in 1837, *The
Elements of Political Economy*; and in 1854, the year before his retirement, *The Elements of Intellectual Philosophy*. In addition to teaching his
own classes, he also visited the classrooms of others (though, here
again, we must remember that the entire faculty numbered only a
handful of men). Before taking up his appointment at Michigan, Angell made clear to the regents of the university that it was important
to him that he have contact with undergraduates in the classroom.
Although he had originally been a professor of modern languages
and literature at his alma mater, Brown, Angell's teaching and scholarly interests ultimately turned to politics and law, and at Michigan
he taught—effectively as far as we know—international law and
treaties, offering one course each semester throughout his career. Such
a shift in disciplinary affiliation, which is difficult to imagine in contemporary terms, is itself a comment on the changed structure of
teaching and scholarship.

I have found no evidence that Charles Eliot taught during his presidency. In his book *University Administration*, where he delineates the
responsibilities of a university president, Eliot never mentions teaching. Of course, this is not to say that he was not concerned with pedagogy. As a faculty member, he had not been regarded as a top-flight
researcher, but he was admired for his innovative classroom practices.
In fact, he made his name by publishing a chemistry text that relied
on the laboratory method of teaching. As president, he drew on his
past experiences to reform teaching practices in the laboratory sciences and also brought about teaching reforms in the law school by
introducing the case method. In many ways, Eliot seems a forerunner
of the more modern full-time administrator, and though he remained
throughout his career a committed advocate of excellence in teaching,
he did not himself continue to teach.

Woodrow Wilson assumed the presidency of Princeton as a faculty
member with a stellar teaching reputation. Indeed, he was often
voted the most popular teacher on the faculty. Throughout his tenure
as president, Wilson continued to teach. His own profound vocation
for the classroom is evident throughout his writings and speeches. In
an essay of 1907, he touches on the intense spiritual relationship between teacher and pupil: "No system of teaching which depends
upon methods and not upon persons, or which imagines the possibility of any substitution of the written word for the living person,
can work any but mechanical effects. The teacher's own spirit must,

with intimate and understanding touch, mold and fashion the spirit of the pupil; there is no other way to hand the immortal stuff of learning on." Yet his lofty ideals for the teaching profession are also tempered by the humor and pragmatism of the true teacher, as in his words to a Jersey City high school class in 1908: "The pathos of the situation [is] that I cannot impart to you from my experience anything that will keep you from being just as great a fool as I was at your age."

For the presidents we are considering, responsibility for the intellectual training of their students was intimately bound up with a personal and direct responsibility for their moral training and sensibility—indeed, the two frequently merge imperceptibly. At Brown, for example, Wayland instituted a system according to which study hours for the community, including both faculty and students, were fixed and enforced. These hours, during which faculty were expected to be found in their offices working, extended until ten in the evening. Each faculty member was also assigned a cohort of students whose rooms he was supposed to visit, for the purposes of checking on their studying, at least twice a day. Students were not permitted to deny access to the faculty member, who was encouraged to kick the door down if such a refusal were offered. Wayland himself assumed oversight for one of these groups of boys. Angell, fearing that his own specialty of law would not bring him into close enough contact with the students of Michigan's Literary (i.e., liberal arts) Department, undertook the decanal duties of registering all students, granting or refusing each excuse for absence, and investigating disciplinary cases. "The result," he notes with pride in his reminiscences, "is that I knew every student and could call him by name."

Moving further toward the realm of purely moral responsibility, we find presidents responsible for not only weekly but sometimes daily religious services, including the delivery of a sermon or at least appropriately edifying remarks. For Wayland, for example, these duties were discharged twice daily, at both morning and evening services. A good deal of the time was also spent meeting with, counseling, and praying with or for the individual boys. (In a 1838 letter to Basil Manly, president of the University of Alabama, Wayland admits that these private meetings with students occupy a significant portion of his time, but he also expresses regret that he has not had an opportunity for a private conference with each and every student before graduation.) Angell had considered the ministry as a career and, having entered higher education instead, carried over to this profession the sense of Christian vocation. He spoke and wrote about Christianity, conducted several surveys on the religious life of state universities, and "continued throughout the first decade of the twentieth century to preach Christ to Michigan."[14] In fact, Angell's explicitly Christian conduct of his presidency led to a complaint against him filed with the state senate, alleging that his views and actions effectively negated the nonsectarian status of the state university.[15]

Eliot's assumption of moral responsibilities was in some ways at the opposite end of the spectrum from Angell's "preaching." Intensely aware of being a lay president in the context of an institution evolving from a denominational to a secular nature, Eliot opens his memoirs, *Harvard Memories*, with the history of lay presidents at the college. He felt that the university was constricted by its Unitarian heritage and worked hard to open Harvard to various religious beliefs. He pursued this goal in part by reforming the Divinity School, ridding it of its Unitarian domination and bringing in scholars of various beliefs. Further, he created a multidenominational board of preachers to oversee chapel services and, in 1887, went a step further by abolishing compulsory chapel services for students. Eliot himself lists his "re-building of the Divinity School on a scientific basis" and "establishment of religious services on a voluntary basis" as two of his greatest accomplishments.

Although Eliot may not have perceived his role as "moral leader" of the institution in the way more clerically minded presidents had, he certainly took upon himself the burden of enforcing standards and upholding strict codes of integrity. One anecdote has it that on a hot spring day, Eliot happened to see law students busily working in the library in their shirtsleeves. Appalled at this breach of etiquette, he demanded that the librarian post a sign, forbidding students to use the library while in shirtsleeves. (Eventually, Eliot consented to having the sign removed.) His moral scruples famously came to the fore on another occasion, when two students were apprehended stealing library books. When caught, they also lied about their names. Eliot immediately suspended them. As it happened, both were to have rowed in the upcoming Harvard-Yale crew regatta. Word of the suspension spread to the White House, and Teddy Roosevelt, himself an alumnus, urged Eliot to reconsider his actions and permit the young men to participate in the event. Students who impugned their own characters and that of Harvard would certainly not represent the school, was Eliot's terse reply, which leaked to the newspapers as the president of the University upbraided the president of the United States.

When Woodrow Wilson described "my ideal of the true university" for a periodical of the time, he spoke of it as "a place intended . . . not for intellectual discipline and enlightenment only, but also for moral and spiritual enlightenment." Himself the son of a pastor, Wilson was the first nonclergyman to preside at Princeton. For him, the university and the moral life were deeply intertwined—indeed, inseparable— and he devoted his own oratorical gifts to both alike. In addition to his many addresses before civic groups, in which he expounded a vision that melded intellectual, moral, and civic commitment, on campus he regularly led the meetings of the Philadelphian Society (the campus religious organization) and the Layman's Conference, as well as the services in Marquand Chapel and at the University Place Presbyterian Church.

On a continuum with the moral exhortation of various types for which presidents took time in both private and public contexts was the responsibility for discipline, which occupied a great deal of faculty and indeed presidential time and effort. Eliot provides a noteworthy exception in this regard. The year before he assumed office, the position of dean of the college was created to ease the presidential burden in disciplinary matters. While Eliot's predecessors spent as much as three quarters of their working time on student discipline issues, he apparently spent little time on them. Again, these duties had both private and public dimensions. Not only was the president responsible for deciding on disciplinary penalties or responses to a student's misbehavior, but he was also not infrequently expected to correspond with students' families and others.

A large number of Wayland's letters are addressed to fathers whose sons were not applying themselves sufficiently to their schoolwork, were too often absent (generally, the president indicates the specific number of absences), or were otherwise misbehaving (as by stealing wood from the neighbors, spending too much time in the city acting like "gentlemen," keeping "spirituous liquors" in the dormitory, or having young women in their rooms at night). Angell, as another example, corresponded with a mother from New York whose daughter has informed her that a Michigan student whom the family befriended has "been the cause of her ruin." (Some things never change.) The mother importunes the president to compel the young man to marry her daughter and save a family from disgrace. Barring that, she maintains, President Angell should certainly expel the student from the college "as a libertine and a liar, unfit for the society of honorable men or respectable women."[16] The personal attention of the president seemed required in another way when a Harvard student died in the infirmary. His parents complained to Eliot that the college administration had displayed little sympathy for their loss. Subsequently, Eliot ordered that student medical records be moved to the Office of the

President so that he personally could respond to the parents of ill students.

Undoubtedly, correspondence was a major component of a president's day (and evening)! In these prexerographic days, there was also the matter of a copybook, in addition to penning the original document. In Wayland's case, for example, at least a portion of his correspondence is copied into the university letterbook in the hand of the college registrar, Lemuel Elliott; but the record shows that his predecessor, Asa Messor, wrote his own letters and then copied them into the letterbook himself. In return for financial donations or gifts of any kind made to the university, Wayland wrote to each person a letter of thanks. To inquiries made about the course of studies, the availability of scholarships for indigent students, or other university policies, the president responded, often enclosing a college catalog as well as providing answers. Until late in his presidency, Angell answered all of his own correspondence as well, including a tremendous volume of correspondence with high schools in the state, since the university had assumed the burden of accreditation for the state's secondary schools.

In 1901, thirty years after assuming office, Harvard's Eliot hired Jerome Greene, a graduate of the law school, to be his secretary. Prior to this, however, Eliot had shared a stenographer with the dean's office and had responded to all letters personally, sending handwritten notes to applicants for positions and presidents of other colleges and universities alike. Having employed Greene as his secretary, however (promoted a few years later to "secretary of the corporation"), Eliot brought an abrupt halt to his habit of responding to all letters. Henceforth, he scribbled only a two- or three-word indication to Greene, who then composed the president's response. When Eliot traveled, Greene served as his eyes and ears on campus, corresponding with him virtually every day. Indeed, when Eliot retired, he hoped the corporation might name Greene his successor, but it chose A. Lawrence Lowell instead.

Wilson also appears to have done without a full-time secretary for the most part, writing many of his own letters.[17] He was a prompt, faithful, terse, and excruciatingly dry correspondent. Business and personal correspondents wrote to him in styles ranging from the formal to the familiar to the jocular; he invariably returned their letters in the same formal, impersonal style in which he wrote both letters of acceptance and letters of condolence. One astounding characteristic of Wilson's correspondence is its rather drab and unemotional character—remarkable from one of the nation's most moving orators. Although Wilson's correspondence yields little hint of his views on the university presidency, he did have the following to say in a 1909 speech welcoming the president of Union College into "the questionable privileges of the fraternity of college president. It is a very happy life, sir, for those who love strife; it is a very interesting life for those who like to tell their fellow men what they really think of them. It is especially a life of an extraordinary demands upon one's energy, one's time, one's brains. . . . College faculties are sometimes touched with as much sensitiveness and personal jealousy as church choirs."

In some ways what is most noteworthy in Wilson's correspondence is actually what is missing. We know, for example, that he was an important collaborator in the ouster of his predecessor, President Patton. Yet none of this appears in his own correspondence. Letters between other faculty leaders and trustees contain repeated requests that the letter "be shown to Wilson" or that his opinion be consulted, but the only letter from Wilson is written late in the negotiations for Patton's resignation and is no more than a critique of one proposal on parliamentary grounds. In the midst of Wilson's tenure, the absence of written correspondence with some of his closest colleagues seems to indicate their very proximity and the frequency of informal ad hoc consultation. Again, as Wilson's Princeton presidency draws to a close, the absence—or perhaps redirection—of correspondence tells a story of its own. As his own efforts at reform and modernization of the university's organizational structure had spurred an administrative apparatus of deanships, standing committees, and increasing self-governance by the departmental faculties, his correspondence with any faculty member below the level of department chair diminished substantially. By 1909, Wilson's memoranda are addressed to deans and chairs rather than to individual faculty, and they request summaries and reports on actions taken rather than breakdowns of figures and recommendations. The absence of the latter signifies that Wilson had moved, in less than a decade, from the administration of the university as an autocratic, nineteenth-century president into the twentieth-century mold of the management of that administration by others.

In a period without telephone communication, of course, the vast majority of business dealings had to be carried out by letter. And to a far greater extent than today, much of the minutia of the college's business was carried out directly by the president. Of greater significance, however, was the direct role of the president in the hiring of individual faculty members, who generally applied directly to, were interviewed by, and were selected or rejected by the president. Indeed, it was one of Eliot's principles of presidential leadership that "the President's judgment should be brought to bear on every question of promotion within the permanent staff, and on every selection for an appointment without limit of time, or for a long term." So absolute was his authority in this regard that the law faculty, at their meeting of June 3, 1898, submitted a written request to the president that "the faculty should be consulted before the appointment of professors and instructors in law." Eliot himself was a member of every faculty at the university, and he made it a point to preside over every meeting of the faculty. During his first year in office, he presided at forty-five meetings of the College Faculty and thirty-nine meetings of smaller faculties (graduate programs, Lawrence Scientific School, and so on). During one long faculty meeting in which attacks on his motives and ideas were especially pointed, Eliot seemed to remain calm and poised. When he left at the end of the meeting, however, the faculty noted that the arm of his chair had broken off from the intensity of his grip.

In addition to the personnel function, the president seems also in many instances to have carried out the purchasing function. Woodrow Wilson is so minutely involved in these matters as to be ordering laboratory supplies. And an importunate Brown faculty member wrote to Wayland requesting new blinds for his office windows. Wayland even advised another university president on what sort of chairs one should purchase for the classroom. Curricular decisions fell to the president as well. When faculty proposed new courses, they didn't submit their ideas to a curriculum committee, department chair, or dean but to him. In the spring of 1877, for example, a young assistant professor of history, Henry Adams, sent President Eliot a long, detailed note outlining a proposed course and asking that he "give this subject favorable consideration."

Presidents also corresponded with one another, seeking information and advice. Angell, for example, queries President Barnard of Columbia about annual operating expenses, President Porter of Yale concerning commencement traditions, President Dwight of Yale about the constitution of academic departments (a new development at this time), and President Eliot of Harvard also about departments, as well as the conditions on which Harvard accepts bequests. Eliot had written of Harvard's finances as well to Acting President Frieze of the University of Michigan, and Frieze sent back a note on March 15, 1871: "Thanks for your letter of information as to the wealth of Harvard. It has helped us materially in securing an appropriation of $7500 for our poverty stricken university."

In addition to their substantial interactions with students, often involving not just academic but also moral instruction; their personal oversight of every faculty appointment and decision and virtually every operational aspect of the campus; and their prodigious output of correspondence, each of the presidents I have been examining was also engaged more or less extensively in activities in the broader off-campus community.

Wayland, for example, was actively involved in a number of community matters. He donated his time and worked for various charitable organizations in Providence. He forged associations with several Bible societies and even began a weekly "ladies' Bible class." He established strong ties with the public school system of Providence and proposed certain reforms, desiring to expand the number of primary schools (which was done) and to create public high schools as both academies and trade schools (which was not). His zeal for providing the largest possible number of people with the opportunity for self-improvement through learning led him to donate to the town of Wayland, Massachusetts—named after him—the sum of $500 to build a public library (with the stipulation that the townspeople raise what we would call today matching funds). This philanthropic act led the state of Massachusetts to pass a law that ultimately enabled a number of free public libraries to be built.

Wayland's evangelical enthusiasm for what he called the "new system" at Brown kept him busy on the topic of collegiate education beyond the campus as well. In 1849, he was invited to open a course of lectures before the Association of Mechanics and Manufacturers. In 1850, he traveled to Charlottesville, Virginia, to observe the university and the way its version of his "new system" worked. That same year, he addressed the Rhode Island legislature on the subject of the new system. In 1851, he delivered the annual address to the Rhode Island Society for the Encouragement of Domestic Industry, tackling the issue of how farmers and manufacturers might raise productivity. And during the winter recess of 1852, he spoke in Albany to a group of people seeking to establish a national university. In a memoir of their father, his sons note that Wayland, working year round from Monday mornings through Saturday evenings without a break, suffered from strain and mental anxiety. Even in the earliest years of his tenure, Wayland's first wife (who died in 1834) noted in correspondence that he was so constantly busy that she feared for his health. When, in 1855, Wayland's physician insisted that it was time for him to resign on account of ill health, the corporation asked him to stay on, with reduced responsibilities. Wayland replied that he would never be able to keep himself to a reduced schedule!

President Angell put a great deal of time and effort into the relationship with secondary schools in the state. Michigan pioneered a system, loosely modeled on the relationship between German gymnasia and universities, whereby the university would agree to accept the graduates of approved schools upon receipt of the school's diploma, without examination. This system entailed visits of a faculty committee to the individual schools around the state; for twenty-five years, Angell chaired the committee. On the broader civic stage, Angell was appointed minister to China by President Hayes in 1880, requiring him to take a leave from the university. He successfully negotiated a new treaty with the Chinese government, dealing with the immigration of Chinese laborers and the wage and job competition concerns this had raised in America, particularly in California. Expecting to serve for a year, he did not in fact return to Ann Arbor until 1882. Later, he took a second, briefer leave from his presidential duties in 1887, when he was appointed to the Fisheries Commission to settle with Great Britain questions relating to fishing rights in "British North America" (off the banks of Newfoundland, Nova Scotia, and New Brunswick). This appointment lasted only a few months, and the treaty he negotiated was in fact rejected by the Senate in 1888.

As indefatigable as Wayland in his zeal to promote ideas of educational reform was Charles Eliot. Not only was Eliot's liberalization and restructuring of the undergraduate curriculum to include "electives" a landmark in American higher education, but he also transformed graduate professional education. Eliot was the first to introduce the notion that professional programs in medicine and law should require students to have completed undergraduate degrees. Prior to this, the only admission standard for most graduate programs was that the young man be "of good character." When Eliot, for example, insisted on rigorous written examinations at the medical school, the dean objected adamantly, stating that "more than half [of the medical students] can barely write."

Much—indeed, most—of Eliot's external activity was an extension of his grand transformative project at Harvard. More than nine hundred speeches, articles, and books by Eliot have been preserved (most of the articles and books are compendiums of speeches). He also wrote regular articles for the *Atlantic Monthly*. This public outreach was, in large part, a strategy to strengthen Harvard's resources. Eliot believed that the president need not engage in personal solicitation of gifts to his university. Rather, financial support could be attracted by institutional integrity and providing information to the educated public.

Woodrow Wilson was one of the foremost orators of an era that produced the likes of William Jennings Bryan. He was a nationally known and widely traveled popular speaker well before he assumed the Princeton presidency. If his correspondence is dry, value-neutral, and matter-of-fact, his oratory is vibrant, witty, moralistic, and always persuasive or instructive—usually both. So well received was a speech he made in Indianapolis, for example, that a newspaper editorial in that city seriously proposed Wilson for U.S. president in 1901, more than a year before his name first surfaced as a possible president of Princeton. Prior to his assuming the Princeton presidency, Wilson's calendar had been heavily laden with public speaking engagements to a broad range of groups, including not only educational interest groups but also boards of trade, various types of Christian societies, and political organizations. On average, these commitments amounted to about sixty days of travel and fifty speaking engagements per year. In fact, when Wilson did become president of Princeton, his external commitments actually declined somewhat. Within a year of his inauguration, however, he made a "grand tour" of the Princeton alumni, speaking at a series of alumni-organized dinner parties, which introduced him to the elites of whatever region he was visiting.

After this initial tour, the nature of Wilson's other outside commitments began to change. As president of Princeton, he began to be consulted by industrialists, politicians, and others on an individual basis, often meeting with local leaders in New York, Philadelphia, and environs for small dinners or task-oriented gatherings. Beginning in 1906, he also began to be extraordinarily active in the work of the Carnegie Foundation, particularly in its role as precursor to contemporary insurance systems for colleges and universities. By 1909, the number of Wilson's commitments involving large groups and the mass public was surpassed by meetings with such smaller, specialized, often privileged groups. Unlike contemporaries in Ann Arbor or Chicago, Wilson benefited from Princeton's central location in the nation's already well-developed rail and steamboat infrastructure. He seems to have traveled to New York as readily as any modern commuter, not infrequently visiting the city two and three nights in succession for dinners and after-dinner meetings. Wilson's engagement and stature as a political and moral, as well as educational, leader are inseparable from his facility with the spoken word, whether at a large religious revival or in tête-à-tête discussion with the cultural elites of his time. He devoted a considerable amount of his time to these encounters, apparently averaging about seventy days of travel per year during his tenure at Princeton.

Now: Where Are the Giants? What Do You Do?

Two issues rise quickly to people's lips when engaging in casual conversations with the presidents of present-day colleges and universities regarding the nature of their curious and perplexing (if not odd
and eccentric) métier. One is an observation, usually nostalgic or
yearning in nature, and the other is a direct question, often desperate
or derisive in nature. The observation has many subtle variations but
typically reduces to the wistful comment that there was a time when
great figures presided over our nation's campuses—intellectual giants
who led their faculty, students, alumni, trustees, and nation with
grace, vision, and moral purpose. In most cases, this observation is
the interlocutor's rather indirect vehicle for informing the listener, a
polite but often harassed leader (scholar, ambassador, manager, fund-
raiser) of some university, that he or she lacks all of these admirable
qualities. Since this latter conclusion is the main point, the reality of
the historical claim is quite secondary.

  If the conversation moves beyond this point and gets businesslike,
the speaker will take note of the lack of real purpose and direction of
today's colleges and universities, their inefficiencies, their self-aggran-
dizing rhetoric, and most revealing, the unwillingness of today's so-
called leaders to do anything about it. In an effort, finally, to force the
accused to provide evidence of his or her own inadequacy, the
speaker may turn from observations and opinions to *the* question:
"Just what do you *really* do?" Presumably, the answer sought refers to
activities besides spending time with individuals interested in such
interrogations. This question is normally aimed at shifting the attack
to the "president's court" to demonstrate that even on friendly turf,
the issue is hopeless. Surely the president's response will be so self-
incriminating that even the president will conclude that the office itself has come to have certain rather dubious properties.

  It is surprising how defensive or tongue-tied most of my colleagues
and I become in the face of such an inquiry. There are, of course,
many ways to begin addressing this question, though very few short
responses that might turn the quiz in your favor and cause the interrogator to thoughtfully scan the many staggering accomplishments of
the modern university that administrative leaders somehow seemed
unable to prevent. Depending on your morale, patience, and objectives, you might consider the following set of alternative responses
that serve to ally the president with that great American folk hero, the
manager.[18]

  "I manage to survive; I manage to plan, organize, staff, coordinate,

budget, report, and make decisions regarding the future of this organization; I manage to serve this organization as part figurehead, part
pastor of interpersonal relations, part spokesperson, part disturbance
handler, part negotiator, part resource allocator and general disburser
of institutional propaganda and positive reinforcement to students,
faculty, alumni and trustees; I manage to be an unprincipled (at times)
promoter and principled (at other times) huckster of the institution
and its objectives; I manage to bring forward the historical traditions
of the institution and give some of them new life and meaning in a
different world; I manage to articulate a set of goals for the institution
that, despite all odds, actually covers all the activities of what increasingly has become a general-service public utility; I manage an organization of bewildering scope with at least a little dignity, respectability,
some authority, and (occasionally) wisdom. I manage to preserve
some sense of community in a sea of independent and fiercely self-
regulating disciplines; I manage to blur the contradictory obligations
the modern university too eagerly assumes; I manage to convince
others that our elitism is not of the unjustified sort; I manage to persuade our patrons that no single university can address all the needs
of modern life."

Unfortunately, most of my colleagues—not being economists,
thankfully!—might miss the distinction between a manager (who
oversees the ongoing efficiency of a continuing but relatively static
process) and an entrepreneur (who may be a manager too). The latter
is characterized as someone who, in contrast to the "mere" manager,
is actually putting new ideas into effect, even if this means, as it usually does, stirring up things a bit. In the economic sector, one associ-
ates such qualities as imagination and leadership with the entrepreneur, not with the manager. Perhaps this is what the partly informed
questioner is really concerned with: that neither university presidents
nor faculty nor trustees any longer expect or will allow the exercise of
leadership and imagination by the administrative head of a college or
university. In view of all this—depending on your objectives—it
might be best at this point to find a way to lob the ball back into the
interrogator's court.

Or you could try to persist for a while longer and, for example,
attempt to describe briefly particular dimensions of the task of most
university presidents. You might note: "Whatever I am doing, the
pace of work is unrelenting, and the demand for my time remains
remarkably high despite the low value some others, especially specta-
tors, place on it. The latter 'economic paradox' is explained by the
simple fact that most people seeking my attention are not charged
anything extra for this 'indulgence'! In any case, my days, therefore,

can too easily become characterized by too large a variety of tasks, brevity of attention to each one, and an almost inevitable fragmentation of effort. As a result, I work continually with the fear of responding and even acting in a rather superficial manner."

On a "difficult" day, the president might even go on to confess that "to alleviate this fear or anxiety, I often find myself focusing on current and well-defined alternatives, if any are available, rather than important long-term issues where uncertainty extends even as to the right question to be considering." Alternatively, on a more reflective note, the president might comment on the constant reality that leadership in higher education involves the difficult task of implementing *new* combinations to achieve old goals in a changed world or newly defined goals, and as long as you are engaged in this process, you are guaranteed to be enraging some who have feelings of affection for a previous time. You are therefore in the business of creating loss as you move ahead or losing ground by standing still!

Alas, when challenged to explain what we do, it is more common for the university president to proceed on a more defensive or exasperated note—showing little faith in the transformative possibilities of dialogue—and ask the interlocutor to distinguish between the common external illusions (focusing on rights, power, and "glory") concerning the presidency of a contemporary college or university and the reality that often consists of a rather more prosaic and limited field of action. A president who has read Arthur Link's majesterial sixty-nine-volume collection of Woodrow Wilson's papers might quote the former Princeton president: "The truth is that there are no more big things in a college president's day than in any other man's, and there is no use in his posing and pretending that his life is not made up of trifles—made or marred by them."[19] Indeed, it is commonplace at this point to observe that, for good or ill, many people believe that the reality for many contemporary university presidents consists of either reacting to the unpredictable or trying to reconcile the conflicting demands of various citizens and patrons of the university community. As a result, many observers have concluded that the university or college president's job is largely symbolic and his or her influence, if any, sporadic, as the pace and direction of activity are determined by events over which the president has little control. Therefore, if the questioner is concerned with the leadership of change (forward or backward), he or she ought to speak to someone else!

If this line of inquiry continues, your visitor may try to help out (i.e., allow the president to maintain some modicum of self-esteem) by posing a more narrowly defined (i.e., easier) question by asking if universities, and perhaps even their presidents, have any well-defined goals that guide the entire institution and a well-understood strategy that moves the university community toward these objectives. For those of us who are both presidents of research universities that have not been overwhelmed by professional schools and not risk-averse, we might sally forth with an articulation of the idealist conception of the university, first developed in Germany, which is based on a "technology" that relies on the organic unity of both teaching and research and the acceptance of a set of scientific values. According to this model, we could go on to explain that students who are taught to locate and operate on the scientific frontier—and thus understand how their knowledge base is changing—develop into autonomous subjects with a unique capacity to serve their society by shaping new ideas and concepts that can transform and enhance social and technological relations. Moreover, since the scientific community is structured around a set of values—the scientific ethos—that exerts its own appropriate discipline and authority, it is to be free of normal forms of public accountability. This ethos has been described in a number of ways, but some of its key values are honesty, free inquiry, an open and critical examination of relevant evidence, an open sharing of results, universalism, disciplined skepticism, tolerance, and a certain antiauthoritarian and antiprovincialism stance. It is, you might boldly state, its own democracy, which serves us best through its own self-direction!

If, however, life's experiences have made you too risk-averse for such an audacious approach, you may be reduced to noting, rather defensively, that the various constituents and patrons of the college have separate and largely inconsistent objectives that they will pursue, as best they can, on their own.[20] It is, you may ruefully report, an illusion to imagine that the university's faculty and students are anxious to behave as a community with a shared interest in education, scholarship, and public service. The reality is that most members of the university community do not care a lot about most communitywide issues since they seem to have little relevance to their immediate highest-priority tasks, which require resources, independence, and disciplinary commitments, not shared interests, not the pursuit of a new vision, and certainly not something as amorphous—and oppressive to some—as the idea of community. In this latter respect, you may go on to note that higher education is simply one of the latest institutions of Western liberal democracies to substitute a kind of self-regulating (one hopes!) individualism for what had previously been an intricate web of mutual responsibilities that sustained the academic community for centuries. Moreover, in recent decades, society's support for higher education has come to be taken so completely for granted that faculty and administrators alike have lost sight of the necessity of ensuring a broad base of support and understanding of the social role of the academic enterprise.

If the conversation is still cordial, the president may exclaim that he or she would like to stand firmly (against the advancing horde) for the old and tested truths or boldly take the institution (against the weight of tradition) toward the top of a new mountain of innovation and pluralism, but the reality is that different parts of the contemporary university community will, depending on their particular concern, view any such initiative of the president as parochial or forward-looking, courageous or cowardly, and in any case convincing evidence that the president was discharging his or her duties without the right (i.e., their) set of fundamental principles! Indeed, some may go so far as to claim that presidential behavior is purposeless, inconsistent, governed by emotion, indifferent to evidence, and constantly being governed by one kind of "group thinking" or another.

Since this type of defensive and exasperated rhetoric is unlikely to serve anyone's interest, it may be that a far superior tactical approach would be to finally get the ball back in the interlocutor's court by asking a question of your own, such as, "What should a transient trustee of an institution's health and purpose do?" or, better still if you are talking to someone from the business sector, especially a CEO, "Just what do you do?" This latter question often helps focus the attention of your visitor in a manner that results in an anxious switch of subject to the weather or, if your inquisitor is still on the offensive, to the football team's inadequate win-loss record!

Conclusion

My preliminary attempt both to examine the day-to-day working lives of an earlier era of university presidents and to characterize the contemporary nature of this distinctive position is by no means comprehensive, but I believe it does yield some fruitful provisional conclusions. First, it seems clear that the tremendous demands for communication and interaction with a president, the intense "busyness" required in his or her day, at least during the academic year, has not dramatically changed from the nineteenth century. Although the phone call, the fax, and e-mail have reduced the tremendous volume of written correspondence passing through the president's office, the high demand for communication with constituencies both internal and external has remained constant. What has changed is the much wider portfolio of both responsibilities and constituencies that the college or university president must now deal with. Foremost among these, of course, is the relationship with the federal and state governments, which has greatly increased the complexity of a president's interactions with both external and internal constituencies. More broadly, however, a single day often requires contemporary college and university presidents' attention to traverse back and forth from alumni concerns to developments in Washington or a state capital, from public policy issues to student discipline, and from faculty appointments to curricular reforms—all in an endless quest to help provide for his or her institution and to help secure the broadest acceptance of higher education's needs and responsibilities.

Another example of apparent evolution in form yet underlying consistency in function is the president's engagement with the full panoply of campus activities. While today's president will probably not be involved in ordering laboratory chemicals, venetian blinds, or classroom furniture (as Wilson and Wayland were), he or she is almost certain to be involved in a broad spectrum of decisions that represent comparable commitments of resources in universities, which have become much larger and more complex administrative entities. Decisions on parking garages, patent and licensing policies, equitable health care and pension plans, safe disposal of chemical wastes, child care facilities—these and many other legitimate university concerns represent, perhaps, the contemporary equivalent of decisions on physical plant or purchasing made by presidents such as Angell or Eliot.

Although the means and the scope for exercising some presidential responsibilities have changed, their structure seems in many ways to have remained relatively stable. Yet despite these similarities, I believe there is at least one area in which we do see a distinct change between the nineteenth- and late-twentieth-century university presidents. That is in our predecessors' traditional responsibility for ethical leadership, which they originally carried out by teaching the college's capstone course in moral philosophy and ensuring an adequate amount of "right thinking" in the faculty. It might be argued that in the more complex modern university, this ethical dimension of presidential leadership has evolved from a more strictly delimited and almost rule-governed activity into a more diffuse but no less significant role of helping set the moral tone for the academic community—and beyond—through the president's choices, policies, actions, and words.

Indeed, it is my own view that the moral requirements of a contemporary university president are no less than in some previous age, but they are of a different sort. It is no longer the president's responsibility to teach other members of the academic community the precise nature of appropriate beliefs and "right thinking." It is rather to act as an example of personal integrity—accepting both the rights and responsibilities of academic life—and to both protect and project the academic vision of the modern American university and the intellectual culture encompassed therein as a social institution that serves the long-term interests of the society that supports it. Moreover, it is critical for the president and any allies he or she can mobilize within the academic community to be able to convey to others the notion that for universities, the future is of great ethical significance.

The issue of integrity, both intellectual and personal, is important. One could look at this question in the negative by focusing on intellectual or personal corruption. It is more helpful, however, to focus on the positive and think of integrity as reflecting such qualities as open commitment to a set of academic and social values; forthrightness, discernment, steadfastness in the pursuit of a vision; fierceness in the defense of the cultural conditions (such as thoughtful debate and reasoned inquiry) required for scholarship and education; compassion and a capacity to compromise (to a point) when that is what is required to move a community forward. It seems to me that one can project such qualities if and only if one acts from a set of principles that helps distinguish between right and wrong and articulates these principles for the entire community. To my mind, too few contemporary college and university presidents actually articulate their perspectives on such matters.

It is certainly the obligation of all members of the academic community to nourish the human qualities among its members and the social and cultural conditions that are crucial to sustaining the vitality of educational and scholarly programs. Once again, these factors include the ability to focus on important issues, a commitment to the thoughtful reexamination of current understandings, respect for evidence, creativity, productivity, and integrity. However, it is surely the task of presidents not only to visibly support this effort but also to be able to grasp the meaning of current events (as in the explosion of information technology or the globalization of economic, demographic, and environmental concerns) for the evolution of higher education, to anticipate transformation, and to pose questions such as the following:

What confidence should we continue to place in human competence?

Should there be any limits to our desire to control all and possess all? Does scientific and technological progress allow us to avoid dealing with issues of values, justice, and interests?

How do we achieve both intellectual autonomy and collective identity?

To what extent are liberal democracy and free scientific inquiry tied together?

To what extent, if any, should trust replace accountability?

What rules, if any, should characterize citizenship or belonging to an academic community?

Only if we engage such questions will we be able to sustain both the social responsibilities of universities and the intellectual authority of new scholarly ideas in the face of a knowledge base that is both exploding and decomposing and dealing with phenomena that pervade our lives and yet are far from our everyday experience. Only by asking such questions will we develop the strength to continue to challenge the familiar, deal with the inevitable criticism and disappointment, build peaceful bridges across cultural divides, and help our society build a new understanding of the role of education and scholarship in a rapidly changing world.

As we think of our nineteenth-century colleagues, it is well to recall that in their world, the building of character—piety, moderation, love of country, and the like—was the chief aim of higher education. Indeed, for our now long-departed colleagues, the responsibility to impart a particular set of moral claims and beliefs suffused the entire educational effort. The emergence of the modern university, however, characterized by a more rigorous, speculative, probing, and less dogmatic perspective, caused not only a certain loss of confidence in the particular moral consensus promoted by our predecessors but also a general reluctance to engage higher education's moral issues. Indeed, once the university's programs shifted from the fostering of a particular moral pose to encouraging students to think more carefully for themselves about complex moral issues, the role of the president and faculty with respect to these particular matters became more ambiguous, even murky. As a result, there was every tendency to avoid some of these difficult and contentious issues in favor of a focus on a rapidly growing set of more easily defined challenges. At the same time, however, an important new presidential obligation arose: creating the conditions for enabling and encouraging this new intellectual autonomy to flourish.

This has been a loss, since it seems quite clear to me that although we were right to welcome and promote a new vision of a liberal education, one that liberated us from the constraints and limits of certain capricious traditions and customs, the modern academic community and its administrative leaders have often lost sight of the fact that a life without a larger purpose has no meaning. Because education remains a moral endeavor in that it deals with the things we believe to be important, it remains essential for university presidents—and other members of the academic community—to engage in a campus-based discourse that centers on the broad set of issues that help students focus for themselves on the meaning and purpose of life and what is involved in moral and virtuous action.

This matter can be considered from the somewhat different perspective of cultural adaptation. Any viable set of cultural arrangements, including higher education, must not simply adapt to changing external circumstances but do so in a manner that allows individuals to feel a sense of attachment to or personal integration in evolving circumstances. It seems to me, however, that although university and college faculty, as well as their presidents, have demonstrated considerable leadership in highlighting the need for societal responses to a changing set of external circumstances, they have been largely silent on the issue of what set of values would be most helpful in allowing individuals to feel a sense of attachment and belonging to a changed world. Assembling a group of very intelligent people and adequate resources is important, but so is a vision that structures the overall effort in a manner designed to give greater meaning to the effort and to society.

In examining the lives and activities of presidents of this earlier age, I cannot help but feel that they both perceived and enacted their moral responsibilities on a different scale, at once more grand and more minute. On the one hand, these presidents frequently seem to have believed that they were both called and empowered to transform an institution that needed transforming on a grand scale. Today's leaders, by contrast, are often more sanguine about the fundamental soundness of the institutions over which they preside, frequently believing that more gradual and thoughtful change, rather than utter transformation, is called for. On the other hand, the nineteenth-century presidents seem to have been much more atomistically engaged with responsibility for the moral and intellectual growth of each individual student within the college, as we see by the time devoted to correspondence with parents, shared prayer with students, and so on. In comparison with this latter focus, today's president often seems to work with a more global sense of duty to promote and protect the soundness of the institution as a whole and its role in society, rather than intervening directly in each individual student's life. Thus the grand transformative schemes of the past seem often to have been coupled with the tendency for quite local intervention in the individual lives of community members, while the more modest transformative goals of many contemporary leaders seem frequently joined with a rather global sense of institutional action, which fre-

quently relies more on the power of new ideas than on direct intervention to affect the moral character of individual lives.

What I perceive as changes in the president's sphere of moral action are explained in part by changes in both the scale and the scope
of higher education and its social transformation. The eight-man faculty of Wayland's day is dwarfed by today's often massive academic
communities, and the interaction of the president with that community must necessarily be quite different. Moreover, the social responsibilities of universities are now interpreted in quite different ways.
Yet I think it is important to recognize that as our colleges and universities have grown and been transformed, there have, despite enormous gains, also been some unfortunate losses. My own feeling, as I
have tried to understand the similarities and the differences in the
lives of great past presidents, is that the specific domain of moral
leadership, for which both they and their communities perceived
them to have major responsibility, is an area for which, in the contemporary university, we have not clearly enough identified, assigned, or
assumed responsibility.

As our campuses, our student bodies, our faculties, and our associations with the extramural community grew, our need for ethical
awareness and understanding did not decrease. Indeed, I would argue that a president's moral leadership is more challenging than ever
when his or her responsibility extends to sustaining the conditions
under which faculty and students are themselves encouraged to think
and act on the basis of moral principles—principles that they themselves can articulately defend. With all due respect, this is a task for
both presidents and faculty that is far more complex than teaching a
required course in ethics or moral philosophy. The more pluralistic
and complex the university, the tougher and the more important this
task of moral leadership. Yet by and large, we have neglected this
growing need. This is a loss, I believe, that we must begin to repair,
perhaps in part through a reexamination of the responsibility of the
university president.

Notes

1. To the surprise of some, I have found my years as a university president—eight years at the University of Michigan and, thus far, more than nine
years at Princeton—to have been enormously fulfilling and a lot of fun. It's a
great job, if you can get it! Certainly there have been moments of discouragement and exasperation, and the pace of activity has been unrelenting; but all

this has been far outweighed by the many satisfactions that have accrued, the friendships gained, and the broadening of my own horizons and understanding. I have not been able to continue my previous research work, and my teaching has declined (in quantity!) to one course a year and the direction of senior undergraduate theses, but I have found new avenues for my writing that have been rewarding. I approach my topic, therefore, with the gratitude of someone who continues to enjoy his time as a university president and continues to learn an enormous amount from it.

2. In this essay, I employ the terms "college president" and "university president" interchangeably.

3. It is of some interest to note the various meanings assigned to these titles outside of academic circles. *Rector* often refers to a ruler of some country, city, state, or people (or even to God as rector of the heavens) but also to the queen bee of a hive. It is also used to refer to the holders of ancient ecclesiastical offices and to others who exercise supreme or directive control. *Chancellor* is also a quite ubiquitous term whose origins are traced to rather petty officials of the court (and operettas!) but one that has come to be applied to more and more important offices (e.g., Lord High Chancellor). *President*, of course, just refers to "one who presides" over something. Although this is the most frequent description for the head of an American university, it has the least picturesque history. It is of some interest to note a number of possible titles for the head of a university that, as far as I am aware, have *not* been officially adopted. Some of these are: shepherd or herder; superintendent or supervisor or steward; bailiff or constable (although warden is used); chief or lord or seigneur; headman or chief; potentate or mogul or sovereign. In some contexts, arguments could be mounted for one of these alternatives.

4. This does not seem to be an issue for the school of thought that considers the "true" role of educational institutions to be providing a mechanism to allocate good jobs and reinforce existing class structures and the authority of the status quo.

5. Nannerl O. Keohane, "Collaboration and Leadership: Are They in Conflict?" *College Board Review*, no. 135, Spring 1985.

6. One can consult, for example, James L. Fisher, *Power of the Presidency* (New York: ACE/Macmillan, 1984); George Keller, *Academic Strategy: The Management Revolution in American Higher Education* (Baltimore: Johns Hopkins University Press, 1983); Michael D. Cohen and James G. March, *Leadership and Ambiguity* (New York: McGraw-Hill, 1974); and Clark Kerr, *Presidents Make a Difference: Strengthening Leadership in Colleges and Universities* (Washington, D.C.: Commission on Strengthening Presidential Leadership, 1984).

7. Milton S. Mayer, "Hutchins of Chicago," *Harper's*, March 1939.

8. William Rainey Harper, "The College President," *The William Rainey Harper Memorial Conference* (Chicago: University of Chicago Press, 1938).

9. William C. Lawton, "The Decay of Academic Freedom," *Educational Review*, November 1906.

10. Harper, "The College President."

11. Harold W. Dodds, Address at the inauguration of President W. A. Eddy, Hobart and William Smith Colleges, 1936.

12. Unless otherwise indicated, the quotes attributed to Wayland, Angell, Eliot, and Wilson are from materials found in their papers. I am grateful to Sara Lindheim at Brown, David Greene at Harvard, Caroline Winterer at Michigan, Chris Mackie-Lewis at Princeton, and my colleague Georgia Nugent for their help in providing and interpreting archival materials.

13. Charles Eliot did much the same at Harvard in his first five years. He doubled the size of the teaching staff—largely, it seems, by appointing friends to various positions, a move that undoubtedly strengthened his political base within the faculty.

14. George Marsden, *The Soul of the American University* (New York: Oxford University Press, 1994).

15. The senate, reluctantly investigating the complaint, concluded that the advancement of "a liberal and enlightened Christianity" was not in fact "sectarian," and that "a school, a society, a nation devoid of Christianity is not a pleasant spectacle to behold." It is worth noting that Angell's own survey in 1896 of about five thousand students at five state universities—Indiana, Kansas, Michigan, Washington, and West Virginia—indicated that only about 165 students, or 3%, were Catholic and only about 44, or less than 1%, were Jewish.

16. Charles Eliot was once paid a visit by an elderly couple from western New York, seeking his assistance in processing an annulment of the marriage of their son, a Harvard student, to his landlady's daughter. The president attempted to reassure the angry parents that the landlady came from a reputable family and "the prospects of a happy marriage [were] not unfavorable."

17. As early as 1897, the Committee on University Affairs of the board of trustees had reported that "one of the most pressing needs of the institution at this time is a University Secretary." Charles Williston McAlpin assumed this post in 1901. In that role he served, as the current secretary of the university does, as the major liaison with the board of trustees, for example, in matters concerning honorary degrees. In addition, it is clear that eventually he directed much of the traffic of correspondence for Wilson—for example, when the latter was traveling abroad or on an occasion when he had to leave campus for medical treatment. On October 24, 1902, the trustees approved a resolution "that the President of the University be authorized to engage a Secretary at a salary of $500 per annum." (The president, at the time, received a salary of $8,000.) From 1906 to 1910, Gilbert Fairchild Close served as secretary to the president, as he did again at the Paris Peace Conference. However, Wilson seems to have employed him on research projects, doing such tasks as compiling statistics on the number of "clubmen" who achieved high academic standing. On several occasions, when Close is responding directly to correspondence on Wilson's behalf, he indicates as much. Both McAlpin's and Close's duties extended well beyond narrowly defined secretarial duties.

18. Henry Mintzberg, *The Nature of Managerial Work* (Englewood Cliffs, N.J.: Prentice Hall, 1986).

19. Link, *Papers of Woodrow Wilson*, vol. 28 (Princeton, N.J.: Princeton University Press, 1978), p. 479. I am grateful to Professor James Axtell for pointing me to this quotation.

20. As Cohen and March observed over two decades ago, the American university may best be considered an "organized anarchy" or an institution with loosely defined and inconsistent objectives and preferences! Cohen and March, *Leadership and Ambiguity.*

On the History of Giants

HANNA H. GRAY

IN HIS excellent and comprehensive essay, President Shapiro has touched just about every base on today's playing field. As cleanup batter, I will raise the questions: when was "then," and what is "now"? with some special attention to the history of the giants. Let us first assume that "then" was a hundred years ago and ask whether the *fin de siècle* belongs more to the nineteenth or to the twentieth century.

One might start by pointing out that a hundred years ago, and indeed well into our own century, presidents were normally expected to have three names. That stately catalog would include Charles William Eliot, Daniel Coit Gilman, William Rainey Harper, David Starr Jordan, Benjamin Ide Wheeler, and later, Nicholas Murray Butler, Arthur Twining Hadley, James Rowland Angell, and Robert Maynard Hutchins.

A yet more refined and impressive category also comes to mind: that of presidents with a first initial followed by two names, for example, G. Stanley Hall, E. Benjamin Andrews, M. Carey Thomas, A. Lawrence Lowell. I heard of a recent candidate for appointment at Harvard who, eager to demonstrate his intimate knowledge of that university's history, talked incessantly about "Larry Lowell." He failed to get the job. Larry Lowell did not in fact exist, any more than did Chuck Eliot, Billy Harper, or Nick Butler.

The candidate was presumably young and therefore innocent of the reverence the trinitarian image once commanded in underscoring the perceived authority of the university president. In our age of downsizing, names are pretty much down to two, and informality is on the rise. These developments can stand for a symbolic shift of status and a change in public attitudes as well. Regard for the office of president, or for the presidents themselves, has descended a few notches. Where giants once walked the earth and now, deceased, look down from their pedestals, smaller folk are seen to scurry about, tin cups in hand, snuffing out fires here and there, preoccupied with committee meetings, dealing with so-called constituents, and hoping to get through the day without having to think too deeply or face yet another political, financial, or public relations crisis.

In the imagined past, the giants meditated and produced inspiring educational visions that spoke to a larger world. They were wise men, better equipped by character and learning and some kind of spiritual force than was the common run, to forecast the future and to lead the present toward its promise, to teach principles and values, to expound issues ranging from the substance of curricular truth to the prospects for world peace, from prescriptions for curing immediate ills to striking exactly the right balance between tradition and change in a restless and rudderless universe. They were, in brief, the leaders of a secular church who were meant to exemplify the pretensions of high thinking and its consequences for whose sake, after all, existed the institutions over which they presided and for which they were accountable.

President Shapiro has rightly described the fictive and nostalgic elements embedded in these prevailing attitudes. They reveal at once a changing view of roles and institutions and an intense longing for the constructed ideal that is thought to have passed—a longing for leadership, clarity of understanding, significance of purpose, heroism in the quest for a civilized world for which the college or university should serve as training ground and microcosm. The desire that university presidents, and thus their institutions, fulfill such expectations indicates the continuing hope for higher education and its works as "creators of the future." The opposite belief, that the university presidency, in its mandate and practice, falls short of past standards, reflects a continuing confusion over the nature of the university itself.

There were indeed giants a hundred years ago, and we still sit on their shoulders, a position that speaks to indebtedness but also to heightened and widened perspectives and responsibilities. We know from the history of Rabelais that Gargantua was a great pathbreaker who matured into a wise old giant; he understood that the cultural environment inhabited by his son Pantagruel had advanced so far beyond the world of his own education that it made his own vaunted accomplishment in learning seem sadly primitive. Here, then, is a younger and larger giant standing on the shoulders of an older one.

The most hulking of the late-nineteenth-century gargantuas were founders. Some, like Gilman and White and Jordan and Harper, created new universities; some, most notably Eliot, re-created colleges as universities. Their work directly influenced all of higher education and the larger debates over higher education, its essence, the quality and purpose of its programs, the place of research and scholarship, the goals of knowledge, and the professions of knowledge. They were unrelenting spokesmen for their causes. These presidents were surely not the typical administrators of their time. They were leaders who inaugurated a new era of American higher education. They were in some ways as different from the average "nineteenth-century" president as from ourselves.

These were men, and occasionally women, intent on moving from the model of the small, often sectarian college, itself not far removed from the academy or prep school, to goals less concerned with inculcating personal and civic virtue (although no one opposed these things). Their goals were directed to advancing intellectual life, intellectual training, and the progressive discovery of knowledge. The institutions they created differed from one another in curriculum and in the mix of ideas informing the curriculum. There was constant and intense curricular controversy roiling around the future of undergraduate education and its impact on academic institutions more generally. Yet the impact of the elective system was to some degree common to all, and if its revolutionary force had to do above all with the undergraduate curriculum, it was equally influential for university programs as a whole.

The introduction of the elective system and its accompanying ideas stimulated the very possibility of combining teaching and research, the opening up of new subjects and new methods of learning, the making of research, scholarship, and specialization central in stating the purpose of higher education. It assumed the existence of an organic connection between research and teaching and so provided the charter of the American research university. As Eliot put it, "The largest effect of the elective system is that it makes scholarship possible, not only among undergraduates, but among graduate students and college teachers." "As long as our teachers," he said, "regard their work as simply giving so many courses for undergraduates, we shall never have first-class teaching here. If they have to teach graduate students as well as undergraduates, they will regard their subjects as infinite, and keep up that constant investigation which is necessary for first-class teaching."[1]

Such ideas introduced the characteristic strains of thought that redesigned the vision of academic space and work as animated above all by a set of requisite and enabling freedoms related to both personal and institutional forms of independence. All this tipped the scale of university educational purpose from the assimilation of a common discipline and spirit of service to the development of autonomous minds and judgments and choices. The precise setting of the scale moved back and forth, both then and in succeeding generations. There were always those who feared that the loss of coherence once situated in a curriculum ordered around unifying truth was a sin both intellectual and social—Woodrow Wilson did, for example, and so, later, did Robert Hutchins. But the institutional framework within which educational goals, however controversially delineated, were to be pursued had altered permanently. The agreement that some basic definition of freedom rested at the core of the collegiate or university enterprise had come to dominate.

A profound change was under way that would construct a new expectation of the presidential role, even though many continued to consider the president the super-headmaster of old or yearned for him to be so—a phenomenon still present in our own day. Eliot's university at the end of his term, as Oscar Handlin has written, had merged the inherited ideal of liberal education with that of scholarship, "ever evolving as knowledge accumulated. Tradition yielded to science as the source of authority."[2]

It is evident that the authority of a president for whom the stewardship of tradition came foremost would inevitably be different from that of a president whose goal it became to serve as steward of a realm where the authority of science reigned sovereign. The source, and hence the nature, of presidential authority had moved decisively.

Not all universities became such in the same way or embraced to the same degree the new movements of professional education and of professionalism and greater specialization in academia. The person of the president mattered, as of course did the institutions' particular histories and traditions and governing boards and alumni sentiment, in shaping the pace and the outcome. But the presidents were out in front, planning and arguing and directing. One has only to think of President Eliot's steadfast translation of educational intention into the reality of a transformed Harvard College and Harvard University or of the detailed blueprint for an entire university forged by President Harper for the University of Chicago or of the remarkable and widely followed public debate between President McCosh and President Eliot over the elective system. There was almost nothing on which McCosh and Eliot could agree. When Eliot criticized Princeton for having only one professor of history, McCosh responded that one was quite enough. "I think," he said, "the numerous narrative histories of epochs is just a let-off to easy-going students from the studies which require thought."[3]

One must remember, too, the power of appointment that rested in the hands of the founding presidents. Harper, for example, picked an entire faculty of well over a hundred in the year before his university opened its doors. In a legendary incident known as "Harper's Raid," he appeared briefly in Worcester, Massachusetts, and left with at least half the faculty of Clark University; he would have taken the president, too, and at a higher salary than he was then earning, had Hall been amenable. These presidents had very busy days indeed, and some had very little wish to pursue the old routines of enforcing discipline or maintaining compulsory chapel. They worked prodigiously, wrote volumes with little secretarial help, and traveled endlessly on long railroad journeys. But if they made do with little support and looked after details unimaginable now, if they persisted in thinking moral discipline a significant dimension of their role in undergraduate education, the founders can scarcely fit under a generic rubric of "nineteenth-century" presidents. The institutional visions they followed and the "university idea" to which they subscribed were set in conscious contrast to the traditions they worked to supersede and to the more conventional aspirations of their contemporaries.

The same presidents, in helping to create the new university, helped also to change the assumptions that had identified their office. Obviously, the rapid growth of numbers (students, faculty, staff, and programs), the proliferation of the disciplines of knowledge and research, the expansion of facilities and of relationships with external entities would guarantee such a result. But more fundamentally, these presidents assisted, with varying degrees of enthusiasm, in developing the forms of governance and shared responsibility that are often seen to have diminished the potential of strong presidential leadership and necessary institutional change and yet are also seen as basic to the idea of a true academic community. A constitutional foundation had been laid, however reluctant the motivations that produced it or partial its actual effects.

Our modern stereotypes of the administrator as academic philistine or failed professor or power-hungry bureaucrat or gutless politician have a long history, too. After all, an academic administrator—the term itself is thought by some an oxymoron—plays a political part (one hopes a constructive one) in a drama enacted by and for purists who are naturally contemptuous and suspicious of anything that smacks of compromise.

Listen to these words of a professor writing in 1902:

Unfortunately, very few of our college presidents have taken a preliminary course to qualify them for the position. Indeed, it must be confessed that ability to superintend educational work has not been regarded in all cases as the essential prerequisite; in some cases that appears to have been thought less important than a supposed ability to collect money. But at the best no one man is able now to understand all the phases of university or even college work. . . . The best of presidents becomes weakened by the overwhelming importance of the financial side and comes to look upon increasing numbers as the sure proof of success. He soon finds himself between the upper millstone of the trustees and the nether millstone of the faculty, the former insisting upon numbers, the latter upon a high standard, so that in an honest effort to perform his duty, he is in danger of receiving censure from both.

The college itself is not the school of thirty-five years ago; the whole system of training has been changed, and there is offered not a narrow but a broad education. Yet one finds in control of the vast institution the same president as in the olden time, with powers like those of an academy principal and often with the same sense of personal ownership.[4]

A long history attaches, too, to modern patterns of consultative governance within a kind of constitutionally protected order, however intensified and elaborated that has become in the present.

President Harper recruited his first faculty almost single-handedly, but he had also to negotiate with them. In a seller's market, they capitalized on what has come to be called free agency. And when he went to Ithaca to soothe the anxieties of two senior professors hooked from Cornell, he was greeted by, and came to agree with, their protest that major matters affecting academic policy in the planned university should not be decided by the three of them, let alone by Harper acting on his own. He set out immediately to design some mechanisms of faculty consultation. Eliot, it is true, had broad power over appointments (or at least nominations to the governing boards, which sometimes proved troublesome). But in practice, he engaged in considerable consultation, and by the last decade of the century, Eliot would normally forward appointments and promotions only after their initiation or approval by the senior professors of the relevant department and on the recommendation of the dean of the faculty.[5]

In short, while the fullness of the faculty's role in the appointment process took some decades to unfold, the understanding of its foundations and strong presidents' acceptance of its desirability had come to be quite well settled in the leading universities of the late nineteenth century. Future arguments and developments were to revolve around the extent, and not the importance, of such faculty participation. In the newly created departmental structure of universities, it is not surprising to find the swift emergence of the belief that educational policy and judgments of academic need, opportunity, and quality should find their point of origin in the organized faculty.

The presidents, whether out of obedience to political necessity or thoughtful concurrence, helped lay the groundwork for those important attributes of university and collegiate governance and therefore also for another important aspect of presidential leadership: leadership in the interest of sustaining the value of process in institutions of higher education, leadership to preserve what might be called the constitutional norms of a healthy academic community.

The late nineteenth century saw several celebrated episodes that raised acutely the questions of academic freedom, its significance for the integrity of academic institutions, and the responsibility of presidents for maintaining the conditions under which it might thrive. Not surprisingly, these cases and others less dramatic tended to involve professors holding what could be considered heterodox views on economics and social policy, boards with views divided on or even hostile to the changing character of university life, or influential outsiders alarmed by the subversive and anarchic dangers of unfettered thought and expression. It is not, to put it mildly, as though the presidents always behaved like giants on these as on other issues. It is certainly not as though the problem went away. The recurrent crises that have spawned the need for the defense of academic freedom—whether freedom from external intrusion and pressure or freedom from internal orthodoxies and conformities, both implicit and explicit—will never go away. Nor will the concomitant need and opportunity to explore and to explicate the complexities of what universities are about and why their preservation matters. At the same time, it had become clear that the sustenance of institutional independence and of intellectual autonomy, the obligation of maintaining the greatest possible freedom of expression and outlook within an academic community in the interests of the long term and for the pursuit of its educational and scholarly purpose, were, together with the protection of appropriate process and the oversight of an institution's academic and material health, the central mandate given to a president.

Following from this point, we may note yet another shift of emphasis in defining presidential responsibility and presidential leadership, one that has developed far more gradually and is still fiercely debated. If the freeing of individuals to pursue their deepest interests—wherever those may lead within a framework of common commitment to that purpose and its myriad outcomes—is combined with the imperative of institutional autonomy and academic freedom in providing the conditions for pursuing that end, then the president must be vigilant in enabling these values as the *raison d'être* of an institution of higher education.

The president's responsibility has its source in the nature of the institution's mission, always imperfectly realized and always vulnerable to controversy and radical misunderstanding. The president has the obligation of spokesmanship and action on behalf of academic purposes. That being the case, the president cannot become an advocate for other causes that are not germane to that mission, cannot presume to speak for the institution on matters that fall outside its own special functions and competence. To do so would imperil both institutional autonomy and individual freedom within the academy.

The temptation to act the secular preacher is powerful, as is that of benign paternalism in providing moral instruction for the young. Were any of this even possible in the midst of the presidential life that has been described, it would still, I think, be inappropriate for presidents to see the function of moral guidance as their rightful role. There are of course a lot of people who want to see presidents doing just this and who deride their pusillanimous caution. The same people are often infuriated when a president does do what they ask, finding themselves in shock and disagreement and castigating the president's college or university for falling prey to such false and disgraceful opinions.

If a university and the responsibilities of its leaders are defined and judged by the purposes distinctive to that institution and no other, it follows that the ethic of the academy, and the teaching of that ethic, must be based in those purposes and the activities to which they give rise. Ultimately, an institution dedicated to intellectual aims is directly concerned with the priority of one virtue in particular, a virtue that it exists distinctively to teach, to support in practice, and to see constantly renewed and expanded. That is the virtue of intellectual integrity, and this is ideally the quality that education and scholarship and serious debate will aspire to exemplify.

Intellectual integrity is not, of course, divorced from other aspects of character. But its nature and assimilation do have something to do with learning, with the aims of learning, and with the vocation of learning. Critical and independent judgment, respect for evidence, openness to other points of view, tolerance of complexity and uncertainty, willingness to undertake reexamination and to suspend final conclusions, patience with rigorous and even painful analysis, refusal to bend to the fashionable and comfortable, insistence on reasoned explanation—these are among the constituents of principled conduct in the realm of intellectual integrity. The quest for thinking and acting along such lines is the identifying vocation of academic existence, the identifying aim of genuine education, the identifying excellence of first-rate scholarship and teaching.

Do presidents have a special role in this form of moral instruction and action? Like all their colleagues in the academic community, they should of course be outspoken and committed adherents of such precepts. More generally, their conduct in fulfilling them will be the means by which genuine leadership can benefit the given institution and its individual members alike. Intellectual integrity will help make possible a vigorous institutional integrity.

It is, in a sense, easy to state abstractly the guidelines for academic freedom or for the distinctions between a president's institutional role and that person's stance on any number of matters that lie outside his or her function as corporate spokesperson for the academic community. It is easy, too, to see the dramatic instances of challenge to core academic values, like those of the early 1950s, of loyalty oaths and McCarthyite terrors, as the ground on which our battles have been fought and won or lost with greater or lesser courage and dignity. But the real tests, I think, come with the persistent, less public challenges that affect the life and work of academic institutions, with the universities' strength and steadfastness of response to those and with their success in applying guiding principles to individual cases that are by nature ambiguous.

It is one thing to assert the distinction between exercising the rightful forms of corporate spokesmanship on behalf of academic policies and priorities on the one hand and the inappropriate taking of social and political positions that come to be identified with the corporate academic community on the other. But exactly where that line is to be drawn is, as we all know, often very hard to discover in concrete and controversial cases, as for example in the matter of endowment investment policy. Similarly, the basic requirements of intellectual freedom and of civil behavior may appear at odds and in need of calibration in crucial instances. It is in the capacity to preside over discussion and decision on such matters in accordance with standards imposed by the imperatives of intellectual integrity and principled attention to long-term goals that the contributions and leadership of presidents may ultimately be judged. The ability to sustain that imperative in the daily routine to the greatest extent, and its consequences for institutional integrity over time, sets the ultimate measure.

I have not, I think, said anything fundamentally different from President Shapiro, only shuffled the cards a bit. Let me now touch on his points as to the multiple roles of presidents and the nature of presidential authority in our day and return once again to our theme of "then and now."

I have argued that while many presidents of the late nineteenth century continued to emphasize a traditional conception of collegiate education and their own preceptorial role, others stood out who in part shared but who also pushed beyond the legacy of the prevailing collegiate culture. This culture was in turn affected by all kinds of burgeoning trends—for professionalization, for women's education and coeducation, for new kinds of growth and service. Some presidents led such movements; others adapted more cautiously to their aims. Some founded and others re-created institutions both public and private. Some acceded less willingly and more selectively to the winds of change. In all circumstances there was conflict. Higher education underwent rapid growth, and presidents became increasingly aware of the limitations inherent in their office, increasingly distracted by a multiplicity of roles they could not escape.

The work of attending to institutional process and autonomy, the collegial conception of educational governance, the need at all times to persuade and be responsive to faculty and boards and external supporters, the function of arbitration among competing interests as well as decisive action and spokesmanship on behalf of the whole— these features of the presidential role were as visible to the presidents of the late nineteenth century as they are to us now. If to us these seem beginnings and if their extent and intensity have grown immensely, that does not diminish the experience of the late-nineteenth-century founders (nor does it mean that all this was simply their work—not at all). For the generation of the founders, the emphasis on such duties was relatively new and the stirring of such beginnings a compelling and not always welcome challenge. These presidents often expressed great frustration over the constraints under which they labored. Men and women whom modern presidents envy because they appear so much closer to the educational direction of their institutions and so much more powerful in getting their way, and— shall I say it?—were accorded so much more respect were often discouraged by feeling how slight an authority they wielded and how small the results they achieved, even when those look monumental to us.

President Shapiro has quoted William Rainey Harper's essay "The College President" and his conclusion that "the office of president is an office of service. Everything good or bad which connects itself with service is associated with this office." Before these words Harper had written as follows:

> A close study of the situation will show that when all has been said, the limitations of the college president, even when he has the greatest freedom of action, are very great. In all business matters he is the servant of the trustees or corporation; and his views will prevail in that body only in so far as they approve themselves to their good judgment. In educational policy he must be in accord with his colleagues. If he cannot persuade them to adopt his views, he must go with them. It is absurd to suppose that any president, however strong or willful he may be, can force a faculty, made

up of great leaders of thought, to do his will. The president, if he has the power of veto, may stand in the way of progress, but he cannot secure forward movement except with the co-operation of those with whom he is associated.[6]

And later:

To what definite thing can the president point, and say—this is my work? Does he not find his highest function in helping others to do the things which he himself would like to do? Yet he must stand aside and see others take up this very work which in his heart he would desire to handle. The head of an institution is not himself permitted to finish a piece of work. It is his business to find ways and means by which others may be helped to do their work.[7]

Some fifty years after Harper wrote these words, a successor whose towering figure still looms over contemporary longings for the second coming of giants in higher education made his own analysis of the trivial authority available to a president and, typically, tried to do something about it. Robert Maynard Hutchins was renowned for his youth, his impatience, and his readiness to speak out on almost every question (including the ruin wreaked on America by the Republican party and the reasons why America should stay out of war). He was known for his scathing attacks on the state of the higher learning and his missionary zeal for expunging the evils wrought by Charles William Eliot and the elective system, which he believed had destroyed all genuine education and scholarship. Equally well recognized as a courageous and articulate defender of academic freedom, Hutchins spoke with dismay of the conditions of the presidency he held so long. Patience, he said, was a terribly overrated quality. It was definitely not one of the virtues a president should seek; President Eliot's belief in its importance was yet another of his characteristic errors. A faculty member (one who was actually quite well disposed toward Hutchins) said of him, "He was incautious and close to arrogant. . . . He took upon himself to try to exercise a function which constitutionally, I thought, belonged to the faculty (or to God); and he did this by methods that often trenched upon the high-handed."[8]

After fifteen years in office, Hutchins allowed his frustration to boil over. Those who attended the annual Trustee-Faculty Dinner of the University of Chicago in the winter of 1944 must have remained unusually alert during the president's after-dinner address. He began by comparing long-serving presidents to flagpole sitters, went on to say that nothing whatsoever had been accomplished in the preceding fifteen years, questioned the reputation for excellence and innovation of his university, decried the credit and course system and its failure to educate, attacked what he called the "farce" of academic rank, asked that all outside earnings of professors be returned to the university, recommended that compensation for faculty be based on individual or familial need rather than rank and seniority, and called for a new Institute of Liberal Studies that would award the Ph.D. as a teaching degree, leaving preparation for research to other programs and new degrees.

Hutchins announced that the purpose of the university was "nothing less than to procure a moral, intellectual, and spiritual revolution throughout the world." "The whole scale of values by which our society lives," he said, "must be reversed if any society is to endure." The means to such a revolution lay through giving voice and effective life to a genuine conception of liberal education. Finally, Hutchins maintained that academic organization as constituted—by which he meant the dispersion of authority without accountabililty and the support this rendered to obstructionism in the face of any change—must give way to granting the president real power of decision on all essential matters (including educational policy and appointments). He proposed some safeguards involving elected terms of office, formal reviews, and provisions by which votes of no confidence could be registered. But, he said, it was urgent that modern universities move beyond the forms of organization that had once been suitable for simple colleges. "All theories of organization based on a separation of powers have broken down," he claimed. "They have paralyzed the executive without protecting his constituents, or they have led to extra-constitutional means of getting things done, such as the party and the patronage of the President of the United States. A university president is a political leader without patronage and without a party."[9]

Hutchins's speech, and succeeding ones that reiterated his points, created a firestorm of anxiety and outrage. His call for a "moral, intellectual, and spiritual revolution" was intepreted as a plan to impose an ideological orthodoxy on the university; his demand for presidential authority, as a dictatorial assault on duly established rights and freedoms; and the proposals relating to compensation, rank, the giving of degrees, and the ultimate definition of liberal education and its proper teaching, as an attempt to get the presidential way at no matter what cost. There followed a prolonged crisis at the University of Chicago, one that could have been, but did not become, destructive, for several reasons: because Hutchins's own respect for constitutional rules, even if he wanted them redrafted, was so great; because the faculty wanted a real resolution and in fact respected Hutchins; and because a board of trustees under wise leadership helped elevate the conflict to the status of thoughtful collegial discussion and constructive outcome.

Hutchins did not, of course, get his way. I would observe that he may have been in some ways the last of the giants to see the academic world in terms of a moral compass that sought to convert and remake the individual and the world. He was a secular preacher and missionary for a faith that believed in regeneration or salvation by grace alone—an intellectual grace to whose acquisition the works of education and reason, mediated through the word of canonical texts, formed a hard and noble path ending in moral renewal. It was, he thought, the president's ministerial responsibility to persuade people of that truth and to that path.

It is also of interest, I think, to note that Hutchins was not entirely one-sided. He represented two strong tendencies in a state of tension: the passionate desire to possess real authority and the equally serious conviction that constitutional and procedural rules, however irksome, should not be violated. He wanted not to undo but to reform and direct an institution for which, despite his impatience with its erring ways and its failure to live up to his grandest visions, he held considerable reverence. He wanted to preserve its fundamental freedom as critic and gadfly together with the freedoms of thought and expression that this required, and no president has ever been more eloquent in stating those values.

The tallest presidents of the late nineteenth or even mid-twentieth century could scarcely have peered so far as to foresee the university of now, of the late twentieth century. The impact of the government relationship, as President Shapiro has pointed out, is probably the single most important element in the complex of developments that have shaped our present state, as always stemming as much from social and political causes of external origin as from the logic of its own internal development. The lives of presidents are inevitably further removed from the direct participation in every aspect of their institutions that once prevailed, and they devote vast amounts of time to matters like large medical centers and to forms of public service and engagement that earlier generations could not have fathomed. The articulation of shared governance and of the systems of tenure and process in appointments has moved to new levels. The problematic dilemmas seen to intervene between managing to stimulate institutional change and doing so while maintaining the traditions of shared governance appear more formidable than ever, especially in an age of contraction and amid the pressures and expectations of an uncertain environment.

Nor does the presidential role described in this situation appear heroic. As the man hired to mow the lawn at the cemetery was told, "You'll have a lot of people under you, but you won't be able to get them to do much."

The past is always more heroic than the present—we know that. Yet could it be, we ask ourselves, that some pasts really *were* more heroic? Were the giants of the late nineteenth century, human and imperfect as on closer contact we see them to be, not really taller? Was the opportunity to be founders not unique?

My own conclusion is that there were giants then and there have been giants since, the latter harder to identify because the rest of humanity has not yet shrunk to scale. Giants may, of course, be founders. Over time, they are still more likely to be steadfast leaders and renewers, generally under difficult and distracting circumstances that will seem threatening to the requirements of preserving and enhancing the conditions and possibilities of the higher learning and its institutions. Their voices may be quiet, their most important works perhaps invisible as they take place, but cumulative and weighty in their consequence.

In my view, the roles of academic leadership relate above all to what President Harper called "service" and what I would call "enabling," an activity never performed by one person alone in our setting. It means enabling people to meet their own highest standards in an environment at once supportive and demanding, enabling institutions to reach, over the long term, toward their goals. Such enabling, at its best, will rest on a foundation of collegial respect, disciplined restraint, constancy of purpose, and old-fashioned courage, on a willingness to pursue what may be unpopular at the moment and speak out against the merely popular, and on faithfulness to the academic calling itself. Such enabling leadership does not presume to rule but is not afraid to lead, to take decisive positions, and to accept accountability. It recognizes that the president's is but one of the many interrelated roles that together give a degree of form and stability and a reasoned sense of common ends to an academic community that is, by its nature, a society of individualists and questioners.

On the subject of giants, Sir Winston Churchill can perhaps provide us with a coda for these reflections. "I did not," he wrote in his memoirs, "suffer from any desire to be relieved of my responsibilities. All I wanted was compliance with my wishes after reasonable discussion."

And that, I suppose, is probably what giants have always thought, both then and now.

Notes

1. Samuel Eliot Morison, *Three Centuries of Harvard* (Cambridge, Mass.: Harvard University Press, 1936), pp. 335–336.

2. Oscar Handlin, "Making Men of the Boys," in *Glimpses of the Harvard Past* (Cambridge, Mass.: Harvard University Press, 1986), p. 109.

3. Morison, *Three Centuries*, p. 349.

4. J. J. Stevenson, "University Control," in Richard Hofstadter and Wilson Smith (eds.), *American Higher Education: A Documentary History*, vol. 2 (Chicago: University of Chicago Press, 1961), pp. 763, 768–769.

5. Morison, *Three Centuries*, pp. 372–373.

6. William Rainey Harper, "The College President," n.d., cited in Richard J. Storr, *Harper's University* (Chicago: University of Chicago Press, 1966), p. 103.

7. Ibid., p. 104.

8. T. V. Smith in Harry S. Ashmore, *Unseasonable Truths: The Life of Robert Maynard Hutchins* (Boston: Little, Brown, 1989), p. 109.

9. Robert Maynard Hutchins Papers (January 12, 1944), box 26, folder 3 (University of Chicago Library).

THE FACULTY

A Neglected Topic: Professional Conduct of College and University Teachers

HENRY ROSOVSKY WITH INGE-LISE AMEER

AN IMPORTANT characteristic of nearly all major professions is the existence of explicit and shared codes of conduct that are part of the training received by those preparing to enter these fields.[1] By codes of conduct we mean a college or university teacher's obligations to colleagues, students, institution, and field of study. Medical schools make an effort to teach the aspiring doctor the norms of proper professional behavior. Every young physician is given a sense of what is or is not permitted or proper in dealing with patients. To give an example, in 1994, every entering student at the Harvard Medical School received a letter that said in part, "Medical school differs from other graduate and professional education in that . . . you will be interacting with patients from your first week in school. For this reason, medical students are expected to demonstrate the behavior of physicians. Honesty, kindness, respect for others . . . are each as important as mastery of the science and skills, and are all evaluated as components of professional development."[2] Both Harvard and Yale medical schools require first-year students to take courses examining professional responsibility and the patient-doctor relationship. Stanford Medical School offers a wide variety of electives about the same subjects.[3]

The legal profession shows similar concerns. Judges enforce standards of conduct, lawyers are responsible to a bar, and one does not graduate from law school without some acquaintance with a code of legal ethics. All law schools have a professional responsibility requirement because it is needed to pass the various bar examinations. In addition, most major law schools offer a wide selection of courses concerned with this topic.

We wish to express our warm gratitude to Derek C. Bok, William G. Bowen, and Dennis Thompson for many helpful comments. We are also grateful to The Andrew W. Mellon Foundation for supporting the project of which this paper is one result.

No one would suggest that doctors and lawyers always adhere to the high principles of their callings—we know better—but at least these professions make an effort to safeguard and propagate an enabling and unifying set of values.[4] In recent years, business schools have also shown an increasing interest in teaching ethics.

For all these reasons, it is puzzling that university and college professors have shown so little interest in studying or teaching issues related to their own professional conduct. University professors teach ethics to doctors and lawyers and businessmen and women. They offer in-depth study of ethical questions in departments of philosophy. But very little attention has been paid to the norms of conduct of their own profession: college and university teaching and researching. Why? Surely our actions have complex consequences and involve much independent judgment. What we do influences the future, fortune, and lives of our students. We can ruin a life just as easily as any doctor or lawyer. Do we assume that an understanding of professional conduct is a genetic trait among Ph.D. students?[5]

Perhaps academic attitudes reflect an insufficient appreciation of social change, as well as the feeling of professors that they are not equipped to teach professional ethics and an exaggerated faith in mentoring. They may also be a reflection of human nature combined with insufficient accountability. In any case, one does not frequently hear of a disbarred professor. Indeed, when professors talk of unprofessional conduct, they often have in mind how they are treated by their institutions rather than their own conduct! Mentoring—as reality and myth—is a strong tradition in all professions. Teachers are compared to parents—as in the very first sentence of the Oath of Hippocrates "I will look upon him who shall have taught me this Art even as one of my parents"—and the ties with pupils stress reciprocal obligations that last a lifetime. Maimonides said that if forgiveness is requested three times from an offended person, and if the individual remains obdurate, no further effort is required. "But if the offended person was that offender's teacher, the pupil has to go to him again and again, even a thousand times, till pardon has been granted."[6] All the free professions initially used this "laying on of hands" model, but is it still valid?

Whatever the situation in the past, our primary concern has to be the present, and we will not find it easy to escape the circumstances of the society in which we live. This is how Dan Yankelovich recently described the "real threat": "Any society that elevates individualism to the highest rank of values and then proceeds to weaken individual responsibility is asking for disaster. It is to be doubted whether any such society can function for very long."[7] Substitute university for society and the shoe still fits. What Yankelovich describes is a far bigger threat to the future of universities than allegedly neglected undergraduates, rising costs, or political correctness. To put it differently, it is a basic ingredient of all of these ills.

Today, there is a conspicuous lack of agreement concerning appropriate standards of professional conduct. Is it proper for professors to date students? Who has jurisdiction over what is taught in the classroom? How far does a professor's authority go in the classroom? Are speech codes that prohibit racial insults either desirable or constitutional? How many authors can reasonably claim credit for the same scientific paper, and what does signing a paper imply in terms of responsibility for content? What are the obligations of a professor to a student? What are proper standards of accountability? All of these varied and not necessarily closely related questions are complicated, and no answer is devoid of controversy.

Of one thing we may be sure: that an individual who joins the academic profession will almost never have received any instruction concerning conduct or the dimensions of a social contract. A law teacher is likely to have some training in legal ethics; a chemist will be informed about standards of research; someone teaching in a divinity school can be expected to understand moral conduct from a religious point of view. The chances are overwhelming, however, that none of these individuals will have ever been required seriously to consider conduct in their capacity as university teachers. We do not know of any university that has this kind of requirement.[8]

Why Now?

MENTORING IN DECLINE

The traditional method of transmitting standards of conduct in higher education was thought to be mentoring: masters (older professors) initiating apprentices (graduate students and younger professors). Of course, the masters were supposed to assume responsibility for the moral as well as the technical development of their apprentices.

Perhaps this was always an excessively romantic model, but there can be no doubt that the rise of what Edward Shils called the "mass university" and the "bureaucratized university" has seriously weakened whatever mentoring impulses may have existed.[9] As long ago as the late 1960s, Jacques Barzun observed, "Nowhere is the Oral Tradition of learning transmitted . . . The thing missed in the present system is not the rudiments of pedagogy, important as they are, but the intangible contents of scholarly succession. The quasi-apprentice system of an older day used to assure this continuity."[10]

Mass and its inevitable companion, *bureaucracy*, imply size, formality, and impersonality. The act of mentoring connotes opposites: one on one, informality, and personal warmth. It is not that "small is beautiful"; it is simply that a master cannot train fifteen apprentices at once while serving on six committees and simultaneously consulting for three corporations. Individual instruction has diminished, and close personal ties between teacher and student have weakened. Disciplinary competence now appears to be the sole measure of professional development.

These tendencies are reinforced by an important demographic and social transformation that became especially noticeable after World War II. "The 1950 census put the number of academics at 190,000. By 1960 the number had grown to 281,000, by 1970 to a whopping 532,000."[11] Today the figure stands at over 800,000.[12]

In the not so recent past, when our society was more closed and hierarchical, large groups were denied entry into the academy by a variety of direct and indirect means, primarily quotas, lack of money for prolonged study, and the inability to penetrate networks. Groups chosen for disfavor included people of color, recent immigrants, Jews, Roman Catholics, and women—a not insignificant share of our population.[13]

In the "good old days," professions had a more patrician cast. Law and medical offices could, without obstacle, pass from father to son. Successive generations of one family that followed academic pursuits were not uncommon, especially if we include the children of ministers. Under these circumstances, moral and ethical training could be a part of growing up. Standards of professional conduct, one might suppose, were absorbed at the dinner table, in church, and perhaps in clubs.

Once entry shifted to a greater emphasis on merit, thereby gradually sweeping away social and economic barriers, considerable changes occurred in the composition of professionals. In the academy, newcomers brought heightened technical skills and raised average levels of competence. What they failed to bring were traditions of professionalism or conduct that extended beyond the narrow confines of the particular subject that they had mastered in school. Their allegiance was to subject rather than to student or institution. Perhaps they could provide mentoring in disciplines, but they were not equipped to deal with broader issues. At the same time, those who had absorbed some standards of professional conduct at the dinner table or in other informal settings were gradually leaving the scene as a simple function of age.[14]

No feelings of nostalgia are intended. The atmosphere may have been more genteel in the past, but there is no reason to believe that it was morally superior. Students and faculties were more homogeneous and professors may have been better institutional citizens, but the intellectual climate surely was less lively. Whatever benefits homogeneity may have had came at a high price: discrimination of many types—a major form of ethical failure.

THE VALUE OF WHAT WE KNOW AND RESOURCES TO FIND OUT MORE

The years after World War II not only caused a social transformation within university faculties but also assigned a much higher value to their research output. Research in the natural sciences became crucial to defense, medicine, and many aspects of manufacturing. Government and industry poured billions of dollars into university scholars because they were the principal source of new ideas and also willing investigators.

This trend was not confined to the natural sciences. Social sciences also claimed more public attention and public dollars. Economists played increasingly important roles in policy formation; survey research had an interdisciplinary base in the social sciences; politicians of all kinds sought the expertise and advice of scholar-experts. Even the humanities were affected as the media and other organs of information transmittal required ever more material as well as those articulate enough to interpret changes in culture.

A greater value placed on knowledge possessed by professors and the resources to purchase research results is not all bad. Society benefits, and for those in universities it is heady stuff: more attention, more money, more travel, more glamour—more of everything except time or inclination to perform what might be called the professor's pastoral duties. The pull between "inside" and "outside" is not a zero-sum game. Outside activities open opportunities not only for teachers but also for students. They may well improve certain kinds of teaching by giving professors richer experiences and material. Nevertheless, the lure of the outside has to undermine institutional citizenship because a professor's marketability as a researcher or lecturer and commentator is largely personal—a function of disciplinary standing. In other words, there has been, in the postwar decades, a declining incentive to concentrate on the intramural community of students and teachers.

SPECIALIZATION AND PROFESSIONALIZATION

Increasing specialization is very closely related to the value placed by society on research. As we know more, specialization becomes necessary and inevitable; resources make it possible. Whether or not specialization has been excessive from an educational point of view is not now precisely the issue. (It is, of course, an overwhelmingly important question.) Rather, we have to ask how specialization and professionalization affect conduct and academic ethics. That most prescient student of higher education, Eric Ashby, stated the problem very clearly. He characterized academics as belonging to two guilds. The first is the guild of university teachers "demanding loyalty to the university he serves and the pupils under his care." The requirements of the first guild are easily overshadowed by those of the second guild to which we also belong: our peers in specialization. Since Ashby wrote those words in 1970, we all know that the shadow of the second guild has continued to lengthen.[15]

COMPETITION

That American institutions of higher education compete with each other for students, faculty, and funding has had positive results. This becomes especially clear when one contrasts the progress of our system with those systems in other countries in which competition is stifled. Most observers agree that the upper end of the American system of higher education sets a standard that others wish to emulate, and this would include quality of faculty (recruited all over the globe), students (actively recruited on the basis of widely ranging achievements), and facilities. Most observers would also agree that institutional competition has played an important role in creating the American advantage. Competition requires the ability to change, to alter direction, to pursue new initiatives. The absence of competition usually means status quo.

At the same time, there is a darker side to competition. Competitive forces will give advantage to some fields and individuals over others. The market is an external force and makes us more likely to respond to the second guild at the expense of the first. The well-known star system—absent in most countries—could not exist in the absence of competition. Stars bring visibility and luster; they also bring special deals, special—in the sense of privileged—rules of conduct, and discord and jealousy.

The point is simple. Intense competition among our universities is largely a postwar phenomenon that has undermined some aspects of professorial conduct. It has greatly increased the power of professors and given many of them immunity from institutional control.

POOR MANAGEMENT

All of the foregoing has been made infinitely more complicated by archaic and inefficient management practices. The background, as we have said, consists of rapidly changing internal and external circumstances, both social and economic. Business has faced similar circumstances, but tight and supposedly efficient corporate practices are rarely appropriate for scholars who require a great deal of independence. Business management assumes the existence of a clearly identifiable bottom line and close control by supervisory personnel. Neither is a powerful or practical tool in universities.

Scholars do have obligations to their institutions, and that is where universities frequently fail to enforce reasonable standards. In the words of Steven M. Cahn, "the first step toward discharging duties is to know what they are,"[16] and that we often accomplish in unforgivably casual fashion. Most professors have little sense of social contract—after all, who or what will give them that sense?—and most administrations lack the basic information needed for even rudimentary managerial efficiency. For example, we believe that every dean should have a desktop computer console where, upon typing in the name of a faculty member, would immediately appear that individual's current and past teaching assignments with class enrollments, number of Ph.D. students, number of undergraduate honors theses under current supervision, salary history, leaves, major committee assignments, absences, consultancies, a list of publications, and other particulars. Nearly all institutions have this information—but hardly ever in readily usable form. Furthermore, faculty members do not necessarily want administrators to have these data readily available: Why give ammunition to Big Brother?

The problems associated with poor management go beyond inefficient practices. Universities also show administrative lack of will, and that is a more damaging weakness. Faculty behavior (e.g., little teaching and frequent absences) has been rational and understandable, given the absence of constraints. For this, administrations should assume a major share of the blame because of a manifest unwillingness to set clear tasks and clear limits. In this matter, deans and presidents have not displayed the required degree of leadership, and their determination has certainly been undermined by all the subjects discussed here: social transformation, professionalization, competition, and so on.

OTHER POSSIBILITIES

In trying to explain why issues of conduct are particularly pressing at this time, two rather more speculative influences can be mentioned.

Shils used a variety of adjectives to describe the current state of universities: *mass, service, politicized, bureaucratized, financially straitened*, and *disaggregated*.[17] All are rather disagreeable terms, and they apply to a greater or lesser extent to nearly all American research universities. Their meaning certainly affects faculty behavior. Bureaucratization in particular tends to transform faculty from "owners" into employees, and employees are more likely to limit commitment physically and psychologically: we put in our nine-to-five, and let it go at that. Such tendencies may be unavoidable in large institutions, and they are reinforced by growing government regulation and our legal system. The second guild—to borrow Ashby's term—is the beneficiary: more time for "one's own" work, fewer annoyances, and greater rewards associated with "peers in specialization."

Closely related is the fact that disaggregation applies not only within institutions but also to individual professors. Most larger campuses are no longer residential communities of teachers and students living in close proximity. At Harvard, for example, professors and other staff have increasingly been forced to move to the suburbs. That is dictated by housing costs and quality of schools, and it clearly contributes to a nine-to-five attitude. A parking space becomes more important than a study in the library. Not all institutions have suffered equally from this factor: Princeton and Chicago are far better off than Columbia, MIT, or UCLA. In general, however, most of our larger research universities have to consider the influence of the real estate market after World War II as negative.

Finally, one has to wonder about the legacy of the 1960s: Did the student revolution strengthen the second guild? Probably only in the short term. An older generation may have been traumatized by building occupations and other forms of disruption. To use Milovan Djilas's famous phrase, a certain amount of "internal emigration" occurred, although those most affected are now leaving the scene.[18] A new generation of faculty is sometimes described as today's "tenured radicals," referring to former student leaders of the 1960s. That description applies only to very few individuals, and it is hard to think of them as in any sense disengaged. After all, they stand accused— usually without much supporting evidence—of politicizing the internal functioning of their schools.

We have now examined various reasons why problems arise if universities continue to rely on informal methods to transmit standards of conduct from one scholarly generation to the next. Paying little attention to conduct and ethics is deeply ingrained in the academic profession. Shils's conclusions are particularly revealing. "Even at the height of the glory of the German universities from the last third of [the nineteenth] century . . . the promulgation of an academic ethic was not taken in hand. *Perhaps it was thought to be superfluous.*" He adds that the same was true in the United States, Great Britain, and France in the first quarter of the twentieth century, because professorial "obligations were accepted as *self-evident.*"[19] The point of this section has been to suggest that neither *self-evident* nor *superfluous* can be applied to discussions of professional conduct at this time.[20]

Can Anything Be Done?

We are neither alone nor the first to make most of these observations. Frequently cited authorities concerning professional conduct would include Burton Clark, David Dill, Donald Light, and Walter Metzger, and there is a fair degree of agreement among these authors.[21] All of them make special note of the fragmented nature of the profession, resulting in little consensus about professional expectations—by institutions of professors, by professors of each other, or by professors vis-à-vis students. Given the large number of diverse colleges and universities that include faculty who primarily teach, faculty who teach and do research, and scholars (often outside universities) who just do research, any notion of a meaningful consensus disappears. Indeed, Light says that "the academic man is a myth" and that "the academic profession does not exist."[22]

The authorities also seem to agree about the reasons for fragmentation: growth, specialization, and an increasing influence by professional schools. Kenneth P. Ruscio, another expert, makes the entirely believable prediction that we will increasingly come to think of academics as belonging to separate professions "taking *profession* to mean different work styles, reference groups, objectives, organization of authority, and attitudes."[23]

Fragmentation also implies that a meaningful professional code of conduct does not appear promising. Perhaps a variety of codes might be more meaningful, but that would still leave us with difficult problems of enforcement. The history of academic administration does not permit much optimism when it comes to that task.[24]

In general, those who write about the subject of academic ethics and conduct appear to be content to describe and analyze the problem. There are very few practical suggestions about improving or reversing what many see as a deteriorating situation. One exception is David Dill, who does propose offering instruction:

> Discussions of professional responsibility are rare, sporadic, and of crude quality . . . To date we have been unable to effectively bring together broad collections of doctoral students or faculty to discuss issues of fact or issues of research, or issues of pedagogy, because the gulfs between different disciplines or fields suggests to us that we have little in common on these issues . . . The ethics of the academic profession . . . transcend the gulfs. All faculty members are faced with similar issues of professional choice, particularly of teaching and there should be potential for emotional and intellectually challenging learning on these issues in, for example, a common seminar for doctoral students.[25]

Both of us share an agnosticism concerning the possibility of promulgating effective general codes of conduct, even though we remain interested in the possibility of creating and administering an academic's analog to the Hippocratic Oath.[26] We feel more strongly about the necessity of developing instruction and agree with Dill that there is enough that binds the profession together so that effective learning can occur. Furthermore, it seems possible and desirable to tailor the instruction to the requirements of specific types of institutions. The bottom line is that all who intend to enter the academic profession—regardless of field, in arts and sciences and professional schools—should be required to take instruction in standards of professorial conduct.

In practical terms we have in mind a seminar or course that might last for a maximum of six weeks and would be a required part of the curriculum for graduate students in all fields seeking teaching positions. The course would consist of "classical" readings on standard topics: professorial obligations to students and to institutions, academic freedom and tenure, research standards, free speech, campus politicization, and so on. Class discussion would feature the analysis of specially prepared cases in each category. We are preparing cases for such a course and in the next sections will discuss highly abbreviated versions of two of these cases to illustrate the nature of the education that we hope will result.[27]

The warnings of professional ethicists have been taken into account in the course design:

> Courses in professional ethics . . . often concentrate on what might be called quandaries in practice, especially those faced by the individual practitioner . . . The great prestige of the case method of study in law and busi-

ness schools, and the clinical method of training in medical school, tend to make practitioners divide the moral life into cases.

The teaching of professional ethics needs to go beyond individual quandaries and problems. It should also include institutional and structural criticism, the clarification of professional character and virtue, and the enforcement of professional standards and discipline.[28]

According to William F. May, using cases as an exclusive method of teaching "resembles acute care more than preventive medicine," and that is why a basic set of readings is included. May's comment is not inconsistent with the view that cases train students "not only to know, but to act,"[29] and that, after all, is one of the purposes of becoming familiar with these issues. Both acute care and preventive medicine have their place: without the former, there might not be the need or the opportunity for the latter.

And that brings us to a last preliminary point. We much prefer the expression "professional *conduct*" (or professorial conduct) to the more customary "professional *ethics*" or (professorial ethics). This may be playing with words, because there is considerable overlap between *conduct* and *ethics*. We are, however, trying to make a distinction. Ethics is the province of philosophers and emphasizes general questions of moral principles and values. The Hastings Institute, for very good reasons, urges that all who wish to teach the subject acquire formal training in philosophy or religion.[30] These requirements, as already noted, seem to have left the academic profession almost entirely out of the picture, and there is no indication that this will change anytime soon.

We are not trained philosophers, and our interests are exceedingly practical. Of course, moral principles and values are key to an understanding of readings and cases, but grasping standards of appropriate behavior may be of even greater immediate importance. Long years of experience in universities lead us to believe that it is possible to discuss and instruct in conduct and behavior without a philosophical specialization. However, when the ethicists decide to address university students, teachers, and administrators, we will be glad to yield to their superior wisdom and analytical powers.

That is certainly what Dean Gutmann would like us to do—just as soon as possible—judging by her essay in this volume. But there is little evidence that the ethics profession has much interest in meeting its responsibilities, judging by the number of courses or programs that deal with university teaching and research. Meanwhile, our more modest emphasis on conduct seems to remain useful.

We now turn to an account and analysis of two very different cases to illustrate how aspects of conduct could be taught to prospective members of the academic profession. Both cases address issues of professional conduct. The Stanford case asks, what are the collective responsibilities of a faculty regarding curriculum revision? The Russell case asks, how much authority does a professor have in the classroom? The Stanford case received much national attention. The Russell case was entirely of internal interest. Both are, however, of equal value from an educational point of view.

Case I: Socrates Shares the Stage: The Western Culture Debate at Stanford

THE HISTORY OF CIV

In 1935, Stanford followed in the footsteps of many other universities and developed a Western Civilization course required of all incoming students. The course included selected works from Plato, Homer, Aristotle, Dante, Machiavelli, and Locke. During student unrest in the 1960s, the course fell to criticism and was eliminated. Al Hastorf, dean of humanities and sciences, explained: "The Western Civilization course had lost its gas and change was good." The change took the form of a history course, not a canon course. It occurred in 1973, when the history department developed a Western Civilization course covering the medieval and modern periods titled History 1-2-3. That course, however, was not required of all incoming students.

In 1980, change occurred again. The faculty developed a new required course for all freshmen called Western Culture. Students were given a choice of tracks—separate courses that lasted for a whole academic year. Each of the eight new tracks was built around a single discipline. The tracks did, however, share a common intellectual experience, a list of approximately fifteen canonical texts.[31]

THE TASK FORCE

By 1982, the new Western Culture course appeared to be a success. Student evaluations were generally favorable, and as later evaluations by the alumni demonstrated, the course was valued as a rich part of their four years at Stanford. Not all corners of the campus, however, were pleased with the new course. By 1982–83, the Black Student Union (BSU) began criticizing the "elite" nature of the tracks exemplified by the fact that no women or people of color were included on the core list. Amanda Kemp, a BSU member, wrote in an editorial for the student newspaper, the *Stanford Daily*, that the "implicit message of the current curriculum is nigger go home." Many faculty teaching within the tracks were unhappy. They felt the common list was restrictive or unsuitable and cheated by adding and deleting texts of their choice. In addition to student and faculty concerns with the course, the president of the university, Donald Kennedy, also saw problems: "I had heard concerns for a long time, from students as well as from faculty, about the Western Culture Program. I thought that the Western Culture Steering Committee [the oversight committee for the program] had not paid a great deal of attention to these evaluations of the program. So, I asked Carolyn Lougee [dean of undergraduate studies and professor of history] to get after the Steering Committee and find out what they were doing."

After investigating the situation, Dean Lougee presented a report to the faculty senate on June 12, 1986, that was critical of the Western Culture program because it did not include any scholarship from women or people of color. After Lougee's presentation, there was discussion within the faculty senate, and then Provost James Rosse appointed a task force to evaluate and possibly make changes in the program. The task force consisted of three students, six faculty members, and Dean Lougee. History professor Paul Seaver was appointed chair.

The task force submitted its proposal for reform on October 12, 1987. It proposed unanimously that "Stanford should adopt a new freshman requirement in Cultures, Ideas, and Values, starting in the fall of 1989." The core list was to be abandoned, and all tracks were to reflect multicultural experiences. Texts were to come from at least one of the European cluster of cultures and from at least one of the non-European cultures.

Mary Pratt and some of the other professors who taught in the Western Culture program were excited by the task force's recommendations and decided to start planning a new course applying the new guidelines, a course that would evaluate Western culture from many perspectives. Pratt recalls, "We thought it was a good proposal, so we started planning for the Americas course [the future Europe and the Americas track]. We wanted to have it ready to go with the new legislation. We were surprised by the opposition that later followed the proposal. We were naive."

The proposed track included the following description, "Europe and the Americas studies the dynamics of culture and history of the Americas from pre-Columbian times to the present. Its goals are two: first, it examines historically some European, Native American, African-American, and Asian-American sources of American cultures. Second, it studies the ways these have coexisted, clashed, and intersected over the past five hundred years in the societies of North America, Latin America, and the Caribbean." Some of the authors included on the syllabus were Willa Cather, Virginia Woolf, Gabriel García Márquez, Rigoberta Menchu, Zora Neale Hurston, Maxine Hong Kingston, Mary Shelley, Frederick Douglass, Alexis de Tocqueville, and Thomas More. Several canonical texts from the previous Western Culture list were also incorporated into the proposed track.

According to academic policy at Stanford, all curricular change proposals must first go to the Committee on Undergraduate Studies (CUS) and then to the faculty senate for final approval. On January 19, 1988, the CUS issued a report backing the Cultures, Ideas, and Values (CIV) requirement. Debate on the faculty senate floor was scheduled to begin on January 21.

Even before the senate debate could start, U.S. Secretary of Education William Bennett went on the attack. He condemned Stanford's administration for caving in to student demands and for diminishing the significance of Western culture in undergraduate education. The *New York Times* (January 19, 1988) ran the headline "Stanford Set to Alter Freshman Program in a Dispute on Bias." After learning about the proposed changes in the Western Culture course, Saul Bellow asserted in the *New York Times Magazine* (June 5, 1988) that "when the Zulus have a Tolstoy, we will read him." *Newsweek* (February 1, 1988) ran an article titled, "Say Goodnight, Socrates: Stanford University and the Decline of the West."

Criticisms were coming from within the campus as well. William Chace, professor of English and vice provost for academic planning, circulated a petition proposing alternative legislation. He wanted to keep the tracks as they were originally structured with the list of core texts but add authors who are women and people of color to that list and include new issues.

THE SENATE DEBATE BEGINS

The debate began Thursday, January 21, as students led a vigil outside the building where the meeting was held. A student coalition of the Black Student Union, the Chicano student organization, the Asian-American Student Association, the Stanford American Indian Organization, and Students United for Democratic Education released a statement in support of the reform. William King, president of the BSU, proclaimed, "Today's vigil is a culmination of eight years of struggle. The same faculty who stress thinking critically refuse to look critically at the program they are forcing us to study." Outside the faculty arena, the president and provost were feeling the heat.

The *Wall Street Journal* (December 22, 1988) published an editorial headlined "The Stanford Mind" condemning the new program: "The new course rides the main hobby-horses of today's political left — race, gender and class. The West is perceived not through the evolution of such ideas as faith and justice, but through the prism of sexism, racism, and the faults of the ruling classes."

THE DEBATE ON CAMPUS CONTINUES

The debate on campus continued to swell, with letters pouring into the *Campus Report* and the *Stanford Daily*. Early in March, it appeared as though the proposal was going to die. Tom Wasow, dean of humanities and sciences, observed, "The sticking point was the core list." Chace and his supporters insisted on a common list similar to the one in the Western Culture course included in the new tracks. Pratt and her supporters wanted no set list.

The March 3 faculty senate meeting was tense. Each side was hitting the other hard and refusing to compromise. The campus was being attacked inside and outside, and the pressure was great. Many left the March 3 meeting wondering if the matter would ever be resolved.

A TIME FOR COMPROMISES

As the debate grew more fierce, Paul Robinson, director of the current Western Culture program, called a meeting at his home of those who regularly taught in the program. Both sides of the debate were represented. The groups discussed the possibility of a compromise. They had a second meeting on March 15. At this meeting, the group composed and endorsed two compromises, one drafted by Clay Carson and William Chace (later known as the Carson-Chace compromise) and one drafted by Clay Carson and Paul Seaver (later known as the Carson-Seaver compromise). Clay Carson taught in the Western Culture program.

The Carson-Chace amendment reformulated the instructional objectives of the proposal as follows:

> To give substantial attention to the issues of race, gender, and class during each academic quarter, with at least one of these issues addressed explicitly in at least one major reading in each quarter. (The incorporation of this amendment means that all the tracks would share at least three common themes. It thus represents, in our view, an important step toward guaranteeing a common intellectual experience.)

The Carson-Seaver amendment assured even further a common intellectual experience by charging the committee that would ultimately
be responsible for overseeing the new program with

> supervising an annual process by which the regular faculty and course co-
> ordinators who will be teaching in the various tracks will meet to discuss
> their syllabuses for the following year and to agree on those common ele-
> ments—texts, authors, themes, or issues—that will be taught by all the
> tracks.

The two amendments provided for common themes and for common
texts. They were adopted by the Senate on March 31.

William King said after the vote, "Two generations of students have
worked for this change." William Chace said, "It was an effective
compromise and a very strong achievement."

Stanford: Analysis

The main issues in this case are three closely related questions:

1. Who is responsible for the content of and changes in the curriculum?
2. Is the nature of the institution a major factor in determining what
group or groups have primary responsibility?
3. What has made this topic a matter of such intense political concern?

Nothing is more normal or desirable than occasional curricular debates and, in many cases, the changes that these debates bring about.
Every academic will go through one or two such episodes in a career.
Years later, one will probably look back on these experiences with
satisfaction because the issues matter greatly and permit faculty
members to discuss intellectual topics of general importance, outside
of their narrow fields of specialization. Modern academic life does not
provide many such opportunities. The ultimate responsibility for the
curriculum is the essence of this case.

This is, admittedly, a debatable conclusion. Many readers of the
case may be influenced by the excitement of current disputes: "multi-
culti," Western civilization under attack by the brigands of political
correctness or perhaps from the other end of the political spectrum, a
traditional old-boy network resisting all change. These remain important issues for higher education, but they are trendy and as such have
relatively short lives. Curricular design and content are nearly eternal
issues: they will confront us for as long as colleges and universities
exist.

The subjects included in a course of study—requirements and electives—make up a curriculum. A curriculum is an announcement of the educational priorities of a faculty: What does a student need to know to be certified, as having majored in a field, to receive a bachelor's degree or a Ph.D., and to be welcomed into the company of educated men and women?

This definition implies both the normality and the desirability of change. To give an obvious example from the field of economics, the curriculum for graduate degrees has undergone basic transformation in the past forty years. Today, all programs insist on considerable mathematical knowledge, while foreign-language requirements have virtually disappeared. The reasons are clear. Mathematical economics and econometrics drive theoretical and applied research, and English has become the lingua franca of research. Over time, a new professional consensus changed the curriculum. Forces that led to change at Stanford were quite different, but their origins were similar: the perceived need by some individuals or groups to alter what students needed to know to be adequately prepared for the present and future.

A few more words about the *desirability* of these discussions. (Desirability and normalcy are, of course, not the same things.) Quite simply, when faculties assemble, all too often the subjects of concern can only be described as petty and unworthy, given the self-proclaimed lofty purposes of higher education. Parking is a favorite topic of lengthy discussion; "how we dislike the administration" is another. To have the all too rare opportunity to exchange ideas about education—about the meaning and claims of disciplines or thinkers or cultures—becomes an exhilarating experience. That is what curricular discussions can be, and they may eventually unify disparate groups and build a consensus. How long the consensus lasts is another matter.

It should not be surprising that curricular discussions will generate a great deal of transitional conflict. Heat precedes light. Curriculum is about priorities and is also about turf—where is *mine*? The relative value of subjects is believed to be involved. A requirement brings status, tenure opportunities, and additional positions. Not to be required can have the opposite effects.[32]

What about the periodicity of curricular reform? Is everything moving more quickly? The answer is yes. Academic fields are changing at unprecedented rates in both content and method. The outside world that provides context for education is also undergoing more frequent alterations. Over the past few decades, for example, we witnessed the collapse of the Soviet Union and end of the Cold War, the rise of East Asia, and rapidly changing demographics in the United States. Whereas the *trivium* and *quadrivium*, initiated during the Middle Ages were used by universities in Western Europe for hundreds of years, today we are surprised when a curriculum remains unchanged for more than twenty years.

These tendencies are well illustrated by the happenings at Stanford. Western Civilization (1935–1973) lasted thirty-eight years, History 1-2-3 (1973–1980)—not required—ended after only seven years, and Western Culture (1980–1989) had about the same life span. Note also the trendiness of what today are called "change agents." The most recent debate might not have started without the Black Student Union, a race-based political and cultural special-interest group of relatively recent vintage. Multiculturalism and Eurocentrism, so prominent in the discussion, are post-1960s concepts, as is the claim that colleges and universities have mounted a concerted attack on Western values. Questions concerning "great" or canonical books have a much longer history, though the feeling that the canon, reflecting authority and tradition, should be more inclusive in terms of race, gender, and cultural origin is specific to the present.

THE UNUSUAL CHARACTER OF STANFORD UNIVERSITY

Institutions, like individuals, can be celebrities, and that status creates exaggerations and distortions. Stanford is a celebrity in American higher education, bringing with it the glamour of selectivity, wealth, a California location, famous professors, and athletic teams featured on national television. Since World War II, no university has risen more rapidly in national rankings. Today, Stanford is on everyone's "top five" list. What that means from the point of view of media attention needs no elaboration for any inhabitant of the United States.[33]

Other factors besides celebrity status increased the notoriety of Stanford's curricular reforms. Beginning gradually with the student disturbances of the 1960s and increasing in fervor to the present day, higher education has been the subject of strong public criticism. Disapproval has been heaped on allegedly lazy professors, costs running "out of control," curricular incoherence, faculty politics that lean to the left, various frauds, and much else.

Both elements created high visibility the moment any kind of controversy erupted at Stanford. There is no other way to explain why something of such inherently parochial interest as changes in general education requirements should have attracted so much media attention. The *Washington Post*, the *New York Times*, and the *Wall Street Journal* all expressed strong views. The *McNeil-Lehrer News Hour* featured Stanford's President Kennedy—on the defensive. The *Chronicle of Higher Education* spoke of "sweeping curricular change," and William J. Bennett used the pages of the *National Review* to issue dire warnings:

> Stanford will be praised for being "forward looking," "progressive," and "innovative." . . . other universities will decide that they should change their programs in the same or similar ways . . . The methods that succeeded in pushing CIV through the Faculty Senate have shown that intimidation works—that intimidation *can* take the place of reason. The loudest voices have won, not through force of argument, but through bullying, threatening, and name-calling. That's not the way a university should work . . .
>
> Stanford will be harmed . . . by these recent events . . . [though] those who deplore what has transpired here will not say so publicly. They know that speaking out against CIV will invite charges of racism—an utterly fake but highly damaging accusation . . . For now the defenders of Western culture will mostly confine themselves to talking quietly with one another about what has happened. But they know what they know and others around the country know it too: that for the moment, a great university was brought low by the very forces that modern universities came into being to oppose—ignorance, irrationality, and intimidation.[34]

Perhaps Dinesh D'Souza reached the hyperbolic peak in his assessment: "[Stanford's] curricular diet now consists of a little more than crude Western political slogans masquerading as the vanguard of Third World thought."[35]

As is their habit, both the media and the social critics were guilty of exaggeration and distortion. After all, what happened besides a change in the title of the program from Western Culture to Cultures, Ideas, and Values? Of course, that very change caused alarm because the use of the plural in connection with culture suggested that there was more than one and that none, judging by the title, occupied pride of place—at the very least a symbolic defeat for the West. The removal of "Western" from the title was even more upsetting.

In fact, the basic structure of the curriculum remained relatively unaffected. The foundation continued to be the eight tracks that were heavily linked to departments and to Western approaches to knowledge. One new track, Europe and the Americas, was created. Although it adopted a greater emphasis on the Third World, Western thinkers remained very much in evidence: Freud, Melville, Marx, Aristotle, and Thomas More, to cite some examples. Dinesh D'Souza, in misleading fashion, titled his chapter on curricular debates at Stanford "Travels with Rigoberta," referring to the autobiography of a Guatemalan Indian human rights activist who is both a lesbian and a Nobel Peace Prize winner. Yet this was only *one item* on the Europe and the Americas reading list—a track enrolling some one hundred students—and it was no more or less representative than Voltaire, Darwin, or Conrad, all of whom appeared on the same list. Mentioning canonical authors would, of course, not have served to convey his intentionally alarmist message.

True, the permanent and common canonical list of fifteen books was abandoned. A new list was to be assembled by a committee of instructors every year. Three comments are in order. First, the old list was, to say the least, odd: a great emphasis on theology, *two* works by Freud out of the total of fifteen, not a single American author, no Shakespeare.[36] Second, in actual practice the list was used selectively and idiosyncratically by teachers in the Western Culture program. Third, the new list of common readings—reduced to six to eight selections—has remained solidly Western and traditional, including the Hebrew and Christian Bible and thinkers representing classical Greece, the Renaissance, and the Enlightenment.[37]

What is left to cause such enormous concern? Primarily the following injunction: "to give substantial attention to the issues of race, gender, and class during each academic quarter, with at least one of these issues addressed explicitly in at least one major reading in each quarter." Many will detect a strong political flavor in this requirement. It is stated very broadly, and one can argue with its wisdom—that would be our inclination. However, we are primarily dealing with three readings—or at most three sets of readings—during an entire academic year. Unless race, gender, and class dominate the remaining readings and discussions, unless white males have been systematically exiled from reading assignments, it is hard to see this as an apocalyptic change.

To repeat an important point: the differences between Western Civilization and CIV were, from the point of view of students' education, very small.

WHO OWNS THE CURRICULUM?

Considerable notoriety associated with the Stanford case tends to obscure its long-term significance. The basic question is, who is responsible for—who "owns"—the curriculum? What role belongs to faculty, administration, students, and perhaps others in determining its content?

The problem of ultimate responsibility is most important. At Stanford, the recent episode of curricular change, as distinct from earlier instances, started with the BSU and a few professors sympathetic to its ideas. President Donald Kennedy and some deans played both out-front and behind-the-scenes roles. Eventually, influential out-siders became involved.

Not all these constituencies have equal claims to authority within the university. All can partake in public discussions, and there is nothing inherently wrong with the BSU assuming a position of advocacy. That this should have sometimes included demonstrations and office occupations is unfortunate and undesirable, though most administrators will admit that direct action helps one concentrate. At the very least, it is good general practice to punish those who violate codes of conduct, and that would certainly include office occupations.

The president and deans are faculty members and obviously should play a leading part in curricular discussions. Yet the ultimate responsibility for curriculum does not belong to students or individual faculty members or to trustees and legislators. It belongs to "the faculty"—a collectivity—and should represent the common wisdom of those whose task it is to educate students. That is the primary responsibility of the faculty, although many others assist in the process, and we would certainly include students in this category.

In the type of institution represented by Stanford, educational policy is "delegated" to the faculty by titular "owners," private trustees or representatives of the state, in recognition of the professional standing of those who profess in colleges and universities. No other group brings the same authority to the table; no other group has sufficient authority to be given a vote—as opposed to a voice—in the final decision. To claim this right for the faculty also means that it has to be exercised seriously and responsibly, paying attention to standards, the interests of students, and the efficient use of available resources. If that is not the case, we would not be disposed to defend these propositions and would consider various forms of "receivership"—removing delegated power temporarily by administrative means, a serious and inevitably controversial action that should be used only as a last resort.[38]

Are we espousing an extreme view of faculty autonomy? What about faculty members in their role as senior administrators? They are facilitators—servants of the faculty and students, in the best sense of the word. Their task is to implement educational policy set by the faculty acting as a group or in groups and to make student learning more efficient. But, someone will ask, what about *leadership*? Well, academic leadership *in these areas* has to be democratic in certain types of schools. Not all aspects of academic leadership are subject to democratic determination. Everything except educational policy is usually handled in much more traditional fashion: the granting of tenure, salaries, benefits, discipline, buildings and grounds, and so on.[39]

"Owners" have not delegated these powers to "the faculty" because it would pose insurmountable conflicts of interest, and professors bring no special expertise to the formation of some of these policies. Imagine faculty setting their own salaries! The power of the purse is hardly ever delegated, and that limits faculty action in nearly all spheres.

Senior administrators can initiate, facilitate, and implement, but they do require—or should be required to seek—democratic approval for their educational plans. A faculty should operate on a collegiate model; no other model is as appropriate, and nothing else makes the task of the administrator more difficult. There is, however, no good substitute for horizontally distributed rights and responsibilities because a faculty consists of scholar-teachers, many on tenure, who come together with equal votes for certain purposes. One of the most important of these citizenship obligations is to set a curriculum.

The events at Stanford illustrate how collective faculty responsibility and leadership can operate in practice. Remember that a principal objection to faculty democracy is that nothing will ever get done. This need not be and is not true. According to the case, some BSU and faculty dissatisfaction with the Western Civilization curriculum started in the early 1980s. That is when President Donald Kennedy, in his role as academic leader, asked Dean Lougee to study the complaints; her portfolio was undergraduate education. By 1986, the representative faculty senate had set up its own task force consisting of faculty, students, and administrators: democracy was beginning to function. In 1987, the task force had reported to the senate through the Committee on Undergraduate Studies. After debate and amendments, a new curriculum was mandated to begin in 1989. All procedures were observed. It is true, of course, that political pressure was present and that some disruptions occurred. To what degree these factors influenced the final outcome will have to remain a matter of opinion. We were not there, but it seems clear to us that alarmist observers like William Bennett and Dinesh D'Souza did not give credit to the democratic processes that prevailed.

CONCLUSION

The purpose of studying and discussing this case is not to reach a conclusion concerning the quality of Stanford's new curriculum. The choice of a particular curricular approach has little to do with professional conduct or ethics. Many possibilities exist, ranging from a program confined to a list of great Western books to one that gives students almost complete freedom of choice. Both can be and have been advocated by wholly responsible and caring academics whose philosophies of education differ. Both points of view can be maintained by individuals whose professional conduct, singly or as a group, is impeccable. Our interest in the Stanford case has to do with the dynamics of curricular change and the professionalism with which it occurs.

By these standards, Stanford did well despite great odds. In an atmosphere that became highly politicized, under the glare of often unfair publicity, and in the presence of strong minority militancy, Stanford's institutions functioned as intended. Faculty debate was serious and addressed real educational differences, and in the end a reasonable compromise prevailed. This may be hard to understand against the background of right- and left-wing political correctness rhetoric, but it is nevertheless true when the *actual* changes are closely examined, rather than the symbolism of Rigoberta Menchu or the alleged canonical monopoly of "dead white males."

Can one *prove* that debate was serious and that compromise was reasonable? We examined over two hundred pages of faculty senate debates and emerged convinced. We can also cite the summary judgment provided by Professor Gerald Lieberman, chair of the senate, later provost, and perhaps best described as a "liberal centrist": "This was the most important and stimulating debate I have ever encountered here. I was proud of the faculty. This is the sort of thing the Senate should be doing."

POSTSCRIPT: BUT VERY IMPORTANT

The purpose of using cases is to stimulate thought and discussion. In the end, there may be little consensus about the main issues in the case and even less about solutions to problems. That should not be disturbing because even without general agreement, discussion will have prepared participants to face difficult issues: they should have a better understanding of what to expect. That is worth a lot, and it may be perfectly obvious.

It follows—equally obviously—that for pedagogic purposes, a large variety of cases could serve equally well to stimulate ideas concerning whatever problem one wishes to study. In general, the fact that the events of this case occurred in Palo Alto should not matter, and that is true for many cases. For example, the student-professor incident at Russell University (discussed next) is relatively independent of the type of institution in which it occurred. However, that is *not* true of the Stanford case; hence this postscript.

Our strong conclusion that the faculty is the ultimate "owner" of the curriculum has to be modified to take account of the great variety of circumstances in American higher education. Stanford is part of a family that has at most fifty members: the best research universities and colleges, public and private. But there are over 3,500 institutions of higher education in this country, and the traditions of faculty responsibility are not flourishing to the same extent everywhere. Generally speaking, faculty "ownership" is most developed in research universities and some liberal arts colleges. It is probably least present in community colleges, where part-time teachers are common. Clearly when powers have not been delegated to the faculty—explicitly or implicitly—other constituencies have to step in, and most likely these will be administrators. One should, perhaps, discuss whether too much or too little power is delegated to professors in different types of schools.

This is an important issue because there are no "professional" standards that apply to undergraduate education with a heavy liberal arts content. All forms of graduate education, even in arts and sciences, prepare students according to certain external criteria, and these act as constraints on faculty choices. Many professions have formal licensing requirements; in others, informal requirements prevail. These are largely absent in colleges, although an increasing number of states are instituting standardized tests to ensure that students have mastered certain designated materials—a clear constraint on faculty control. We may question the desirability of this trend and its appropriateness for all institutions, but few can doubt that faculty "ownership" will be increasingly challenged in the future. One way to meet that challenge is to treat curricular matters with care and seriousness and to give full attention to the interests of students rather than the convenience of professors.

We should also note that the Stanford case had nothing to do with resources: the issues were intellectual and political. The faculty could deal with these quite effectively because they did not present serious conflicts of interest.[40] Stanford's wealth makes it most untypical. At more representative schools, discussions concerning curriculum are more likely to involve enrollment shifts, significant reallocation of resources, and perhaps even the employment status of current faculty members. Would faculty debate yield a solution in a tuition-driven school that needs to make changes to attract students, when jobs are at stake? Not very likely.

There are other obstacles to faculty self-government. Professor Richard Chait of the Harvard Graduate School of Education uses the expression "unweeded curriculum" to describe our tendency to add specialized courses without ever removing anything. He quotes an insightful comment by Donald Kennedy: "Sunset is an hour that rarely arrives on college campuses." Given the most likely economic future of higher education (increasing shortages of funds), we may anticipate further changes in governance. Trustees and administrators may have to force sunsets on all types of institutions, and that may mean that faculties will have to include other powerful voices in their deliberations.

The point of this postscript is to underline variety and complications. The lessons of Stanford do not apply with equal force everywhere in American higher education. At many, if not most, colleges and universities, educational policy is less directly delegated to faculties, and change will therefore come about in different ways. Beyond that, we do not wish to leave the implication that deans, presidents, and trustees are cast merely in the role of cheerleaders and observers. When the reallocation of resources is a requirement, their leadership is paramount.

Case II: A Question of Fairness at Russell University

My problem was having missed that first day of class, I didn't get the information about absences until it was past the point of being able to vote with my feet. I would have had no qualms about shifting courses. It became an extremely frustrating time in my life. I was working full time, barely seeing my wife, and then two nights a week was at school until 10:00 P.M. The nights I wasn't at school, I was either doing homework for the three or four courses that I was taking or trying to do the work I was getting paid for at my job. It was just a seven-day-a-week, twenty-hour-a-day grind for two years. And then something like this is thrown up in your face when you're killing yourself to get all the work done. It was just unbelievable. And not to find a rational way out of it, any sort of common ground. I would have done a handstand if he had wanted me to.

These were Steven Burton's feelings of frustration during the fall semester of 1987.[41] He was pursuing a part-time M.B.A. at Russell University in the Northwest while working full time for a five-person investment management firm in downtown Seattle. His life at this time was hectic, but his two worlds had not collided until he enrolled in ACC 1420, Management Accounting, with Professor Lyle Simmons.

PROFESSOR SIMMONS AND THE TWO-CLASS-ABSENCE RULE

Professor Lyle Simmons was scheduled to teach the fall 1987 evening section of ACC 1420. He was a twenty-one-year veteran of the Russell

University College of Business faculty. Simmons had taught ACC 1420 since his arrival at the school. During his time at RU, he had become concerned about what he called "diminishing academic standards" that seemed to him increasingly prevalent in the M.B.A. program. To address this problem, Simmons announced to all of his classes that no grade would be given if two or more classes are missed; there would be no exceptions.

To date, Burton had completed six M.B.A. courses and was doing well—three A's and three A – 's had translated into a cumulative grade point average of 3.84. Burton had also been experiencing professional success. He had been asked to assume sole responsibility for managing the firm's Corporate Forum program. The job required considerable coordination and travel to ensure that all constituencies were satisfied with these high-stakes encounters. One of the forums coincided with the first ACC 1420 class; consequently, Burton missed it. He attended the second class meeting; reviewed the syllabus, which did not state the absentee policy on it; and appeared thereafter to be on track with the course. He then recalls the following:

> I think it was the third or fourth class, Professor Simmons made some reference to it again [his policy of not issuing a grade if two or more classes are missed], and that's when my ears perked up and I said, "What?" The problem was that it was too late at that point to change courses. I went up to him and said, "Professor Simmons, I have a problem. I'm going to be out of the country on this date and won't be able to make class." He said, "Well, I very clearly laid out in the first class that I won't give a grade if you miss two classes." I said, "I missed the first class and I know that looks terrible, but these will be the *only* two classes that I will miss. What can we do? At this point, I can't add another course." He said, "That's just the way I work." I offered to do whatever I could.

All attempts to work directly with Simmons failed. Burton saw no alternative but to bring the issue to the attention of the university administration.

PRESSING FOR A RESOLUTION

Burton pursued various administrators for resolution to his problem. Joyce Kingston, associate dean of the Graduate School of Business, advised Burton that his only option was to appeal Simmons's decision to the Committee on Graduate Programs, a faculty committee.

No official policy was set forth in the faculty handbook of the College of Business regarding what is and is not required to be included on every course syllabus. The undergraduate faculty handbook did require faculty to include any major classroom policies on their course syllabi. Prior to the committee meeting, several faculty members on the committee asked Kingston to find a "precommittee" solution. They were uncomfortable about getting involved with another faculty member's classroom policies. Kingston was unable to find a solution prior to the meeting, and she remembers the occasion:

> The committee struggled with the conflict a lot. I believe we discussed all the angles—faculty standards, Simmons's academic freedom, the struggles of part-time students. We debated all points. Some faculty argued for the student and others for Simmons on the grounds that they did not want to breach academic freedom. We decided not to act on it. I knew we needed something more clear than "not act." I gave Steven the news verbally. I knew that the graduate student handbook for all graduate students at RU provided the option of going to the provost's office. In the almost ten years that I had been at RU, very few cases had been advanced from the business school to the provost's office.

WEIGHING THE ALTERNATIVES: WHERE TO GO FROM HERE

If anything, the committee's finding seemed to strengthen Burton's resolve to achieve a fair settlement to what he firmly believed was a very legitimate request: "I made a $20,000 decision based on the way the university was marketed to me. I understand that academia has certain moral and ethical issues that are sometimes above the fray of commercialism. But when all is said and done, I am a paying customer."

Professor Simmons continued to believe that his absentee policy was fair and should be upheld by the university: "My view is, well, damn it, this is a fair thing. This makes sense. In terms of my value system and what we're trying to do here, it seems to me anything less than this—if students can miss three classes or just show up for exams—then what the hell have we got here? [The university] has the attitude that I am a bad guy. How dare I make these students come to class or force them to do things that they don't want to do? How dare you tell me how to teach this stuff?"

Although the graduate school's formal responsibilities had been fully discharged with the October 22 action of the Committee on Graduate Programs, Kingston still felt she wanted to find a resolution for Burton and for Simmons. She called Associate Provost Catherine Rosenthal shortly after the committee's October 22 meeting. Having received copies of prior correspondence on the Burton matter, Rosenthal was somewhat familiar with the particulars of the case.

THE ROSENTHAL-SIMMONS MEETING

Shortly after Kingston's phone call, Rosenthal arranged a meeting with Simmons in his office to discuss the Burton situation. Simmons recalls that meeting in these terms: "She made an appointment to see me. I'm telling you, she infuriated me. I almost threw her physically out of the office. Because she was absolutely, as far as I'm concerned, the stake in Dracula's heart. My whole attitude about this place changed from that day on." Rosenthal remembers the meeting differently:

> I became involved with this situation through my responsibilities in the provost's office. After getting some background from Joyce and others, I called Simmons to see if I could come up and see him. At no time did I accuse him of anything, but I remember upon leaving his office being shell-shocked at his attitude. I remember telling someone afterward that I have just had the most unbelievable meeting, that I had never been so attacked before. The Graduate Student Handbook details the procedure of involvement by the provost's office for appeal, and I was just investigating the possibility of a solution.

AN INFORMAL MEETING OF THE MINDS

Surprisingly, the Rosenthal-Simmons meeting seemed to prompt Simmons into rethinking his position. His reconsideration ultimately led to an informal resolution of the dispute. Simmons describes what happened:

> Eventually I see the kid is pretty smart, the kid is doing the work, he's very serious about what he's doing, he had a good attitude in class, he wasn't belligerent at all. So I felt better about [Steven]. I knew that this kid wasn't really shirking, and this rule that I had was not intended for a guy like him because [he's] working. But we had come to this loggerhead. So the kid came to me and wanted to know what I was going to do. I looked him in the eye and said, "You got me into this, you get me out. I don't want this problem anymore in my life. You don't want this problem anymore in your life. What can we do?" He said, "Professor, how about we do this—I'll take the course and take the final. Then next semester when you give this course again, or whenever you give this course again, I'll show up for the class that I missed." I said, "That's fair. I'll tell you what I'll do. I'll even give you a grade since the grade is based strictly on the exams, and if you show up, that's fine. If you don't, that's OK too. Give me your word you'll show up, and we're done." Jesus Christ, I give the kid the grade—he gets an "A"—

and next time I give the course and I'm giving the class he missed, the kid showed up! Came up, shook my hand, and that was the end of it.

Steven Burton graduated in June 1989 with a 3.88 cumulative grade point average. His degree was conferred at university commencement exercises. Immediately following commencement, at a reception, College of Business Administration Dean Arthur Daniels presented him with a plaque recognizing him as the student with the highest GPA among the part-time M.B.A. graduating class.

Russell University: Analysis

Most cases examined in connection with professional conduct deal with questions perceived by nearly everyone to be weighty. No one doubts, for example, that free speech and content of curriculum are at the heart of, as we like to say, "what universities are all about." The entire institution, the media, and the public can all become actors in cases that attract national concern.

Highly publicized cases tend to be macroscopic and may not be the most typical incidents that inhabitants of a university encounter. The Russell case is microscopic and more typical: it starts with one student and one professor in a classroom—the most basic and fundamental educational interaction. During the second meeting of the class, the student becomes aware of an announcement made by the professor at the first meeting, which he had to miss. Most unexpectedly, this turns into a complex situation that raises basic questions concerning relations between teachers, students, and institutions.

The main issues are these:

1. Were the rules in Professor Simmons's class reasonable and administered in a professional manner?

2. Is a challenge to Professor Simmons a violation of his academic freedom?

3. Should the nature of the institution affect its rules, and does "I am a paying customer" adequately describe the relation between Steven Burton and Russell University?

REASONABLENESS AND PROFESSIONALISM

Disagreement can exist about the reasonableness of Professor Simmons's rules. A case could easily be made for the inappropriateness of attendance rules in higher education—especially in graduate programs. Students in higher education are adults and enroll voluntarily, hoping to gain various benefits. In primary and secondary schools, where attendance is mandated by law, it represents a decision made by society on behalf of children and not an individual decision of a mature person made on his or her own behalf. As Steven Burton believed with considerable plausibility, understanding the content of the course is the main (perhaps only) thing that should matter, and this can be adequately demonstrated by examination. Indeed, that is the most common practice in postgraduate education. In its extreme European form, there are no course requirements of any type—the student's primary obligation is to pass a series of general examinations. (Sometimes there is a supplementary requirement to submit a thesis.) If these criteria are met, the student will be granted the degree.

But other points of view can also be defended. Surely professors have the right to go beyond the minimum standard of only grading an examination. Class participation is frequently part of evaluation. Attendance rules, in the Russell case, could be perceived as a laudable effort to maintain standards that Professor Simmons believed to be slipping and also to bring more seriousness to the evening program.

We have never made use of these types of rules; we agree that understanding is all that really matters in a lecture course. However, we are not inclined to call the rules in this class "unreasonable." In their own classrooms, teachers should be able to use a wide range of pedagogic options, and attendance rules fall well within the limits of reasonability. If Professor Simmons's requirements were particularly disliked by some students, it was probably possible to find another alternative—another professor and another course.[42]

Reasonable, yes; professional, no. An announcement in class that some students might miss or might hear too late to make other arrangements is unforgivably casual, especially since Professor Simmons clearly believed that attendance mattered. His way of providing information represented a serious lapse in meeting obligations to students, a problem compounded by the inability or typical unwillingness of the administration to broaden sensible rules concerning due notice. As the case makes clear, a policy already existed requiring all *undergraduate* syllabi to state "the basis for grading including such items as . . . attendance expectations." A greater awareness of these rules—they should really have been mandated for all schools at Russell University—would have greatly strengthened the hands of administrators during the difficult and unpleasant negotiations with Professor Simmons.

Unfortunately, this kind of administrative carelessness, combined with rather too much respect for professorial autonomy, is all too common in higher education. It is, perhaps, related to misunderstood notions concerning academic freedom.

ACADEMIC FREEDOM

Whenever a conflict arises that includes members of the faculty, sooner or later someone will ask whether the question of academic freedom has to be considered. We know that many readers of the Russell case believe it is one of the main topics to be explored. No one can doubt that academic freedom is a "hot button" issue; it comes up in many conduct cases. But what about this case?

We are not aware of any all-purpose definition of academic freedom. The best general statement that we have come across was made by Sir Eric Ashby in 1969.

> It is . . . a right of all citizens in this country to say, teach, and publish what they think, subject only to limitations set by the law of the land. Academic freedom does not exceed this right; but it does exempt academics from constraints upon this right such as are imposed by many other professions; indeed it empowers a university teacher to carry this right into the actual discharge of his contract with the institution he serves. Within the easy constraints set by a [dean] or the head of a department (and even those constraints are arguable) he fulfills his contract by devising his own teaching program and choosing his own research projects; and outside his contract he can promulgate his views—whether or not they lie within his expertise—without endangering his job. He can, with impunity, upset the theories of his professor by his research, and embarrass the vice-chancellor by his letters to *The Times*. This is a greater degree of freedom than is allowed to men belonging to some other institutions, such as the civil service, the army, or the priesthood of the Roman Catholic Church.[43]

Ashby adds that there are two concomitants to academic freedom: the familiar security of tenure and control of standards.[44]

This statement and its amplification can lead to only one conclusion: the events at Russell had little to do with academic freedom. Professor Simmons's rights to express his ideas were never an issue. His tenure was never in the slightest danger. No one questioned his authority to set standards in the classroom. The only relevant issue was the implementation of these standards, and that was not remotely related to academic freedom. Administrative standards and fairness are the root of the problem, and unfortunately that is not a "hot button"—although it should be!

Of course, Professor Simmons would not agree with this conclusion. We can infer that he believed that his academic freedom had been violated. Among other things, he said, "How dare [the dean] tell me how to teach this stuff?" But Steven Burton's assessment was more to the point: "There's a difference between academic freedom and administering freedom." The root of the problem was administrative, *not* academic. Academic freedom protects the expression of ideas and not the institution of rules.

There is, however, a perverse way in which academic freedom may have affected this case. Members of the committee to whom the Simmons-Burton dispute was about to be referred asked Dean Kingston to resolve the matter before it came before their group. The explanation may simply be an understandable desire to avoid a nasty domestic dispute—but the reasons may have been much more perverse.

Faculty members generally display little reluctance in evaluating each other's research. We do it all the time as referees, reviewers, and judges in hiring and promoting colleagues. In contrast, the sacredness of the classroom is almost never invaded by the opinion and judgment of peers. Instead, less reliable student evaluations are widely encouraged. We say that it is extremely difficult and imprecise to judge what is happening in the classroom but at the same time seem content to let (undergraduate) students perform this task! The Simmons-Burton situation that was blown all out of proportion could have been avoided if the chairman knew what was going on in Simmons's classroom and if a reasonable policy concerning syllabi was enforced by the department. Even after the impasse was reached, direct involvement of colleagues would undoubtedly have prevented the conflict from escalating.

The fundamental reason for faculty timidity is, in all probability, a partial function of yet another misunderstanding concerning academic freedom that needs to be corrected. Academic freedom does not absolve colleagues or administrators from assuming responsibility for what are essentially matters of procedure, management, good order, and—above all else—legitimate student needs.

NATURE OF THE INSTITUTION

In devising academic rules, the nature of the institution should play a major role. One would expect great differences between, say, Bennington College, West Point, and Princeton in some, though not all, matters. For example, there is no obvious reason why notions of plagiarism, cheating, or sexual harassment should differ among these schools. They pertain to general moral principles that apply in all settings of teaching and learning. Differences between institutions usually do occur in specific administrative situations.

In 1994, Russell University ran an advertisement in the local newspaper under the following heading: "At Russell University we don't do everything by the book." Underneath a smiling professorial face on a computer screen, the text says, in part:

> Accounting Professor Joel Garrison has been known to stray from his textbook. . . . he uses a variety of innovative methods . . . his students are adults and many of them haven't been in a classroom for ten, sometimes more than twenty, years. If you're thinking about going back to school but are afraid you've been away too long, consider Russell University where professors like Joel Garrison go a step beyond to provide the support and encouragement to keep you going.

The emphasis is on adult students, and the subliminal message is *flexibility*. That was also the message in the president's letter of greetings to incoming graduate students: "Many of you have already launched promising careers, committed yourself to mortgages, begun families of your own. As adults you must juggle many responsibilities, and the demands on your time are many. We understand that at Russell."

Most of these communications would not easily suit Bennington, West Point, or Princeton, but they do touch the essence of Russell: older students and working students, and throwing away the rule book without too much fuss. Good administration and teaching should reflect these circumstances. The right words used in advertising or welcome speeches is not a substitute.

At the same time, it is extremely difficult to accept Steven Burton's notion that "when all is said and done, I am a paying customer." Is that an adequate description of the student-teacher relationship? Is the fact that the student pays for an education crucial in this interaction?[45]

Paying is not at all the issue. At some schools students pay a great deal; other students pay nothing. In general, most schools like to claim that all students are subsidized in some form or other. That is also beside the point.

Customers expect service that bears some proportion to what they spend. More is expected of a meal at a five-star restaurant than one at a fast-food joint. The same applies to nearly all other purchases, from automobiles to apartments. These are commercial transactions, and they are not perfectly analogous to professional or spiritual ties. One should, of course, not be naive. Rich people can purchase better medical care and legal advice than those with smaller resources, and yet the doctor-patient or lawyer-client relationship is not exclusively commercial. Professional ethics require doctors and lawyers to do their absolute best for those to whom they render service, even if payment is small or entirely absent. No seller of clothing or groceries has the same moral obligation. Needless to say, when it comes to priests and their communicants, commercial considerations are also largely absent.

The tie between teacher and student should resemble that ideally existing between doctor and patient or priest and parishioner. That is the goal, perhaps only rarely achieved. We teach all students with equal care and fervor, whether they pay tuition or not. We do not "close the store" at five o'clock. Russell University did not owe Steven Burton flexibility or clearer and more sensible practices because he paid tuition. It owed him these things because professional excellence demands these standards.[46] Claims of academic freedom cannot be allowed to become the last refuge of the irresponsible teacher.

Conclusion

The conclusions of this essay were stated in the introductory sections: all professions pay more attention to questions of conduct than our own; this should change as soon as possible because problems related to conduct are becoming more serious. One small step in the right direction would be a required seminar for all graduate students. We have tried to illustrate one possible version of such a seminar.

Problems of implementation remain great. Very few faculty members feel inclined or qualified to teach such courses. Training a core group of instructors is made more difficult by little consensus about the content of courses or major principles that need to be taught. But other professions have made progress in facing these challenges. Can higher education afford to do less?

Notes

1. The introduction relies on Henry Rosovsky, "Appearing for the Defense Once Again," *Bulletin of the American Academy of Arts and Sciences*, vol. 49, no. 2, 1995, pp. 25–39.

2. Can anyone imagine a Ph.D. candidate getting a similar letter?

3. The following is a typical course description: "The objective of Patient-Doctor I is to provide a series of society-based experiences to enable all Year I students to consider topics relating to patients' experiences of illness, to begin to master basic communicating skills, to discuss social, ethical, and psychological aspects of the physician role, and to develop an ongoing relationship with a preceptor clinician." *Harvard Medical School Course Catalog, 1995*, p. 49.

4. The seriousness of that effort is a matter of debate. The task is imposed by the professions that hire the graduates of these schools. As is the case with many imposed tasks, a certain lack of enthusiasm seems to be commonplace.

5. These are not novel observations. In assessing the report of the Hastings Center Project on the Teaching of Ethics, David D. Dill observes, "The Hastings Center staff deliberated at length over the feasibility of a study on the ethics of the academic profession, but concluded that the area lacked appropriate research material and was not of sufficient current interest to warrant investigation . . . Thus, the ironic situation exists of a group of academics with a professed interest in values and ethics openly questioning the integrity of their own institutions, and advocating university-based instruction in ethics for seemingly every profession but their own." "Introduction to Ethics in Higher Education," *Journal of Higher Education*, vol. 53, no. 3, 1982, p. 245. The same point is made by Donald Kennedy in "Making Choices in the Research University," *Daedalus*, vol. 122, no. 4, Fall 1993, p. 146.

6. See Maimonides, *Mishneh Torah: The Book of Knowledge*, ed. and trans. Moses Hyamson (Jerusalem: Boys Town Jerusalem Publishers, 1962), p. 83b.

7. Daniel Yankelovich, "Three Destructive Trends: Can They Be Reversed?" Paper presented at the National Civic League's 100th National Conference on Governance, November 11, 1994.

8. William E. Fassett at Drake University, Stephen Cahn at the City University of New York, and Donald Kennedy at Stanford offer some formal instruction, as we do at Harvard.

9. Edward Shils, *The Academic Ethic* (Chicago: University of Chicago Press, 1984), pp 12–17, 27–29. Shils defines a mass university as having more than twenty thousand students, and most major graduate programs take place in that kind of setting.

10. Jacques Barzun, *The American University* (New York: Harper & Row, 1968), p. 255.

11. Walter P. Metzger, "The Academic Profession in the United States," in Burton R Clark (ed.), *The Academic Profession* (Berkeley: University of California Press, 1987), p. 125.

12. National Education Association, *Almanac of Higher Education, 1994*, p. 19, n. 5.

13. Metzger observed that "prior to World War I, the academic profession took its membership from a relatively narrow band of society . . . Professing in America remained socially and ethnically exclusive until it became a more common activity in the period following World War II." "The Academic Profession" p. 154. To this day the profession remains predominantly white and male.

14. See Seymour Martin Lipset and Everett C. Ladd Jr., "The Changing Social Origins of American Academics" in Robert K. Merton, James S. Coleman, and H. Rossi (eds.), *Qualitative and Quantitative Social Research* (New York: Free Press, 1979), pp. 319, 321. More recent data are supplied by Metzger, "The Academic Profession," pp. 154–155.

15. See Eric Ashby, "The Academic Profession," *Minerva*, vol. 8, no. 1, 1970. More than a decade earlier, Jacob Viner made a very similar point in a charm-

ing essay, "A Modest Proposal for Some Stress on Scholarship in Graduate Training," in *The Long View and the Short: Studies in Economic Theory and Policy* (Glencoe, Ill.: Free Press, 1958), pp. 378–381.

16. Steven M. Cahn, *Saints and Scamps: Ethics in Academia* (New York: Rowman & Littlefield, 1986), p. 7.

17. Shils, *The Academic Ethic*, pp. 12 ff.

18. More slowly than one might wish in view of uncapped retirement.

19. Shils, *The Academic Ethic*, p.12. Italics supplied.

20. Skeptics may ask, is there hard evidence in support of the assertion that conduct has deteriorated since, say, World War II? Can one *prove* that, for example, research misconduct, sexual harassment, or neglect of students are, on a per-professor basis, more common today? Statistically robust time series do not exist: definitions of misconduct lack consistency, and the degree of public and institutional concern with issues of conduct was smaller. But there is no shortage of impressionistic accounts that almost uniformly support the thesis of deteriorating conduct—from the point of view of the institution. Too many of our critics have called attention to the same transgressions: nostalgia alone is an implausible explanation. Our impressions are recorded in Harvard University, Faculty of Arts and Sciences, *Dean's Report*, 1990–91, under the heading "Citizenship."

21. Dill, Metzger, and Clark have already been cited. See also Donald Light, "The Structure of the Academic Professions," *Sociology of Education*, Winter 1974, pp. 2–28.

22. Ibid., pp. 12, 14. His argument is quite close to Ashby's observation concerning the "two guilds."

23. Kenneth P. Ruscio, "Many Sectors, Many Professions," in Clark, *Academic Profession*, p. 333.

24. It is interesting to note that the AAUP has been much more interested in academic freedom than in questions of conduct. That was not true of one of the association's early leaders, John Dewey. "Dewey felt that faculty members were not entitled to any special kind of autonomy or freedom unless they disciplined themselves and regulated their own conduct . . . To Dewey, the concept of academic freedom made no sense without a concept of academic responsibility." David D. Dill, "Introduction," *Journal of Higher Education*, vol. 53, no. 3, 1982, pp. 243–245.

25. Ibid., pp. 252–253.

26. See Rosovsky, "Appearing for the Defense Once Again," pp. 38–39.

27. The cases used for actual instruction are much more detailed. Each case also has a series of appendixes: study questions, an annotated bibliography concerning the main issues raised by the case, and documentary backup materials such as letters and copies of regulations.

28. William F. May, "Professional Ethics: Setting, Terrain, and Teacher," in David Callahan and Sissela Bok (eds.), *Ethics Teaching in Higher Education* (New York: Plenum Press, 1980), pp. 211, 212, 219.

29. C. Roland Christensen with Abby J. Hansen, *Teaching and the Case Method* (Boston: Harvard Business School, 1981), p. 23.

30. May, "Professional Ethics," p. 301.

31. The texts were divided into three categories: Ancient, Medieval and Renaissance, and Modern. In Ancient were the Bible, *Republic, Iliad, Odyssey,* and one Greek tragedy. In Medieval and Renaissance were *Confessions, Inferno, Utopia, The Prince, Christian Liberty, The Starry Messenger,* and *The Assayer.* In Modern were *Candide, The Communist Manifesto,* and selected works by Freud and Darwin.

32. The current climate in higher education may make curricular discussions more difficult than in the past. Eric Ashby cites Herbert Butterfield, who said that when he was a young tutor at Cambridge, faculty members were interested in the whole intellectual development of their students. They acted as supervisors. Today, "when we are discussing the syllabus, I believe we [are] each of us a little more concerned to look after the fortunes of his own branch of the study." They are acting as researchers. See Ashby, "The Academic Profession," p. 93.

33. One lesson concerning celebrity and publicity could be less obvious. It is not necessary to be Stanford or Yale or Michigan to attract press attention. Every school is prominent in its own sphere, and media interest does not have to be national to cause problems. Even regional schools can be the object of national attention. An example would be the Citadel in 1995 in connection with the admission of women.

34. William J. Bennett, "Why the West?" *National Review,* May 27, 1988, p. 38.

35. Dinesh D'Souza, *Illiberal Education* (New York: Vintage Books), p. 92.

36. Shakespeare was not on the required list but was, however, "strongly recommended."

37. D'Souza makes an interesting point when he questions the competence of most Stanford faculty to teach Third World materials. He implies that they were willing to do it because the readings were ideological and therefore did not call for special training. As he points out, teaching the Upanishads would be a task undertaken with greater hesitation. True enough, but the nature of most general education programs necessarily stretches instructors beyond their full expertise, and that certainly applies to the canonical list used in Western Culture or CIV. We cannot imagine that the instructors in Technology and Culture brought a lot of specialized knowledge to the Bible or to Freud. See D'Souza, *Illiberal Education,* p. 74.

38. Receivership may appear to be a slightly esoteric concept, but the rare withdrawal of delegated authority by administrators from the faculty in the name of the governing bodies is a necessary reserve power. A typical example would be a department so divided by dissension that it was unable to make decisions concerning appointments. An administrator might then decide to appoint a receiver committee—a term borrowed from bankruptcy law—to act on behalf of the department until such time as order was reestablished.

39. Educational policy is certainly not exempt from possible conflicts of interest. See the section "Postscript: But Very Important."

40. We are especially indebted to our colleague Richard Chait for very insightful comments he shared in private communication relevant to this and the next two paragraphs.

41. The incident and events of this case are entirely factual. The name of

the institution and the individuals have been changed. Joseph Zolner, a doctoral student at the Harvard Graduate School of Education, prepared the original version of this case.

42. We do not intend to suggest that teachers have an unchallenged right to determine the content of their courses. We use the expression "pedagogic option" to describe something much more circumscribed. When it comes to content, there are collective responsibilities, interests, and rights. To give an example, a professor teaching a basic introductory biology course should not, as a matter of right, be able to devote a significant portion of the classes to creationism. At the very least, this would be of legitimate concern to a department, an administration, and an academic senate.

43. Ashby, "The Academic Profession," p. 90. Given that Sir Eric wrote these words in the 1960s and in England, we have not attempted to make his language gender-neutral. It is, after all, a historical text.

44. There are many other ways to formulate academic freedom, but most authors would agree with the essence of Ashby's text. Deans and chairs might have some trouble with the freedom to devise one's own teaching program, although it is certainly a very common practice. For other formulations, see *AAUP Policy Documents and Reports*, 1977, p. 2; Russell Kirk, *Academic Freedom: An Essay in Definition* (Chicago: Regnery, 1955), p. 1; and Sydney Hook, *Heresy, Yes — Conspiracy, No* (New York: Day, 1953), p. 195.

45. In the United States, this is not a new idea. "After his visit to the United States in 1904, Max Weber said of the American student that he took the same attitude towards his teacher as a customer towards a merchant: 'He sells me his knowledge and his techniques for my Father's money.'" See Walter Rüegg, "The Academic Ethos," *Minerva*, vol. 24, no. 4, Winter 1986, pp. 398–399.

46. The most complete recent survey of ethical issues in higher education can be found in William Edmond Fassett, *Doing Right by Students: Professional Ethics for Professors* (Ann Arbor, Mich.: UMI Dissertation Services, 1994). See especially "Current Models of Ethical Behavior," pp. 63–79. Nowhere is there a suggestion that the relationship between student and teacher can be described by the term "paying customer." While not rejecting the analogy of the doctor-patient relationship, Fassett pointed to certain limitations. See pp. 135–138.

How Can Universities Teach Professional Ethics?

AMY GUTMANN

CAN UNIVERSITIES teach the ethics of academic life? If so, how? In its broadest sense, the professional ethics of university life includes the principles, rules, and procedures of individual and institutional conduct that enable universities to carry out their valuable social purposes. (The ethics of university life is a subset of professional ethics, which includes the principles, rules, and procedures that enable professions to carry out their valuable social purposes.) The valuable social purposes of universities include creating and disseminating knowledge and understanding at its highest levels; educating for leadership, citizenship, and living a good life as one sees fit; and sustaining diverse associational communities that are willing and able to transform themselves by their own best lights over time.[1]

This essay focuses on the general challenge of teaching the ethics of university life in liberal arts universities and the particular challenge of teaching the ethics of university teaching. Universities are centrally engaged in offering professional education to the next generation of college and university teacher-scholars, and they are therefore responsible for the professional education of future generations of professors. Although liberal arts colleges do not serve this purpose directly, many university professors were educated as undergraduates at liberal arts colleges. Almost all of what I say here about the ethics of university life applies with modest modifications to liberal arts colleges as well.

In debates about moral education, one often hears arguments as to whether moral education in schools should focus on teaching moral reasoning or teaching moral conduct. I have argued elsewhere that this is a false dichotomy.[2] The falseness of this dichotomy may be nowhere more evident than in higher education. The valuable social purposes that universities serve—pushing forward the boundaries of human understanding; learning for leadership, citizenship, and living a good life—require us to conceive of the ethics of the academic profession as entailing both moral reasoning and moral conduct. Whereas faculty and administrators who are adept at reasoning but unable to act according to their reasoning threaten to teach hypocrisy rather than virtue, those who consistently do the right thing without ever articulating reasons for their actions threaten to dictate or indoctrinate rather than to teach.

Many people take it as self-evident that universities can and should teach ethics, personal as well as professional. Others, probably a minority, disagree. In the face of reasonable disagreement over whether professional conduct of university teachers can and should be taught by universities, those of us who defend its teaching would do well to admit that the affirmative answer is not self-evident. I am reminded of one of my favorite *New Yorker* cartoons, which depicts a small boy tugging on the coattails of Thomas Jefferson and asking, "If you take these truths to be self-evident, why do you keep harping on them so much?" This essay therefore pursues some problems as well as prospects of teaching the ethics of academic life, and practical ethics more generally, in universities today.

Whether or not one takes the need for universities to teach ethics as a self-evident truth, it is worth harping—a least a bit—on the reasons why the teaching of professional ethics is important yet difficult to accomplish. If we overlook the most common challenges and greatest obstacles to teaching professional ethics, we are far less likely to succeed in moving forward in the teaching of professional ethics, since many thoughtful people do not now accept this aspiration as either possible or desirable, let alone self-evidently true. I'll therefore say something about why teaching the ethics of university life is desirable, despite the difficulty of teaching it effectively. Since the point of both personal and professional ethics is to help us act in ways that contribute to the well-being of others, I'll focus on trying to figure out how members of universities—especially faculty and administrators—might work to overcome the greatest obstacles to teaching the ethics of the academy in the academy.

There are many reasons why some people think that ethics in general, and therefore the ethics of university life in particular, is impossible or undesirable for universities to teach. One reason, perhaps the primary one, is that many people disagree, and disagree quite reasonably, about what the ethics of the university life should be. Some people take such disagreement about many issues of professional ethics as a clear sign of moral relativism. They voice a version of the familiar relativist refrain: "You have your opinion and I have mine, and who's to say who's right?" (Still other people reject the very claim that there exists reasonable disagreement on ethical issues precisely because they believe that conceding reasonable disagreement implies the false doctrine of moral relativism.) We need not subscribe to moral relativism—or its opposite—when we recognize and respect reasonable disagreement. There is reasonable disagreement over ethical questions as diverse and difficult as, for example, who should determine a university's curriculum and what that curriculum should be, who should determine the rules that should regulate the relationship between professors and students and what those rules should be, and how university trustees, faculty, and administrators should react to public demands for more external accountability and what the internal and external demands for accountability should be.

Suppose that there are correct answers to each of these questions and every other ethical question that arises in academic life and that these answers would be self-evident to a Platonic philosopher king or queen. None of us here and now can credibly lay claim to having all those answers or to having the authority to indoctrinate our students or colleagues (assuming that such indoctrination were even possible!) into believing what we take to be self-evident truths. Nonetheless, we fallible members of imperfect universities still should harp on what we consider the most defensible responses to the difficult ethical issues of university life and act consistently with those responses. Why? We have no better alternative but to offer our best reasons for our imperfect responses if we are committed to reasoning, to teaching through reasoning rather than by relying on indoctrination, and to encouraging people to use their own powers of reasoning in arriving at what they, too, can defend as ethical action. There are no commitments more central to university life than these.

One way of engaging our students and colleagues in ethical reasoning is to present them with case studies along with philosophical readings that articulate and defend relevant principles of ethical life. Having taught ethics and public policy for two decades by this method, I am convinced that it effectively engages students in trying to discern what constitutes ethical action and in evaluating the importance of acting ethically. (The case studies make vivid, as abstract principles cannot, the nature and consequences of unethical action.)

But, a skeptic might ask, can we effectively teach ethics merely by reasoning with our students and colleagues? Does ethics not rely more on habit and emotion and less on cognition than this pedagogical method assumes? Some of the most basic ethical principles and actions no doubt rely as much, if not more, on habit and emotion as on cognition. Most of us learn the habits of honesty and nonviolence, for example, when we are very young, even before we understand the reasons for being honest and nonviolent. But most of the ethical challenges facing professors—and other professionals—cannot adequately be addressed simply by relying on such basic habits as honesty and nonviolence. Without these basic habits, we would not be willing or able to begin to address the more difficult ethical issues that universities face. But with these basic habits, we still need to draw heavily on our cognitive capacities and draw out the cognitive capacities of our students, to think through issues as complex as the content of an undergraduate curriculum, the responsibility of different members of the university for determining that curriculum, the university's response to "hate speech," and the value and limits of compromise in the face of different kinds of disagreement. Habits learned in childhood and reinforced later in life, however essential, will not suffice to address the challenging issues that arise in academic life, or in professional life more generally.

When asked, "Can virtue be taught?" Socrates replied that he could not answer without first posing the prior question, "What is virtue?" No less than in Socrates's time—indeed in all likelihood far more than in Socrates's time—do we reasonably disagree about what virtue is. So, too, we reasonably disagree about what constitutes ethical action in university life. The skeptic may therefore claim that the pursuit of practical ethics through teaching is hopeless. This is a non sequitur. If we measure the success of teaching the ethics of university life by whether we can achieve agreement on the answers to every difficult issue universities face, then academic ethics probably cannot be taught. But agreement on the answers to difficult ethical issues is a misplaced goal for teaching professional or personal ethics. Reasonable disagreement over difficult ethical issues is not good grounds for concluding that professional ethics cannot be taught. Quite the contrary, it is a reason to teach ethics in a spirit of liberal inquiry—in an open-minded, intellectually rigorous way, which invites arguments for and against our own considered judgments, with the aim of arriving at the most defensible answers of which we are now capable. The teaching of the ethics of university life should encourage and enable us to support the principles and practices that we find most defensible after careful reflection and to reject those that do not stand up to critical scrutiny. In the spirit of free inquiry, our reasonable disagreement gives us good grounds for carefully deliberating among ourselves, in a Socratic manner, about the principles and practices of our professional conduct.

The teaching of the ethics of university life must not presuppose easy answers to hard questions and then simply try to find the most effective means of convincing our colleagues and students to act in accordance with those answers. Yet neither can universities simply stand by and wait until everyone agrees on who should control the curriculum, whether there should be codes regulating hate speech, or what the obligations of faculty are to students (and students to faculty) before deciding whether to institute rules and procedures in each of these areas. There is no morally neutral ground on which universities can stand while their members deliberate about rules and procedures. Every university must take some stand here and now, provisionally and subject to change by its members' deliberations.

The rules and procedures of a university are part of its ethics. Every university also encourages or discourages its members to think and act ethically in areas beyond the reach of its rules and procedures. One way of encouraging ethical reasoning and action is to offer high-quality courses in practical ethics in the curriculum, thereby sending the signal that the university takes ethics seriously enough to be an important part of a liberal education. The deliberation of university members about academic ethics, at its best, is therefore an ongoing trial-and-error enterprise. New and better answers to some old questions may be found along the way. But a final destination, the "ideally ethical university," will never be reached. As universities arrive at a consensus on better resolutions to ethical issues that were once hotly contested, new issues will arise that challenge both our individual and our collective understandings. Ethical inquiry, like every other area of intellectual inquiry when it is working well, is an iterative process. Progress is possible, but progress opens up new challenges at the same time as it settles some old issues, which we then tend to take for granted. For example, universities like Princeton made moral progress when they decided to admit women and minorities. Yet the question of what counts as a relevant qualification for university admission is no less challenging today than it was in the decade when coeducation was hotly debated at Princeton and other all-male Ivy League institutions.

This is not to say that all change has been for the better or in the direction that ethical deliberation would lead a university were ethics actually in the lead. Over the past several decades, for example, increased competition among universities for the most eminent scholars, a decrease in faculty teaching loads, and an increase in outside professional activities by faculty may have created an imbalance among teaching, scholarship, and outside professional activities that does not further the university's most salient social purposes. I do not pretend to know precisely what the best balance is, and I suspect that there would still be a substantial degree of disagreement after we all

carefully deliberated together about this issue. Nonetheless, we probably can agree that all universities should carefully attend to this issue rather than let the market or other (external or internal) pressures
inadvertently lead the way. If within the university we do not hold
ourselves to account for doing our best to fulfill the university's most
important social purposes, we will have little defense against outside
intrusion, having failed to articulate, let alone enforce, our own highest standards.

I have suggested a response to the skeptic who takes our ethical
disagreement over difficult issues as a reason for setting professional
ethics aside as impossible or undesirable. Even if members of universities disagree about the difficult issues, we can begin holding ourselves accountable by creating internal forums for deliberating over
ethical issues (much as universities create forums for deliberating
over other practical issues, such as the design of auditoriums and
stadiums) and by acting on the provisional consensus that emerges
from these forums. This is one important way by which universities
can demonstrate the possibility and desirability of teaching the ethics
of university life—by putting ethics into practice. Some of the rules
and procedures so instituted will be controversial and subject to reasonable disagreement. Others—such as rules against academic fraud
or rules requiring faculty to meet their teaching obligations—are so
basic as to constitute part of what it means to be a university.

A second and equally important way that universities can be more
morally accountable is by creating courses on practical ethics, including the ethics of the academic profession, courses that encourage creative and rigorous thinking about the many dimensions of practical
ethics. Putting the ethics of the academy into practice and putting it
into the curriculum are two distinct yet complementary ways of assuming responsibility for putting our own educational houses in ethical order.

This is all well and good in theory, a critic might say, but how do
you propose to put either proposal into practice? Let me begin with
the proposal that is the focus of the Rosovsky-Ameer essay: add a
required course on the ethics of university life to the graduate curriculum. How can we teach such a course when departments of philosophy shy away from the subject, preferring "purer" and more theoretical subject matters such as logic, metaphysics, and epistemology?
Universities, Rosovsky–Ameer argue, can create mini-courses on professional conduct outside of regular departmental curricula, courses
that are required of every graduate student who is planning to pursue
an academic career. These courses would be taught by the case study

method, coupled with relevant readings in the ethics of, say, academic freedom, free speech, and professional responsibility.

Who will teach such courses? Ideally, teacher-scholars who themselves have been educated in moral or political philosophy and the practical ethics of the academy. Should such teacher-scholars be in short supply, universities might enlist others who take an interest in this area of practical ethics and are eager to educate themselves in the relevant intellectual disciplines. But if universities are to be dedicated to teaching the ethics of university life in as thorough and rigorous a way as they teach other important and difficult subjects, they must work to increase the supply of scholars who are educated to teach practical and professional ethics. The skills and habits of ethical analysis are no more easily or automatically absorbed with our upbringing than the skills and habits of scientific, literary, or aesthetic analysis. To suggest otherwise is to deny the intellectual challenge of the ethics of intellectual life.

Specialization among scholars in the practical ethics of university life, however, is unnecessary and may even be undesirable. The ethics of higher education is not an entirely distinct discipline from the ethics of medicine, law, and most other professions. True, each of these professions serves different social purposes, but the principled means of serving such varied professional purposes are often remarkably similar. For professors and physicians alike, for example, we count on honesty in research, industriousness in the pursuit of new knowledge, mutual respect in professor-student or physician-patient relations, and responsibility in carrying one's fair share of institutional work. All of these basic principles and the virtues on which they depend—honesty, industriousness, mutual respect, and institutional responsibility—have practical counterparts in almost every profession. How to refine these principles and put them into practice in the context of the complex challenges of professional life constitutes a central part of the subject matter of professional ethics, regardless of the profession. Whatever our own profession or professional aspirations, we probably have an interest as citizens, clients, patients, or students in understanding how all kinds of professionals can best live up to these challenges.

Consider the institutional responsibility of professionals, the neglect of which is a serious moral concern for many universities today in light of the increasing external activities of scholars, which include consulting for government, industry, and nonprofit organizations and editing, writing, and refereeing for scholarly (and semischolarly) journals. These activities, which have been on the rise for at least a century, take professors away from teaching and advising, but they also serve some important social purposes. It is no easy matter for universities to figure out what constitutes a justifiable balance between the internal and external demands on a professor's time. What can universities do in the face of increasing external pressures on the professoriate and disagreement about how best to cope with such pressures?

Teaching courses in professional ethics would focus the attention of more educated people (and not only future professors) on this and other issues of professional responsibility long before the issues turned into crises of professional neglect, whether it be of students, patients, or clients. Although no one could reasonably object to a course that helps future professors, physicians, lawyers, and citizens think more clearly and carefully about the institutional responsibility of professionals, few universities offer such a course, which would examine the meaning, value, and implications of moral responsibility for professional life. If only a single course tries to teach the ethics of professional conduct, far better that it be a general course in practical and professional ethics that teaches students, regardless of the career they will pursue, to think broadly about the meaning and conditions of moral responsibility. One aim of such a course would be to ensure that everyone who enters professional life—or whose life is likely to be affected by the conduct of professionals—would have reflected on the classical understandings of responsibility for an action or inaction. On one important understanding, which can be gathered from the *Nicomachean Ethics*, we are responsible to the extent that we have the capacity to be the cause of an action, the ability to know its consequences, and the freedom to act or not to act.[3] The considerable power of professors (as well as university trustees and high-level administrators) in all three of these senses—cause, knowledge, and freedom—makes our moral responsibility for the well-being of our universities very great.

The conditions of moral responsibility that I have just roughly outlined are of course contestable (as are many issues), but this understanding stands up remarkably well under critical scrutiny, and without some understanding of what moral responsibility is and why it is important, I see little hope of teaching ethics to future professors and other professionals (as opposed to indoctrinating or coercing people to do the right thing). The actions of professors like those of all professionals, as Rosovsky–Ameer write, "have complex consequences and involve much independent judgment." Actions that have complex consequences are typically the subject matter of highly challenging courses and rigorous intellectual disciplines. Teaching professional ethics, or ethics of any kind, is at least as intellectually demanding as teaching any other subject in higher education. Because it is intellectually demanding, universities cannot come close to fulfilling the promise of professional ethics of any kind by trying to teach these subjects quickly to students and then certifying them as having passed an ethics requirement. If universities settle for quick and easy courses, they may even end up doing more harm than good, both to the intellectual integrity of the university and to the moral practice of the professions.

Practical wisdom, after all, entails knowing how much one does not know. Professors who teach any complex subject—whether it be practical ethics, economics, endocrinology, etymology, or English literature—have a choice. We may convey to our students the intellectual challenge of thinking clearly and creatively about our subject matter, or we may convey a sense of our subject matter made easy by teaching it at the level of the least common denominator. This is not to deny that an elementary education in ethics, as in economics, is nonetheless necessary, even at the university level. But it is to emphasize that universities should not convey the message that an elementary education in ethics or economics suffices for educated professionals upon whom society relies to carry out complex social purposes. Universities should therefore be committed to teaching ethics in as intellectually rigorous a way as they are committed to teaching economics. When they fail to do so, they risk discrediting the enterprise of taking ethics or economics seriously. How ironic (i.e., unethical) it would be to have professional ethics taught unprofessionally, in a way that does not stand up to serious intellectual scrutiny.

Many professional schools once did precisely that—they taught practical ethics made easy rather than practical ethics taken seriously. But over the past two decades, the caliber as well as the quantity of teaching in professional ethics has increased significantly at our leading law schools, medical schools, and business schools. The challenge to teaching professional ethics has not disappeared. The critical ground has shifted from the claim that professional ethics cannot be taught by professors to the claim that it cannot be learned by future professionals because they are too busy to think through ethical arguments before they act. It is incumbent on anyone who advocates the teaching of professional ethics to address this practical challenge, which has enduring resonance in American life.

The challenge is not new, nor is it to be taken lightly. It is most eloquently captured in Tocqueville's observation in *Democracy in America* that "in a democratic state of society, the habits of mind which are suited to an active life are not always suited to a contemplative one. The man of action is frequently obliged to content himself with the best he can get. . . . The world is not led by long or learned demonstrations: a rapid glance at particular incidents, the daily study of the fleeting passions of the multitude, the accident of the moment and the art of turning them to account, decide all its affairs."[4] Professionals, including professors and university administrators, have so many important and pressing purposes that it is practically difficult to stop to think about ethical principles before acting.

As if in support of this view, American culture has the image of the strong, silent hero—the Gary Cooper of *High Noon*, the Humphrey Bogart of *Casablanca*, or more recently (and less lastingly) the Keanu Reeves of *Speed*, and the Sandra Bullock of *The Net*—people who behave morally without articulating or reflecting on the precepts by which they act. It would be foolish not to find the silent hero and heroine attractive. As Michael Walzer has pointed out in defense of teaching practical ethics: "One would not want Humphrey Bogart to stop in the middle of *Casablanca*, say, and deliver a lecture on just and unjust wars. But it is important to understand that his gut feelings and his instinct for the good are parasitic on other people's lectures, [or at least] on the whole tradition of moral discourse. It is also important to understand that his silence is at least in part unauthentic and historically false. . . . Men and women face hard choices, and have to think about them. And since those choices are not only personal but also collective, they have to think out loud, to argue, to criticize, to persuade. On these occasions, it is not all that helpful to be heroic but inarticulate."[5]

Nonetheless, Tocqueville's suggestion that the lives of most "men [and women] of action" are not well suited to moral reflection is as accurate today as it was when he wrote. But the need for moral reflection by professionals is today at least as great and probably far greater than in Tocqueville's time. Professionals have far more power over other people, and the social purposes that they are called on to carry out are far more complex—all the more important that universities educate more professors ("people of inaction"?) whose specialty it is to teach practical ethics and to encourage future professionals to reflect ahead of time on the ethical principles, practices, and precepts that enable various professions to fulfill their social purposes. Many general skills and habits of moral reflection will serve most professionals very well. Universities should teach these skills and habits of moral reflection early in the academic careers of students. Specialized courses for every professional discipline are also important but far less critical than high-quality courses that teach students to think systematically about ethical principles and their relationship to practical problems, whether they be the problems of political or professional life or life more generally.

Both general and specialized courses in practical ethics are part of a comprehensive ethics education, but together they are only a partial response to the challenge of realizing the ethical promise of higher education. An equally important part of the challenge is to put ethics into the practice of higher education by instituting and enforcing rules, procedures, and practices that help universities fulfill their most important social purposes. To appreciate the importance of bringing together both ways of realizing the ethical promise of higher education, we need only imagine two ideal types of universities, each of which pursues only one way to the exclusion of the other. The two ideal types that I sketch here are intended only as a thought experiment; no university represents either ideal type. However hypothetical, the two universities each suggest rather vividly what is wrong with following either way to the exclusion of the other.

Alpha University offers its students the very best set of courses in all areas of practical and professional ethics (business, legal, and medical ethics as well as the ethics of higher education). The courses are by all accounts excellent, and all of Alpha's students, undergraduates and graduates alike, take at least one course in practical ethics, some considerably more. Undergraduates take at least one broad-based course in practical ethics, which supplies the foundation for pursuing more specialized courses in the ethics of a particular profession, law, medicine, business, or higher education. Graduate students are required to take at least one course in the ethics of their chosen profession.

Alpha amply rewards its faculty for excellent research but not for teaching or university service. Its professors of practical ethics just happen to be dedicated teachers, but Alpha offers no incentives for teaching and asks for no information regarding teaching at salary review time. It enforces no rules regarding faculty absence from campus or engagement in outside professional activities. It exempts its faculty from any decision-making role with regard to the curriculum and most other matters of university governance. Its faculty thereby have more time to spend on their research and outside professional activities, and many gain a great deal of external eminence, bestowing it on Alpha. Alpha therefore does not shy away from recruiting eminent scholars by offering them little or no teaching, especially of undergraduates.

Beta University, in contrast to Alpha, requires all its faculty to teach undergraduate courses, and it rewards its best teachers each year with highly publicized teaching awards. Every Beta faculty member must submit a report each year at salary review time of his or her teaching, advising, committee service, outside professional activities, and publications. These reports are reviewed by a faculty committee that makes salary recommendations to the president, who sits with the committee. Beta enforces rules regarding absence from campus during term time and offers financial incentives for faculty to live close to campus. Elected faculty committees also review all new course proposals and every new faculty appointment and promotion.

But Beta, again in contrast to Alpha, does not offer any courses in practical or professional ethics. Although its faculty may serve as role models of responsible professionals, its students graduate without having been taught to think rigorously about the demands of practical and professional ethics. Undergraduates routinely leave without having taken a single course in practical ethics, and graduate students are not required to take any course in the ethics of their chosen profession. Few, if any, such courses are even offered.

One might be tempted to ask, which university, Alpha or Beta, is likely to do a better job teaching the ethics of higher education. But this question makes little sense if our aim is to learn as much as we can from the ideal types of Alpha and Beta. Alpha's ethics curriculum is excellent, but it is unsupported—indeed, potentially undercut—by the rest of Alpha's institutional incentives and culture, which send the message that teaching and institutional service do not count for much. Beta's incentives, rules, and procedures are well designed to recruit and retain faculty members who are dedicated to teaching and institutional service, but Beta's faculty fails to fulfill its professional responsibilities to teach the next generation of professionals, who should be taught to articulate and rigorously reflect on the responsibilities of university professors and other professionals. A university is not forced to choose between instituting ethics in its curricula and creating an institutional ethos, with suitable rules and procedures, that supports the day-to-day practice of professional ethics by its faculty. As the models of Alpha and Beta suggest, something important is missing from any university that pursues one course of action, however excellently, to the exclusion of the other. Both are necessary and neither is sufficient for supporting the ethics of university life. Universities can and should do more to offer courses in practical ethics and to institute rules and procedures that ensure that all faculty teach and assume their fair share of responsibility for the university.

This analysis suggests three mutually supportive courses of action for university faculty members and administrators. First, we should do more to instantiate the ethics of higher education in our institutional rules and procedures. Faculty members and administrators have a responsibility to place our professional efforts where our professed ethics are. Second, universities should create rigorous broad-based courses on practical ethics in the undergraduate curriculum. Without such courses in the undergraduate curriculum, we cannot realistically expect graduate students to take practical ethics seriously or to have learned enough about moral reasoning to appreciate and understand the complexities of professional ethics. Third, universities should offer equally rigorous but more specialized courses in professional ethics to graduate students in their chosen profession. Courses that combine case studies and readings in practical ethics are probably ideal, since such courses challenge students to relate moral principles to professional practices and to develop ethical perspectives on their professional lives that are publicly defensible.

Rosovsky–Ameer's Stanford case raises many ethical issues that are central to the social purposes of the university. Their analysis focuses on the issue of who is responsible for the curriculum. Their answer is that primary responsibility rests with the faculty. They suggest that this is a major lesson to be conveyed by teaching this case study. For the sake of teaching the case study to future faculty members, however, we need to address the strongest challenges to this reply. Why are faculty members the primary agents of responsibility with regard to university curricula? How well does this (or any other credible) answer hold up under an analysis that draws on a defensible understanding of moral responsibility and responds to the strongest critiques leveled at it? A primary aim of this exercise in practical judgment would be to help develop the skills of moral reasoning of future faculty members, since understanding the conditions and implications of moral responsibility in university life well enough to articulate and defend them before one's peers is surely an important attribute for anyone who shoulders a substantial degree of responsibility in university governance.

Other issues raised by the curriculum debate at Stanford are as central to the ethics of the academy, and of professional life more generally, as the question of who is responsible for the curriculum. Rosovsky–Ameer say that the Stanford faculty should be commended for their willingness to compromise on this issue. But they do not say why this particular compromise is commendable. Surely not all compromise is commendable. We would not have commended a faculty for compromising with racists, anti-Semites, or misogynists who called for the ouster of books written by blacks, Jews, or women. So much may be obvious, but less obvious are the reasons why one may think that compromise is commendable in some situations, defensible

(but not commendable) in others, and despicable (or at least indefens-
ible) in still others. If the outcome of the Stanford debate was, as
William Chace said, "an effective compromise and a very strong
achievement," it is important to understand why this compromise
was commendable while some other compromises would not have
been. If we do not understand why (or why not), then our discussion
of this case study will not have produced any generalizable and
hence practical understanding to help guide us in future deliberations. Since a lot of intellectual work remains to be done on the ethics
of compromise, who better to undertake such work than professional
educators who commend each other for compromise?[6]

Connected to the question of whether this was a commendable
compromise and, if so, why, is yet another critical question raised by
the Stanford case study: How do we assess the quality of the arguments offered by faculty members for and against Stanford's new curriculum? Part of any assessment of the ethics of higher education
should depend on the quality of the arguments offered by educators
for and against controversial issues that arise within universities. If a
primary aim of our profession is to create and disseminate knowledge
and understanding at the highest level, then it is a central part of our
professional responsibility to offer the strongest arguments on all
sides of a controversial issue, even if we do not agree on the "all
things considered" answer. If the arguments offered by different sides
in the Stanford curriculum debate enriched our understanding of the
important values that are at stake in the undergraduate curriculum,
then the debate served an educational purpose even apart from the
decision itself. Good case studies of controversial deliberations within
universities encourage us to evaluate the quality of the arguments
offered in the process of reaching a decision as well as the quality of
the decision itself. (We also value the process, of course, for its capacity to produce justifiable decisions.) Were there alternative ways of
framing the argument (about the entire curriculum, for example,
rather than only one course) that would have been more educa-
tionally illuminating?[7] What was the educational value—inside and
outside the university—of the faculty's debate over the required
course? A challenging course on the ethics of university life that inte-
grated excellent case studies with readings in the philosophy of
higher education would effectively address such questions.

Were universities to do more to put ethics into practice in their
rules and procedures, were they to create more rigorous broad-based
courses on practical ethics in undergraduate curricula and equally
rigorous but more specialized courses in professional ethics in graduate curricula, there would still be a lot of other work to do—for exam-

ple, figuring out how to finance higher education in times of decreasing public support. Universities that seriously pursue such a three-pronged approach to professional ethics would sometimes find themselves swimming against the social tide of market competition and moral cynicism. Nonetheless, universities would probably find many more excellent faculty members and students who appreciated than who criticized their efforts and far more support than cynicism among the educated public. Although it is impossible for any single university to transform the entire system of higher education, it is surely possible for universities together to do substantially more than they are now doing to teach high-quality courses in practical and professional ethics and to put our precepts into practice.

Notes

1. I examine these purposes of higher education along with issues of university governance and admissions in *Democratic Education* (Princeton, N.J.: Princeton University Press, 1987), pp. 172–231.

2. Ibid., pp. 50–64.

3. For an excellent analysis of the moral responsibility of public officials, which applies with similar force to most professionals, including professors, see Dennis F. Thompson, *Political Ethics and Public Office* (Cambridge, Mass.: Harvard University Press, 1987), pp. 40–65.

4. Alexis de Tocqueville, *Democracy in America* (New York: Anchor Books, 1969; originally published 1835).

5. Michael Walzer, "Teaching Morality," *New Republic*, June 10, 1978, p. 13.

6. For an informative collection of essays on the ethics of compromise, see *NOMOS XXI: Compromise in Ethics, Law, and Politics* (New York: New York University Press, 1979).

7. I address these questions in the introduction to *Multiculturalism: Examining the Politics of Recognition* (Princeton, N.J.: Princeton University Press, 1994), pp. 13–24.

Unity or Fragmentation, Convergence or Diversity: The Academic Profession in Comparative Perspective in the Era of Mass Higher Education

OLIVER FULTON

IN THE PAST few years, European higher education systems have reached an intriguing point in their development. Numerically, virtually all of them have made the formal transition—at different times and at varying speeds—from elite to mass scale, in Martin Trow's well-known formulation. And as Trow forecast, that transition—the process of "massification"—seems to have challenged many of their traditional assumptions and practices and now threatens to dilute both the resources and the prestige previously assigned to students and staff in the elite systems. At the same time, social and economic change (toward the knowledge-based, globalized economy) have evidently succeeded, as in the United States, both in underlining the central importance of the functions that universities perform and, at the same time, in creating new forms of competition that threaten the universities' monopoly of these functions and put new pressure on their costs. It is a time of change and uncertainty, especially for the academic profession.

The 1992 Carnegie survey of the academic profession, a questionnaire-based sample survey of academic staff in fourteen countries (including the United States and the four European countries of England, western Germany, the Netherlands, and Sweden) was prompted by just such considerations. It aimed to compare working conditions, work roles, and practices, including involvement in governance; to elicit faculty attitudes both on issues internal to higher education and on higher education's relationship with the wider society; and to mea-

A shortened version of this paper has been published in Rob Cuthbert (ed.), *Working in Higher Education* (Buckingham, England: Open University Press, 1996).

sure the extent to which academic staff were engaged in international activities. A descriptive account of some of the findings at the national level is given by Boyer, Altbach, and Whitelaw.[1]

My intent here has a slightly different focus. The brief sketch of pressures for change relies implicitly on two commonly held assumptions. The first is that higher education everywhere in the developed world is subject to the same or similar pressures and that each higher education system is likely to respond in broadly similar ways. In other words, theorized accounts, such as those of massification or globalization, should be universally applicable. As far as the academic profession is concerned, the implication is that there are commonalities, presumably derived from the nature of the work itself, that link academic staff across national boundaries and tend to create a common, or at least convergent, academic identity. The second, parallel assumption is that *within* national systems it is possible to generalize about the academic profession as a whole; in other words, for comparative purposes, the international commonalities apply not to an elite group of international scholars and scientists at the top of the selective and status hierarchies but across the board. It is these assumptions that I will test, using the Carnegie data to examine both commonalities and differences within the structures of the academic profession in the four European countries surveyed in 1992. I will begin by laying out the primary dimensions by which the profession is structured and across which, according to some views, it is so fragmented that it makes no sense to talk of a single profession. I will then draw directly on the empirical data.

The idea that there is a single, cohesive academic profession is both powerful and contested. Of course, academia has long been stratified—into "noble" and "less noble" disciplines, ancient and parvenu universities, professors (or their chairs) and lesser staff. But the notion of the collegium—the "guild," united in the common purpose of the formation of youth and equal before the courts of pure reason, discovery, or exploration—has deep roots.

There was an intriguing outbreak of debate in the United States in the 1960s. Talcott Parsons and Gerald Platt, in a somewhat neglected study of the academic profession, endorsed the by then undeniable description of U.S. higher education as "this highly differentiated system" with an "exceptional . . . range of dispersion of quality" but nevertheless purported to discover "unity" in it—a unity sustained, in best Parsonian style, by the overriding value orientation of cognitive rationality.[2] Cognitive rationality in turn implied (in fact, functionally required) collegiality, autonomy, and the synergy of teaching, training, research, and consultancy. Perhaps untypically for Parsons, this was not just a functional inference: empirical evidence was offered, in the form of faculty attitudes and preferences, as measured by a questionnaire survey, to show that right across the United States' "differentiated system," from the leading research university to the most modest four-year college, there was a common interest in both teaching and research.

In a riposte to Parsons pointedly titled "The Structure of the Academic Professions" Donald Light firmly argued that the claim of unity has no merit.[3] The broad academic profession, in Parsons's terms, does not exist. For one thing, Light claimed, if one takes any of the standard defining qualities of the professions, each discipline logically constitutes a separate profession: each has its own separate body of knowledge, each trains its own new members, and each licenses, admits, and regulates its own recruits, judging its members according to different norms and expectations. There is thus a clear *horizontal* differentiation. But in any case, Light argued, there is a second and even more crucial *vertical* dimension: the real "scholarly professions" are distinguished not by their espoused values or interests but by active involvement in research and scholarship and, specifically, by publication. He described three occupational groups in the United States: the scholarly professions of producers of research and scholarship, a minority (he claimed) of whose members work in universities and colleges; "the faculty," the paid employees of higher education institutions; and a small subset where these two sets intersect, which he defined as the true "academic professions." As for the rest of the faculty, they are "teachers" who do not advance knowledge, who might better be described as members of a "semiprofession," whose status is low and who "do not have democratic departments, though they say that they do" (no evidence is offered for this last claim). After all this, it is a trifle ironic to find Light describing Parsons's theory as "elitist."

As a debate, this one looks, in retrospect, just a little simplistic (though the arguments were of course both subtler and more balanced than my brief summaries allow). But it has the merit of allowing us to ask some simple questions. Theoretically speaking, these are of two kinds. The first concerns what constitutes or defines a profession. For Parsons, it is the values internal to the occupation; for Light, it is primarily the occupation's practices; for others such as A. H. Halsey and Martin Trow, it would be both of these but also structures, working conditions, and what some would call social construction and others, more modestly, public perception.[4]

The second question concerns the lineaments of the occupational group. There are four possible axes of differentiation, only two of which were referred to in this debate. If we think, worldwide, about the occupational group that Light calls the "faculty"—people with academic positions in universities and colleges—we need to add to discipline and "sector" (to use the pre-1992 English phrase) the two other dimensions of rank and national system. These four dimensions are the main analytic focus for my colleagues and myself in our joint analysis of the Carnegie survey, the first (so far as I am aware) international study of the academic profession.[5] I will now briefly discuss each of these dimensions in turn.

Academic Discipline

As far as disciplines are concerned, after Tony Becher's dissection of "academic tribes and territories," it would be hard to deny the existence, *in research universities of the kind he studied*, if not of all the structured differences Light described, at any rate of a cultural diversity, stretching over both values and practices, which Becher convincingly links with the different intellectual projects and epistemological assumptions of the various disciplines.[6] Clark Kerr's well-known description of the modern research university as "a series of individual faculty entrepreneurs held together by a common grievance over parking" may be a deliberate exaggeration, but substitute *departments* for *individuals* and you will be expressing a commonly held belief.[7] And as Burton R. Clark has often demonstrated, the accelerating process of knowledge specialization leads to constant disciplinary fission and hence, presumably, to a steadily increasing fragmentation of academia.[8] (But it could be said that Clark's account deals less thoroughly with the processes of recombination, which seem to characterize both interdisciplinary research and "modularized" undergraduate education.)

Nevertheless, even in formal terms, Light's statement is at best only half true. Of course, each discipline has its own body of knowledge, and the only people who can make fully informed judgments that depend on that knowledge, whether these concern training and licensing, recruitment and promotion, or the quality of academic "output," are other members of the same discipline. But the "faculty" of any institution, across the disciplines, are fellow employees, subject to common working conditions, including recruitment, assessment, and promotion procedures and—in the European context, at least—pay scales; they and their departments are managed and judged by committees and other structures that in almost all institutions draw in representatives of both neighboring and remoter disciplines;[9] and in state-controlled or state-financed systems, there are regulations and structures that relate to the occupation of higher education teaching as a whole and are mirrored by transdisciplinary unions and associations. Even from the viewpoint of the general public, there can be little doubt that the single profession has a strongly perceived reality. It is a moot point whether a professor of biology, let us say, is seen primarily as a "professor" or a "scientist," but there can be little doubt that to be a professor carries a generalizable public weight, independent of the subject which he or she professes. It is not just the exigencies of subediting that lead the British press to label all of us in the U.K. as "dons."

As far as the disciplines are concerned, therefore, there is evidence of increasing intellectual fragmentation over time—disputable in detail but clear enough in the long-term outline. However, the consequences of this dimension of differentiation are less clear. The mere existence of *more* disciplines may not in itself reduce the cohesiveness of the already fragmented profession or professions that they make up.

Institutions and Sectors

On the institutional or sectoral dimension, it is easy enough to construct a case for differentiation. It was probably the work of David Riesman that first illuminated the full diversity of American higher education, that most diversified of systems—a diversity that, *pace* Parsons, is expressed in practices, structural conditions, and, if institutional missions are any guide, many elements of values as well.[10] In the U.S. case, there is room for debate over how far this diversity has developed in response to market pressures, and how far in response to government regulation and prescription (as in the "master plans" of California and other states). In the emerging mass systems of Europe, by contrast, sectoral differentiation has normally been imposed, as in Germany's or the Netherlands' binary structures or the British pre-1992 binary "system," and it is only recently, if at all, that the market (generally well regulated) has been permitted to play a substantial part in diversification. And as Martin Trow has often pointed out, while the market may give (some) institutions some leeway to position themselves on the basis of their own characteristics and strategic choices, external imposition and regulation inevitably problematize the relationship between structures (which the state dictates), practices (which it aims to control), and cultures (which are the property of the organization itself).

Nevertheless, there seems to be a general view, even in the North

American context, that while it is possible to imagine genuine diversity in the *missions* of different colleges and universities—serving a wide range of students and other clients in many different patterns—there is much less diversity in the academic staff. Indeed, there is far more hierarchy than diversity. This hierarchy is expressed through two mechanisms: the renewal of the profession through training and recruitment and the maintenance of the profession's values through the processes of peer review. On the training side in particular, doctoral programs feed their products downward from the most selective institutions and out across the profession as a whole. The typical U.S. faculty member has a postgraduate qualification from an institution a little higher in the academic hierarchy than the one in which he or she is employed; and it is assumed that faculty are likely to bring with them from their doctoral institution certain values into which they were socialized, even if these do not fit well with the mission of the institution that receives them.

This assumption seems to underlie the design of both North American and European binary systems. Binary systems appear to be imposed in order to control sectoral functions—in other words, to constrain institutions' missions through forms of regulation, governance, and funding that work mainly as constraints on the aspirations of the nonuniversity sector, that is, as barriers to "academic drift." This analysis, implicitly if not explicitly, points the finger at the academics—though the mission may be the institution's, most of the aspirations are carried by the faculty. And one of the most common means, internationally, of specifying sectoral missions is to regulate faculty working conditions in such a way as to restrict their role expectations, notably by limiting or even eliminating their time and resources for research and scholarship.

This implies that if unregulated, all members of "the profession" would wish to engage in research and publication, would aspire to teach postgraduates rather than undergraduates and better-qualified rather than worse-qualified undergraduates, and so on. This is essentially Parsons and Platt's claim for the universally necessary values of higher education, and Light—whatever his own prejudices about practices in the nonelite sectors—could well be correct to call it elitist, in the sense that it fails to question the applicability of elite values to other parts of the system. An alternative approach, which parallels Huber's approach to disciplinary differences, is to take the idea of different missions seriously and to investigate what actually discriminates between the faculty in different sectors.[11] Halsey, for example, looked at social and educational background and qualifications and provided evidence, for the U.K., of what he saw as a clear hierarchy of institutions on these dimensions: not only were the staff of the former polytechnics less well qualified than those of the "old" universities, but the latter too were hierarchically structured, especially if we interpret, as he does, the experience of working or studying at Oxford or Cambridge as bestowing an additional component of cultural capital.[12] However, this analysis, too, both depends on and duly confirms a view of institutional status that suggests that all institutions aspire to higher levels by recruiting the best-qualified staff they can find and that, in general, academics aspire to work in the highest-status institution in which they can find a job; and not only this, but they bring with them, and will do their best to retain, the values and aspirations of the sector in which they obtained their own degrees.

We surely ought at least to ask whether there may not be (or have been) features of the nonuniversity sectors that are viewed positively by recruits to these institutions. If this is the case, career choices across the academic professions might have a larger element of positive self-selection than is generally assumed by those who work in and write from the perspective of the traditional university sector. This is not really a question that can be helpfully asked, let alone answered, using the Carnegie surveys. But current ethnographic work on the "new" universities (former polytechnics) in the U.K. suggests that many of the staff of these institutions quite self-consciously espouse an emergent set of values and practices, including a distinctive view of both vocational and liberal undergraduate education, that are distinct from those of the old universities and correspond neither to the rather banal objectives of institutions' mission statements nor, necessarily, to the ambitions of institutional managers. These emergent values are under considerable pressure, not only from the quest for status and market advantage in the U.K.'s newly unitary structure, but also from the current funding regime. But that is another story.[13]

Academic Rank

The dimensions of discipline and sector are the classic components in the literature on the academic profession or professions—the two main axes, for example, of Clark's "master matrix." However, if there is one respect in which it might be most legitimately argued that academia is not a classic profession at all, it must be its internal ranking system, that is, its management and career structure and its conditions of work. As with other "guilds," the idea of the collegium implies partnership on terms of formal equality—if not equality of earnings or of the authority of experience, certainly equality of status as a member of a self-governing and self-regulating occupation. There are relics of this pattern in the relatively democratic and participative governance structures of traditional universities, at least as regards academic decision making, but the rank structure is far from egalitarian. With few exceptions, modern academia abandoned the collegiate model a long time ago and replaced it with a hierarchy of appointments that command different material rewards, different status, and different power. In some systems—notably those based on the German tradition—one could try to rescue the guild ideal by claiming that, symbolically at least, the professor (even though a civil servant and not simply an appointee of the guild itself) is the only true member of the profession, while all other ranks represent at best apprenticeships for that position. But as we shall see, the tension between this symbolic interpretation and the reality of rank in the German university seems to make this view less than convincing to the non-professors.

In fact, rank and career structures are under pressure in most European systems.[14] The process of massification, which has resulted in big increases in the number of academic staff and hence in the salary costs they represent—by far the biggest single cost in university budgets—has led not only to pressure on salary levels and on conditions of work such as student-staff ratios but also to attempts to change staffing structures, either as explicit national policy (as in Sweden or the Netherlands) or inexplicitly (as in the U.K., where the incidence of short-term contracts and part-time employment has increased dramatically).

In recent years, a number of authors have begun to deploy terms such as *proletarianization* and *deprofessionalization*. Generally, these terms are used as a shorthand both for the increased "casualization" of the academic labor force and for the loss of academic autonomy as a consequence of loss of trust and increased demands for accountability (see Trow in this volume, who goes so far as to describe the effects in the U.K. as "a degradation ceremony"). Some writers ascribe the change to the consequences of ("hard") managerialism, which may be seen as simply pursuing the state's ideological or economic agenda or, perhaps more unexpectedly, as taking advantage of the alleged commodification of knowledge, which is said to be creating changes not only in the curriculum itself but also in the kinds of staff needed to deliver it.[15] But in Halsey's version, deprofessionalization also refers to a process in which academics themselves have connived—notably, in the British context, through the decision of the Association of University Teachers to affiliate to the trade union movement.[16] In other words, the process of deprofessionalization, if such it is, may be not just an imposed degradation of working conditions but a defensive and subjective response to the fear of degradation.

The debate about deprofessionalization is not one that the Carnegie survey can fully illuminate, especially since there are no reliable timeline data with which it can be compared. For the present purpose, my question would be whether any such process has affected, objectively or subjectively, the whole range of academic staff or whether it has been more selective. There have been suggestions in the U.K. by present and former academic managers that the status of academics could best be preserved—or even restored—by paying twice as much to half as many people.[17] In other words, an elite group of staff—presumably professors and professors-in-waiting—would be singled out for good working conditions and continue much as before, while the bulk of routine work would be carried on by a force of proletarianized assistants. There are signs in all four of the European countries involved in the Carnegie survey that this is at least a possibility in policymakers' minds.

National Systems

The concept of the "invisible college" of leading researchers in a discipline knows no state boundaries. In the "small world" of academic fiction, or in Burton Clark's research communities, leading academics not only read and write for international journals but move easily from country to country, for conferences or for career moves. Anxieties about the "brain drain"—from Europe to the United States, from Eastern Europe to the West, from South to North, and from developing to developed nations—are a symptom, and a clear indicator, of the globalization of academic work. We know, of course, that this is not the whole truth. Incompatibilities of language and national culture certainly interact with disciplinary characteristics. In some disciplines, there may well be a global network centered on multinational laboratories, disciplinary associations, or journals, but in others (and not only in modern languages and disciplines with a traditional nation-state orientation such as history or law), there are persistent national differences that make globalization less straightforward.

But leaving aside the problems of communication, let alone of transfer, across national boundaries, a functional analyst might well argue that the nature of academic work must require similar patterns of practices and values, at least in all those systems at roughly the same stage of development. In the U.K., I have little doubt that over the past thirty-five years, since both policymakers and the academic community took their first tentative steps toward numerically mass higher education, there has been a very widespread assumption that for better or worse, mass higher education meant that the future was already available for inspection in the United States. Whatever the ambiguities, evasions, and resistances (and there have been plenty of each) and whatever the often self-indulgent assertions of a distinctively English idea of a university, these have been set against the underlying assumption that, for the reasons sketched out in my introduction, massification has and will generate huge forces for convergence on an American ideal type—not least in the structures, practices, and values of the academic profession itself. Indeed, any European who reads much of the more prescriptive recent literature on American higher education will be struck by the number of themes that resonate very clearly with their own country's current domestic anxieties: several of the essays in this book illustrate the point very clearly.

Nevertheless, it is also possible to construct a set of counterhypotheses that take seriously the historic variety and persistence of national structures, notably in their approaches to sectors and ranks. It is at least arguable that these long-established patterns have their roots in deep social and cultural differences and not just in stages of economic development or of the massification of higher education. If so, it would not be surprising if they showed considerable resistance to the homogenizing forces of globalization, or to the admiration and envy that the U.S. higher education system so often inspires in the U.K.

A Note on the Survey

The Carnegie survey, carried out in 1992, included academic staff in both universities and other institutions of higher education in four European countries: universities, polytechnics, and colleges of higher education in England, universities and *Fachhochschulen* in the former West Germany, universities and *hogescholen/HBO*s in the Netherlands, and both research and nonresearch universities and institutes in Sweden.[18] In each country, the samples were designed to include, as far as possible, both permanent and nonpermanent staff and those in research posts as well as conventional academic positions. The number of usable responses ranged, in round numbers, from 1,100 in Sweden to 2,000 in England and the Netherlands to 2,800 in Germany.

Inevitably, this study can give only limited and indirect purchase on the inner life of higher education. Like any questionnaire-based survey, it emphasized the measurable and the quantifiable—inputs, outputs, and fairly crude expressions of opinion—at the expense of the subtleties of process, whether cognitive or affective. The main elements that can help us here are three sets of questions. The first set is concerned with working conditions (including hours of work on different activities, categorized as teaching, research, and administration, both in and out of teaching terms); salary and other remuneration; whether the respondent's work is appraised or evaluated; and a set of opinions including both satisfaction with different aspects of the job, including the resources provided for it, and commitment to the discipline, department, and institution. The second group contains questions about professional activity, including values (for example, preferences for teaching or research); responsibilities (undergraduate and postgraduate teaching duties, number of courses and students, research involvement and research grants); and outputs (publications). A third section concerns institutional governance, including perceptions of where decisions are made, personal involvement in or influence on decision making, and opinions of institutional governance. But in a brief review of this kind, only a few highlights of the results can be given.

Disciplinary Differences

In the four Western European countries, there is (as far as our work has so far revealed) little evidence to support a Kerr-like description of autonomous or independent disciplines loosely coupled into an institutional structure. The strongest evidence in *favor* of such an interpretation comes, in fact, not from any analysis of disciplinary differences as such but from answers to a single direct question about the importance to respondents of their discipline, their department, and their institution, respectively. As Table 1 shows, in all four countries and in each sector, "the discipline" evokes extremely high positive responses (90% in virtually all categories rating it "very important" or "fairly important"), followed by "the department," with "the institution" in third place. This is consistent with a number of earlier surveys that found that when academics are asked to choose in this way, most are inclined to emphasize their disciplinary loyalties: in Alvin Gouldner's terms, they evidently see themselves primarily as "cosmopolitans" and only to a lesser extent as "locals."[19] These statements are a fairly good indication that academic women and men identify themselves with and through the discipline they practice and in

TABLE 1
Importance of Discipline, Department, and Institution, by Sector
and Country

	Percentage of Respondents*		
	Discipline	Department	Institution
England			
University	65/93	41/84	19/65
Nonuniversity	62/94	39/83	16/62
Sweden			
University	56/89	46/86	19/65
Nonuniversity	50/88	42/89	19/76
Netherlands			
University	64/95	31/76	8/47
Nonuniversity	64/94	40/72	10/54
Germany			
University	62/90	15/51	8/34
Nonuniversity	64/95	20/59	8/36

*Number to the left of the slash indicates percentage responding "very important";
number to the right of the slash indicates percentage responding "very important" or
"fairly important."

Source: Carnegie Foundation for the Advancement of Teaching, *International Survey of
the Academic Profession, 1991–93*, Princeton, N.J.

which they have been trained. Insofar as they describe their departments and institutions as of lesser salience (and, as Table 1 shows and
we shall discuss, this varies), one could argue that the hypothesis of
disciplinary primacy is confirmed. But to say that people identify
with their discipline more than with the immediate organizational
context is not the same as saying that they are primarily shaped by it.

In a survey of this kind, there are difficulties of both analysis and
interpretation. It would be impossibly unwieldy to analyze each of
some hundred disciplines separately, even if the number of respondents permitted it. So the subjects have been grouped into five main
areas: natural sciences, applied sciences, medicine and health sciences, social and behavioral sciences, and humanities. Combining
them in this way is rough justice within any one context and much
rougher across national systems and sectoral divisions, in which intellectual traditions differ and the balance of numbers varies considerably. Of course, there are disciplinary differences. But with all due
caution, most of those that can be identified seem to be related to
differences in practice that are well known and to differences in op-

portunity that are easily understood. In research in the university sector, for example, there are quite substantial variations, but broadly of a kind that would be expected: in input, or access to research grants; in process, or norms of collaboration versus lone scholarship; and in output, or publication rates and types of publication (e.g., books versus articles). And there are also differences in patterns of work. In England, for example, staff in the library-based disciplines (the humanities and to a lesser extent the social sciences) have quite polarized work patterns, with heavy teaching loads during the term balanced by a sharp switch to research in vacations, while the laboratory subjects are more evenly balanced throughout the academic year.

But these are differences of practice around common norms. For example, although the calendar of work may differ from discipline to discipline, there are no consistent or substantial differences between the disciplines in the total number of weekly hours that their members work, either during the term or the vacations. Overriding the internal dynamics of the discipline, which undoubtedly determine how the workweek is spent, there seems to be a strong and shared norm that determines the length of that workweek.

Equally striking are the results of what was the key question for Parsons and Platt: whether academics' primary interests lie in teaching or research. As in their survey, and in many others since then, the clearest result is simply that the overriding norm for academic staff across disciplines, even when taking academic rank, sector, and country into consideration, is that *both* teaching and research are of subjective importance. For simplicity, Table 2 controls only for country and sector and *includes* staff who hold research appointments; even so, it can be seen that there is only one group—natural scientists in HBOs in the Netherlands—in which significantly fewer than half of all respondents answered "both"; for most other groups, the proportion ranges between two thirds and three quarters.

This is not to deny that there are disciplinary differences. For example, the table shows that in the university sector, staff in the humanities in each country and in the social sciences in all but the Netherlands are more likely to say "both" than their colleagues, especially those in the natural sciences. Moreover (and not shown in Table 2), there are variations *within* the groups answering "both," with the natural sciences in universities "leaning toward" research for example, and the humanities toward teaching. And the same pattern can be discerned at the extremes, with some subgroups of natural scientists— but by no means all—considerably more likely to declare their interests as "primarily" in research, and some of the humanities staff in teaching; and indeed, the social sciences generally tend to follow the

TABLE 2

Percentage of Respondents Whose Interests Lie in *Both* Teaching
and Research, by Disciplinary Group, Country, and Sector

	Natural Science	Applied Science	Health	Social and Behavioral Science	Humanities and Arts
England					
University	66	73	60	78	80
Nonuniversity	66	72	73	76	78
Sweden					
University	57	64	63	63	76
Nonuniversity	*	58	*	76	*
Germany					
University	63	73	73	83	84
Nonuniversity	76	69	*	66	*
Netherlands					
University	54	64	58	64	77
Nonuniversity	32	49	68	50	49

*Insufficient cases.

Source: Carnegie Foundation for the Advancement of Teaching, International Survey of the Academic Profession, 1991–93, Princeton, N.J.

humanities, and applied science and health the natural sciences. But these differences in preferences are, we would argue, relatively small: we have not found the stereotypical research prima donna, hostile to teaching, concentrated in any one broad area of the disciplines. The general conclusion must be that, whether or not we choose to follow Parsons in ascribing the unity of teaching and research to the functional imperative of cognitive rationality, this unity is broadly shared across the academic disciplines in the European systems surveyed by the Carnegie questionnaires.

As has just been suggested, there are distinct technical difficulties, not least the complexities of multivariate modeling with nonlinear variables, in producing a cross-national analysis of disciplinary effects. However, we have explored one area, institutional governance, more fully, using advanced statistical methods. Here, too, it seems reasonably clear that the effects of academic disciplines are small, even when they are statistically significant. There is nothing to suggest that members of particular disciplines are consistently more or less involved in governance and administration, feel themselves to be more or less influential, or see their institution's administration to be more or less effective or autocratic. Nor, indeed, would it be easy to construct any set of general hypotheses that might predict otherwise: we all know of institutions where the members of a few departments seem to dominate, but it is perhaps no great surprise that the influence of particular disciplines varies from one institution to another.

Sectoral Differences

At the theoretical level, it is quite possible to analyze sectoral differentiation in its own right. In the foregoing discussion, for example, I suggested, first, that there have been common motivations for governments to structure and regulate the different sectors of higher education systems in broadly similar ways and, second, that there may be common value patterns motivating academic staff to aspire to "university-like" status and working conditions even when they find themselves working in the nonuniversity sector—or, alternatively, that some may choose the nonuniversity sector as their preferred place of work. In practice, however, when we turn from discipline to sector, we inevitably need to shift from first-order to multivariate relationships. This is because the nature of sectoral differentiation varies from one country to the next.

There are some common features of the four national systems. In all four countries, the teaching load of nonuniversity staff is considerably higher than that of the universities; outside the traditional universities, research is either not supported by central funds or is funded only to a very modest extent; and a different pattern of qualifications is offered, with the bulk, if not all, of postgraduate education provided in the university sector. However, the detail varies from country to country. Germany and the Netherlands are more sharply and formally differentiated than Sweden and, especially, England: in Germany, for example, the two sectors provide, by law, completely different qualifications in sharply different subjects, while at the opposite extreme, the English polytechnics were able to base their academic case for university status in large part on the increasing convergence of both their degree courses and their subjects of study.

However, the Carnegie survey clearly showed the persistence of very sharp differences in teaching loads between the sectors in each country, with teaching hours up to double in the nonuniversity sector, depending on the other characteristics that are "held constant." But to compensate for this, there are sharp differences in the nonuniversity sector's favor in each country in total working time. There is little difference between the sectors during the teaching term, but in each country, while the hours of work for university staff do not change during the vacations, those of nonuniversity staff drop off by a factor of more than 25%. To make the point clearly, although in both sectors the staff spend substantially more time on research during the vacations, the increase is much smaller for the nonuniversity sector. This is a consistent difference in all four countries.

If we turn to value orientations, we have already emphasized, and partially shown in Table 2, that the majority of staff in virtually every combination of discipline, sector, rank, and country describe their preferences as being for *both* teaching and research. However, it should be no surprise, given their different patterns of activity, that *within* the group that emphasizes both teaching and research, university staff are much more likely to "lean toward" research than nonuniversity staff, who predominantly "lean toward" teaching. Equally, virtually no nonuniversity staff in any of the four countries describe their preferences as primarily for research. But significantly, there is a substantial but variable proportion of nonuniversity staff in each country whose preferences are primarily for teaching: this proportion averages out, holding the other dimensions constant, at just under 25% in England and Sweden, approximately 30% in Germany, and just under 50% in the Netherlands. This difference is both confirmed and further explained by Table 2, which shows little or no consistent difference between university and nonuniversity staff in England, modest differences in Germany and Sweden, and a sharper difference in the Netherlands. We must conclude that a real difference in the structures in each country is reflected in the cultural norms that staff espouse: in the Netherlands, and to a lesser extent in Germany and Sweden, it seems that many staff accept the reality of the constraints on what they can do, whereas in England—where the constraints are undoubtedly less severe—far more of the nonuniversity staff seem to have adopted much the same values as their university counterparts. If we take Parsons's criterion of values as primary, we could even claim that England does have a single, unitary profession, while at the other extreme, the Netherlands arguably has two.

It is clear that this difference in values is reflected in, or reflects, role attributions. In all four countries, university staff with few exceptions agreed with the statement that "in my academic position at this institution, regular research activity is expected." In England, a majority of nonuniversity staff also agreed,[20] followed by Sweden with a little less than half. The proportions in Germany and the Netherlands were far lower. A similar pattern can be seen in research involvement: once again, there were sharp national differences to be found in nonuniversity staff's replies to a question on whether they were currently engaged in a research project. But this national pattern does not show up to the same extent in publication output. Certainly HBO staff in the Netherlands have the lowest publication rates (standardizing for discipline); but in this respect, there is little to distinguish between nonuniversity staff in the other three countries, all of whose publication rates are far lower than their university counterparts'.

Finally, it is possible to shed further light on these patterns if we combine disciplinary and sectoral differences in a single analytic frame. It turns out that in the nonuniversity sector, members of the natural sciences are the least research-oriented discipline. Recall that in the universities, it is the natural sciences that are most consistently active in research throughout the year. In institutions where this is impossible because of heavy teaching loads, natural science inevitably becomes a different activity, whereas staff in the humanities and social sciences can and do still aspire to be members of the research community.

Turning to other aspects of working life that were covered by the survey, the differences between the sectors are generally quite modest. In their ratings of facilities and resources, the English stand out in both sectors as the least satisfied; and in this case, there is a clear difference between universities and polytechnics, with nonuniversity staff in England notably dissatisfied across the board, even by the relatively low standards of their university counterparts. In the Netherlands and Germany, for some resources (quality of classrooms and offices, secretarial support, research equipment) there are real differences between the sectors, while for others (laboratories, teaching technology, computing, libraries) there is little to choose between them. In Sweden, however, there are very few sectoral differences of any size. Of course, these are subjective ratings, and the question remains how far staff in the different sectors share a common set of expectations. But if we turn to more general measures of satisfaction, such as ratings of income, job security, and overall professional situation, we find rather similar patterns: high discontent in England, especially with salaries, and even greater discontent in the polytechnics and colleges than in the universities; near-English levels of dissatisfaction in Sweden, but little to choose between the sectors; greater satisfaction in both sectors in Germany, except with respect to income, where the Fachhochschule staff are not satisfied; and still higher levels of satisfaction in the Netherlands, with quite modest differences between the sectors.

With respect to governance, where full multivariate analysis has been carried out, we have concluded that there are small but fairly consistent differences between the sectors across the four countries, with the nonuniversity staff more likely to describe their institutions' decision making as centralized, to feel that their own influence—at each level from department to institutionwide—is lower, and to regard their institution's administration as less competent, more autocratic, and less effective at communication than their university counterparts. However, these effects are really quite small in comparison with national differences.

To summarize in other words, we find here some consistent sectoral differences—in vacation workloads and in publications, to cite the two clearest examples. But in most other respects, it would be hard to generalize about the sectoral divide in the four countries. If anything, there seems to be a continuum across countries with softer and harder boundaries between the sectors, a continuum ranging from England—whose formal boundaries were about to be removed—through Sweden to Germany and, finally, the Netherlands. The claim that non-university academics retain the values and hanker after the conditions of their colleagues in the university sector cannot be sustained as a universal truth but appears to be qualified by the specific characteristics of the national binary system. These findings suggest that "soft" binary systems are associated (whether as cause or consequence) with greater convergence and a consequently stronger tendency toward hierarchy.

Differences in Academic Rank

The difficulties of comparing sectors in four countries pale next to the problems of comparing ranks. Each country has its own rank structure—indeed, in each case except Sweden, there are quite distinct structures for the university and nonuniversity sectors.[21] In Germany, the Netherlands, and Sweden, the university ranks have fairly recently been reformed, in the latter two countries with a view toward creating separate teaching and research positions in the lower or middle grades. Thus the survey results, which have only been fully analyzed, as far as academic rank is concerned, for the university sector, reveal a varied and complex picture, which can only be discussed in the most general terms for the four countries.

However, it should be no surprise by now that the general value preference for a combination of teaching and research holds true right across the members of different ranks in universities, with the only substantial exceptions being staff in explicitly defined research posts in each country on one hand and Dutch and Swedish staff who are in explicitly designated teaching posts on the other. At least as far as the traditional core of the profession is concerned, the dual value orientation survives at all levels. And leaving aside the kinds of appointments just mentioned, the occupants of most ranks also achieve some kind of balance in their working time between research and teaching. But here there is far more variability between countries.

In England, the university ranks are fairly close together, and there is relatively little internal differentiation. In particular, a similar amount of research activity, by any measure, is the norm for all grades of university staff. But teaching and administration vary quite substantially. The junior ranks have the highest number of teaching hours and professors the lowest—but this is explained by the fact that English professors have the highest time commitment to "administration" of any groups in the sample.[22] This is almost the exact opposite of the situation in German universities, where professors have strikingly low administrative loads but make up for this with larger teaching commitments than any other rank. On the whole, in Germany, junior staff are more heavily involved in research and less in teaching than their seniors. In the Dutch universities, teaching hours are comparatively high across the board, but the pattern is more like England than Germany, with the lower ranks more involved in teaching and the senior more involved in administration—though far less than the English professors. In Sweden, however, yet another pattern prevails. Here, the more senior the rank, the more research is emphasized: Swedish professors spend far more of their time on research than any other rank except contract researchers.

The three time categories are crude, especially "administration." We do not know of other data that could replicate these findings in all four countries, let alone indicate trends over time, although there are a number of single-country studies. But it does appear that the four countries' approach to academic rank is not just a matter of differently named rungs on a standard ladder: these figures suggest quite different approaches to the shape of the academic career and the academic division of labor.

With respect to satisfaction, there are few substantial differences across the ranks in ratings of resources and facilities within each country. But income, job security, and professional satisfaction tell a different story. We have already referred to the sharp national differences here between England and Sweden on one hand and Germany and the Netherlands on the other. Broadly speaking, these differences are reproduced for each rank within these four countries' universities. But despite this, there are variations in rank effects within countries that seem to tell us something important about the internal structure and culture of the profession in different systems. Most notably, the junior and even middle-rank staff in German universities do not share the professors' contentment, with income, promotion prospects, or their professional situation in general. There are elements of the same pattern elsewhere: understandably, few of the most junior staff in any country—defined for this purpose as those not having any form of tenure—are as confident about their promotion prospects as those in more senior ranks. But in other countries they are, relatively, not so discontented in other respects. The peculiarities of the rank (and apprenticeship) structures in German universities—particularly, we assume, the exceptionally long period of study and the double doctorate—clearly create a particular problem.

Conclusion: National Differences

This brief account of variations in two key elements of the academic role—value orientations and research and teaching involvement—coupled with some brief references to satisfaction and governance, has increasingly emphasized the persistence of national differences, whether in sectoral differentiation or in the structure of ranks. Indeed, one of the main purposes of the Carnegie survey, as originally planned, was to examine national differences in what was at first called the "condition of the professoriate."[23] Some of the cruder comparisons between whole samples—for example, in satisfaction and morale—seemed to differentiate the four European countries very sharply, with high levels of satisfaction in Germany and the Netherlands and much lower levels in Sweden and, especially, England.

Multivariate analysis of the kind briefly illustrated here can help qualify these comparisons and explain them. Thus, for example, we have noted that German professors indeed are (or were) exceptionally contented—to the indignation, incidentally, of the German public when these results were first released to the press—but that there is a very sharp polarization between the professors at one end of the spectrum and the junior staff, whose apprenticeship is longer than in any other European country and whose conditions of employment are particularly insecure.

I referred earlier to academics' notable commitment to their discipline in all four countries. It is shared across all of the ranks in the university sector in each country, although there is a modest tendency for staff in higher ranks to be increasingly identified with both their institution and their department. But the national picture as regards commitment to the department and the institution is more complex, as further inspection of Table 1 reveals. In England and Sweden, we see broadly similar patterns, whereby in each case, the department scores nearly as highly as the discipline, and the institution, though in third place, is still regarded fairly positively by most academics. In the Netherlands and Germany, by contrast, the order is the same, but the levels of identification with department and especially institution are far lower, particularly in Germany. This seems to tell us something important about the culture of academic life: if we combine this lack of commitment to the institution with the wide gap in satisfaction between senior and junior staff in that country and the relative lack of involvement of senior German staff in administration, we may begin to understand why the German public seems to regard university professors as irresponsible and even smug. It may also suggest that English and Swedish academics have larger reserves of collegiality to call on in the hard times they both see ahead.

Earlier I asked, somewhat frivolously, whether we might want to describe English and Swedish academics as belonging to a single profession, whereas the Netherlands—and Germany, too, if we take rank into account—may have two or more. This would be an oversimplification of a complex set of differences that I have only briefly illustrated. When I first received the Carnegie survey data, I began by analyzing the English system on its own.[24] Looking at the English responses, I drew a number of conclusions, some of which may need to be reconsidered in the light of the comparative analysis I have just described. I suggested that, whatever the considerable evidence of serious discontent and even of subjective deprofessionalization, English academics retain a set of attitudes and values that could be benevolently described as both professional and collegial. In particular, many of the differentials—whether by discipline, by sector, or by rank—were smaller, I felt, than most observers might have predicted. In terms of the sectors, of course, this could be seen as evidence of the very well developed aspirations of the polytechnics, which were about to be fulfilled, to join the university club—though it could also be described, less benevolently, as a form of "academic drift." But in fact I concluded, from a variety of evidence, not all of which has been referred to here, that English academics could almost be described as hankering after a long-lost collegial culture and style. I claimed (and I am far from the first to do so) that British academics have now adopted the *principle* of mass higher education without fully accepting or understanding the consequences that must surely follow. In other words, I accepted the idea of the kind of supranational convergence, overriding the historic differences of national systems, which I described at the beginning of this essay.

The variations in national structures and cultures that my colleagues and I have begun to explore, with the help of the Mellon Foundation, ought at least to make us pause over this diagnosis. There can be no doubt whatsoever that practices and values that could survive relatively unscathed in an elite system have been sharply challenged by the exogenous changes of recent years, changes that have much in common from one European country to another and even further afield. But there is also evidence—more than has been shown here—of the persistence of powerful national assumptions and practices. The challenges and even the governmental prescriptions may be common, but the responses will not be.

But it would be a mistake to conclude on a wholly negative note. In their chapter in the present volume, Rosovsky and Ameer both agree and disagree with Donald Light, whose skeptical comments on the very existence of the academic profession they join me in citing. It is clear from their account that even in the United States, few norms of professional conduct are routinely imparted to future faculty members in the course of their professional preparation—perhaps they never were. But although the fragmentation of the profession, the lack of a clear professional identity, is one of their keys to understanding the weakness of academic "professionalism," they go on to campaign for a change, insisting that the tasks of teaching and research demand certain minimum standards of behavior, regardless of institutional setting or individual specialization. In other words, at the normative level at least, there are integrative forces at work. To claim that we are all one profession is plainly wrong; but to deny it altogether would be equally foolish.

Notes

1. The survey, initiated by the Carnegie Foundation for the Advancement of Teaching was supported by both the Carnegie Foundation and The Andrew W. Mellon Foundation. See Ernest Boyer, Philip Altbach, and Mary-Jean Whitelaw, *The Academic Profession: An International Perspective* (Princeton, N.J.: Carnegie Foundation for the Advancement of Teaching, 1994), pp. 1–4.

2. Talcott Parsons and Gerald M. Platt, "Considerations on the American Academic System," *Minerva*, vol. 6, no. 4, 1968, p. 497.

3. Donald Light, "Introduction: The Structure of the Academic Professions," *Sociology of Education*, vol. 47, no. 1, pp. 2–28.

4. A. H. Halsey and Martin Trow, *The British Academics* (London: Faber & Faber, 1971); A. H. Halsey, *Decline of Donnish Dominion: The British Academic Profession in the Twentieth Century* (Oxford, England: Clarendon Press, 1992).

5. I would like to thank the Carnegie Foundation and The Andrew W. Mellon Foundation for their generous support for, respectively, data collection

and analysis; my colleagues Jürgen Enders, Peter Geurts, Peter Maassen, and Ulrich Teichler for their collaborative contributions to our study, on which I have drawn extensively for this paper; participants in the Princeton Conference on Higher Education, especially the discussant Dr. Jules Lapidus and Jürgen Enders for their helpful comments on the first draft of this essay.

6. Tony Becher, *Academic Tribes and Territories: Intellectual Enquiry and the Culture of Disciplines* (Milton Keynes, England: Open University Press, 1989). There is a debate, however, about the origins of these differences—between Becher, who places a higher weight on internalist explanations, and Ludwig Huber. See Tony Becher, "The Counter-Culture of Specialisation," *European Journal of Education*, vol. 25, no. 3, 1990, pp. 333–346; and Ludwig Huber, "Disciplinary Cultures and Social Reproduction," *European Journal of Education*, vol. 25, no. 3, 1990, pp. 241–261.

7. Clark Kerr, *The Uses of the University* (New York: Harper & Row, 1966), p. 20.

8. Burton R. Clark, *The Higher Education System* (Berkeley: University of California Press, 1983).

9. Like many others', my own university's constitutional arrangements require most major subject- or department-based committees to include representatives not only of allied disciplines but of at least one "noncognate" area as well.

10. See, for example, Christopher Jencks and David Riesman, *The Academic Revolution* (New York: Doubleday, 1968).

11. Huber, "Disciplinary Cultures."

12. Halsey, *Decline of Donnish Dominion*.

13. Oliver Fulton, "Mass Access and the End of Diversity? The Academic Profession in England on the Eve of Structural Reform," in Philip Altbach (ed.), *The International Academic Profession: Portraits from Fourteen Countries* (Princeton, N.J.: Carnegie Foundation for the Advancement of Teaching, 1996).

14. Maurice Kogan, Ingrid Moses, and Elaine El-Khawas, *Staffing Higher Education: Meeting New Challenges* (London: Jessica Kingsley, 1994), chap. 4.

15. Henry Miller, "States, Economies and the Changing Labour Process of Academics: Australia, Canada and the United Kingdom," in John Smyth (ed.), *Academic Work* (Buckingham, England: Open University Press, 1995), pp. 40–59; Richard Winter, "The University of Life plc: The 'Industrialisation' of Higher Education?" in John Smyth (ed.), *Academic Work* (Buckingham, England: Open University Press, 1995), pp. 129–143.

16. Halsey, *Decline of Donnish Dominion*.

17. Douglas Hague, *Beyond Universities: A New Republic of the Intellect* (London: Institute of Economic Affairs, 1991).

18. Technically, all the Swedish institutions surveyed were universities or university institutes. There is, however, a clear distinction between those "with" and "without research." The English polytechnics and some of the larger colleges became ("new") universities later in 1992, after the survey was completed. For my comparative purposes, both the Swedish universities without research and the English polytechnics and colleges will be referred to as the "nonuniversity sector."

19. Gouldner suggested that in the single college he studied, "cosmopolitanism" and "localism" were polar opposites on a single dimension. In other contexts they appear to be independent attributes. See Halsey and Trow, *The British Academics*, pp. 526–532.

20. The strength of the English response must undoubtedly be related to the pressures of the four-yearly Research Assessment Exercises, in which polytechnic departments were allowed for the first time to compete alongside the universities in 1992, the year of the survey. Success in this assessment was rewarded with both prestige and resources, and most polytechnic managers encouraged their institutions to aspire to success.

21. One of the few commonalities across European countries is the use of the term *professor* to designate the academic leaders of university departments or disciplines. In European universities, the title of professor was traditionally reserved, unlike full professorship in the United States, for the holder of a single chair in each discipline. The number of university chairs has been increased in recent years, if to varying extents in different countries, and in most countries there are now also a small number of professors in the non-university sector. Below the professorial level, there is no uniformity of names or roles.

22. My Dutch colleagues have attempted to quantify the costs of administration by academic staff across the four countries by combining time commitments and salary costs. They claim that England is spectacularly extravagant in its administrative costs because of its insistence on demanding large amounts of administrative time from its most senior staff.

23. Boyer, Altbach, and Whitelaw, *The Academic Profession*.

24. Fulton, "Mass Access."

THE PLANNING AND OVERSIGHT OF SCIENCE

A Time for Audacity:
What the Past Has to Teach the Present about Science and the Federal Government

DANIEL J. KEVLES

THE END of the Cold War has opened a new and so far troubled era in federal patronage of science. This post–Cold War transition differs sharply from the transformation in the relations of science and government that followed World War II. That watershed was precarious because of its connection to nuclear weapons, yet what was dangerous to the world generated good fortune for science in the United States. The country had emerged from the war singularly strong compared with the once dominant technical enterprises in the devastated countries of Europe, and its prospects were enhanced enormously by the federal resources that the demands of national security were making available to it. Federal investment in research and development grew steadily until the late 1960s, turned flat for a decade, and then burgeoned in the 1980s to levels higher in constant dollars than the munificent heights of the late 1960s. The end of the Cold War has dramatically diminished the nuclear danger, but in tandem with that happy fact, the American technical community, which now faces stiff competition from abroad, can no longer take for granted the federal resources for science on which it has counted during the last half century.

The demise of Cold War competition severely disadvantaged research in the physical sciences and engineering. In 1993, Congress killed the project to build the Superconducting Supercollider, a gargantuan machine whose estimated cost had reached $11 billion. Senator Dave Durenberger, a Minnesota Republican, explained, "If we were engaged in a scientific competition with a global superpower like the former Soviet Union, and if this project would lead to an

I am grateful for the research assistance of Peter Neushul; the comments of Evelyn Fox Keller, Maxine Singer, and Frank Press; and the support of The Andrew W. Mellon Foundation.

enhancement of our national security, then I would be willing to continue funding the project. But . . . we face no such threat."[1] Declining military budgets prompted recommendations to close almost a dozen Army and Navy research centers and called into question the future of the nine national laboratories in the Department of Energy whose activities were related to national defense and which employed twenty thousand scientists and engineers.[2]

In the summer of 1994, Congressman John Murtha, of Pennsylvania, chairman of the House Appropriations Subcommitee on defense, moved to slash 50% of Defense Department support of basic research in universities, insisting that the government should not be increasing basic-research spending "when there's not enough money to pay and outfit the troops." Political infighting reportedly accounted for Murtha's attack, but the House was initially disposed to go along with him; in the end, both the House and the Senate agreed to a reduction of $79 million, almost 8%. Congressman Julian C. Dixon, an appropriations committee member from Louisiana, expressed the widespread sentiment on Capitol Hill that since every other sector of the military was taking hits, it was time for universities "to take their fair share, too."[3]

The peace dividend predicted to come from the end of the Cold War was not paid into federal research and development (R&D) accounts. Although after 1989, appropriations to the National Science Foundation and the National Institutes of Health (NIH) went up in constant dollars, analysts reported that many worthwhile research proposals—at NIH, some 85% of them—went begging for want of sufficient funds (see Figure 1 and Tables 1 and 2).[4] In constant dollars, federal expenditures for R&D turned downward in 1989, were driven lower by the recession of the early 1990s, and in the budget passed for 1995 were only some 80% of what they had been in 1987 (see Figure 2 and Table 3).[5] By then, the federal share of R&D spending in the United States had fallen from slightly less than half the total to only a little more than a third of it.[6]

Both practitioners and friends of science found reasons for apprehension in trends outside the budgetary figures. Thoughtful scientists pointed to the beliefs that fraud was pervasive in American research and that universities commonly chiseled the government on overhead costs. They lamented the facts that bookstores devoted far more shelf space to works of astrology and the occult than to books about science and that respect for competent scientific authority seemed gone. No amount of scientific expertise could convince many home buyers, legislators, and influential journalists that radiation from high-voltage power lines did not threaten public health. The popular film *Lorenzo's*

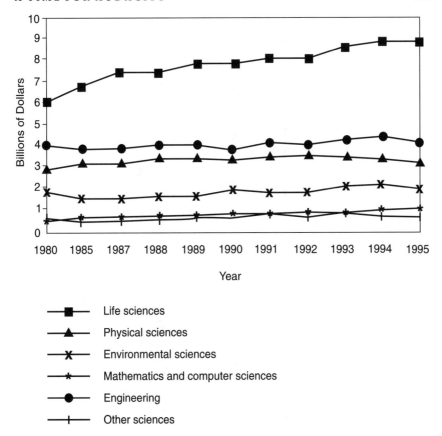

Figure 1. Federal Obligations for Research, by Field of Science, 1980–1995 (in billions of constant 1987 dollars, for fiscal years ending in year indicated)

Sources: U.S. Bureau of the Census, *Statistical Abstract of the United States, 1994*, 114th edition (Washington, D.C.: U.S. Government Printing Office, 1994), p. 613, U.S. Bureau of the Census, *Statistical Abstract of the United States, 1996*, 116th edition, (Washington, D.C.: U.S. Government Printing Office, 1996), p. 607.

Oil—the story of how a family, by treating their son with an allegedly salutary oil, defied medical prognosis of his debilitating disease—was interpreted by the bioethicist Arthur Caplan to express several myths, including the belief that "mainstream science" cared only for its power and privilege and was "indifferent" to the sufferings of patients and their families. The playwright and AIDS activist Larry Kramer indicted NIH as a "research system that by law demands compromise, rewards mediocrity and actually punishes initiative and originality."[7]

TABLE 1

Federal Obligations for Research, by Field of Science, 1980–1993 (in millions of constant 1987 dollars, for fiscal years ending in year indicated)

	1980	1985	1987	1988	1989	1990	1991	1992	1993	1994	1995 (est.)
Life sciences	5,938	6,747	7,341	7,457	7,851	7,884	8,245	8,251	8,758	9,051	9,013
Physical sciences	2,834	3,230	3,253	3,424	3,424	3,401	3,626	3,696	3,599	3,548	3,400
Environmental sciences	1,786	1,489	1,512	1,639	1,639	1,941	1,842	1,838	2,120	2,258	2,089
Mathematics and computer sciences	341	610	641	679	679	751	775	966	996	1,124	1,185
Engineering	4,009	3,836	3,906	4,105	4,105	3,871	4,237	4,144	4,471	4,546	4,370
Other sciences	495	362	438	593	593	593	774	673	921	809	819

Sources: U.S. Bureau of the Census, *Statistical Abstract of the United States, 1994,* 114th edition (Washington, D.C.: U.S. Government Printing Office, 1994), p. 613; U.S. Bureau of the Census, *Statistical Abstract of the United States, 1996,* 116th edition, (Washington, D.C.: U.S. Government Printing Office, 1996), p. 607.

TABLE 2

Federal Obligations for R&D, by Selected Agency, 1975–1995 (in millions of constant 1987 dollars, for fiscal years ending in year indicated)

	1975	1980	1985	1988	1989	1990	1991	1992	1993	1994	1995 (est.)
Department of Defense	18,935	19,803	31,592	34,024	34,729	33,275	27,536	30,083	29,146	28,429	27,117
Percentage of total	47%	47%	62%	62%	61%	59%	52%	55%	53%	51%	50%
Department of Health and Human Services	4,792	5,354	5,780	6,909	7,304	7,505	8,360	7,484	8,414	8,797	8,914
Percentage of total	12%	13%	11%	13%	13%	13%	16%	14%	15%	16%	17%
NASA	6,437	4,581	3,528	4,180	4,985	5,833	6,238	6,376	6,520	6,990	6,665
Percentage of total	16%	11%	7%	8%	9%	10%	12%	12%	12%	13%	12%
Department of Energy	4,300	6,733	5,266	4,861	4,799	5,028	5,127	5,139	5,691	5,207	4,946
Percentage of total	11%	16%	10%	9%	8%	9%	10%	9%	10%	9%	9%
National Science Foundation	1,250	1,249	1,427	1,480	1,543	1,509	1,530	1,555	1,530	1,620	1,723
Percentage of total	3%	3%	3%	3%	3%	3%	3%	3%	3%	3%	3%
Total Federal R&D	39,998	42,253	51,283	54,796	56,753	56,846	52,524	54,615	54,727	55,498	53,856

Sources: U.S. Bureau of the Census, *Statistical Abstract of the United States, 1994,* 114th edition (Washington, D.C.: U.S. Government Printing Office, 1994), p. 609; U.S. Bureau of the Census, *Statistical Abstract of the United States, 1996,* 116th edition (Washington, D.C.: U.S. Government Printing Office, 1996), p. 603.

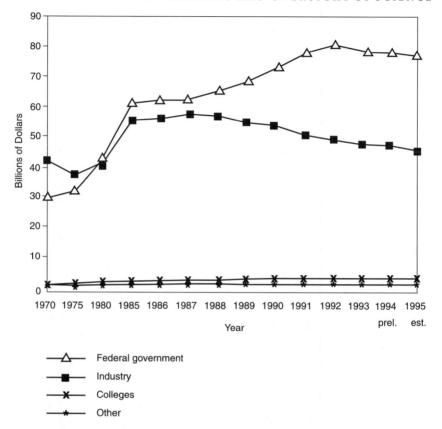

Figure 2. R&D, Source of Funds and Performance Sector, 1970–1995 (in billions of constant 1987 dollars, for fiscal years ending in year indicated)
   Sources: U.S. Bureau of the Census, *Statistical Abstract of the United States, 1994*, 114th edition (Washington, D.C.: U.S. Government Printing Office, 1994), p. 607; U.S. Bureau of the Census, *Statistical Abstract of the United States, 1996*, 116th edition (Washington, D.C.: U.S. Government Printing Office, 1996), p. 601.

   Lay dissenters challenged scientific control of federal research programs. Activists like Kramer demanded that NIH spend more on AIDS research, while women's advocates insisted on increased funds for studies of breast cancer. Fran Visco, president of the National Breast Cancer Coalition, averred, "For too long, funding decisions have been made at the expense of women's lives. We have to make up for being ignored for so long."[8] Between 1989 and 1994, federal funds for breast cancer research rose by almost 400%, while AIDS challenged cancer as the chief recipient of NIH money.[9] Congressmen

TABLE 3

R&D, Source of Funds and Performance Sector, 1970–1995 (in millions of constant 1987 dollars, for fiscal years ending in year indicated)

	1970	1975	1980	1985	1986	1987	1988	1989	1990	1991	1992	1993	1994 (prelim.)	1995 (est.)
Federal government	42,622	37,396	41,385	55,245	55,966	57,913	57,386	55,275	54,587	51,407	50,002	48,876	48,569	46,989
Industry	29,673	32,162	43,118	61,418	63,009	62,643	65,492	69,169	73,604	78,652	81,641	79,069	79,031	78,381
Colleges	1,335	1,574	1,878	2,512	2,867	3,192	3,343	3,624	3,865	4,143	4,496	4,155	4,266	4,270
Other	966	1,105	1,268	1,425	1,453	1,628	1,770	1,958	2,079	2,183	2,407	2,328	2,426	2,437

Sources: U.S. Bureau of the Census, *Statistical Abstract of the United States, 1994,* 114th edition (Washington, D.C.: U.S. Government Printing Office, 1994), p. 607; U.S. Bureau of the Census, *Statistical Abstract of the United States, 1996,* 116th edition (Washington, D.C.: U.S. Government Printing Office, 1996), p. 601.

from scientifically have-not or have-less parts of the country obtained appropriations earmarked for special projects in their states or districts. The maneuvers flouted the peer review process, supplying monies to enterprises that stretched the meaning of "meritorious." Senator Ted Stevens of Alaska earmarked $37 million for a study of the aurora borealis as a potential energy source—a project that its referees had rightly called "wacky" and "crazy."[10] In 1993, earmarking took an estimated $1.7 billion from the scarce R&D funds available, more than doubling the amount it had captured two years earlier.[11]

The power of scientists to set the federal agenda of basic research was questioned even by one of its most sympathetic friends in Congress, the California Democrat George E. Brown Jr., who was chairman of the House Committee on Science, Space, and Technology. Brown was a relentless enemy of earmarking, but a report released by his committee in September 1992 revealed that he was not an uncritical enthusiast of the priorities embraced by the academically centered basic research community. The report found an increasing "mismatch"—a "discord"—between the community's demands and the multiple needs of a troubled society.[12] According to Brown, it was no longer justifiable for academic research to operate as an autonomous "black box into which federal funds are deposited, and from which social benefit is somehow derived."[13] In an op-ed column in the *Los Angeles Times*, Brown made clear his belief that the social returns from science had been inadequate, having done little to overcome "a failing education system, decaying cities, environmental degradation, unaffordable health care and history's largest national debt."[14] Brown ventured the heresy that "the research policy designed forty years ago may no longer be suitable for addressing the problems of today's world," that change was clearly needed, and that a key feature of change should be the forging of "explicit linkages between the conduct of federally funded research and the achievement of national goals." Federally supported science, he summarily told readers of the *Times*, was "down to the last blank check."[15]

Some scientists retorted to Brown that he was blaming science for what were in reality failures of the political system. Others echoed the oncogeneticist Robert Weinberg's tart prediction that the targeting of breast cancer at NIH would "bring American leadership in biomedical research to its knees and prevent the glorious successes we have had over the years."[16] But whether the issue was earmarking or targeting, it was clear to many observers that a struggle was under way over the federal research agenda—particularly, as Edward David, who had been science adviser in the Nixon White House, put it, over

whether the agenda was to be controlled by "scientists" or by "politi-
cans and social engineers."[17]

Whoever controlled it, its prospects seemed bleak. Leaders of
American physics variously declared the Supercollider's death to
mean that high-energy physics had no future in the United States,
that the country was relinquishing its role as a scientific leader, or
that, as the head of the project remonstrated, "curiosity-driven science
is somehow frivolous, and a luxury we can no longer afford."[18] Academic administrators worried with Cornelius J. Pings, president of
the American Association of Universities, that the overall R&D trend
threatened to end "an era of extraordinary growth and prosperity for
basic science and engineering in the nation's major universities."
Ellen Williams, a physicist at the University of Maryland, caught the
mood of many workaday faculty: "A lot of people are scared stiff that
the funding will just dry up, and life as we know it will end."[19]

Students at a select high school in San Francisco frankly told a distinguished local biologist that they saw no point in entering scientific
careers because no grant money was available to support research.
Certainly not enough could be found to absorb the torrent of new
doctorates that were emerging from the nation's graduate school
pipelines. Observers of trends in scientific manpower proclaimed that
universities were producing an oversupply of scientific Ph.D.'s and
that they had to cut back—forever. The "good times for science will
never return," David L. Goodstein, a physicist and the vice provost
of the California Institute of Technology, warned. "We stand now on
the threshold of our new and future condition: the permanent era of
constraint."[20]

The bad times threatened to become unimaginably worse when the
Republican-dominated 104th Congress rolled into Washington in January 1995, ferociously committed to the enactment of its balanced-
budget Contract with America. In June, the Republican majority
drove through a budget resolution that would maintain military research at roughly its current level but that was estimated to slash
nondefense R&D, not including biomedical research, by some 30% by
2002. Biomedical research was slated to fall slightly, then level off,
which meant that at even moderate inflation rates, its buying-power
budget would be reduced by 25%. The proposed cuts threatened an
earthquake in federal science, including extensive reductions in the
programs of space, energy, and atmospheric research, a sharp contraction in the number of grants that the National Science Foundation
could afford, and the outright abolition of the United States Geological Survey.[21] The Survey, already feeling the squeeze, soon announced

that it would fire five hundred of the employees in its geological division, and the Bureau of Mines was in fact abolished.[22]

The *New York Times* called the proposed cuts "shocking," and even George Brown was prompted to snap, "We're dominated by fools."[23] Know-nothingism appeared in vogue on Capitol Hill. Congressman Dick Chrysler, a Republican from Michigan and spearhead of a drive to abolish the Department of Commerce, was asked about eliminating the Commerce-housed Weather Service. Not everyone thought he was joking when he replied, "We don't need the government; I get my weather from the Weather Channel." Leaders of the federal Centers for Disease Control and Prevention, in Atlanta, Georgia, predicted that the proposed reductions would severely hamper the CDC's ability to identify and track epidemic diseases. Susan Tanaka, vice president of the Committee for a Responsible Federal Budget, a bipartisan group devoted to eliminating the federal deficit, suggested that the CDC's leaders were indulging in unjustifiable special pleading, explaining, "Diseases grow and wane. Some have gone away and we don't have to worry about them anymore."[24]

Even before the Republican upheaval the advent of a new era in federal science policy had prompted a search for navigational bearings—reports, studies, and symposia seeking to come to grips with the realities of post–Cold War science. Some offered sober strategies for the future, but few exploited the past except to invoke what is taken to be the charter document of the relationship between science and the American government since 1945, Vannevar Bush's celebrated report, *Science — the Endless Frontier*.[25] Yet in 1947, in the middle of the post–World War II transformation, the chemist James B. Conant, who was president of Harvard University and a key figure in science policymaking, had remarked, "You have to get the past straight before you do much to prepare people for the future."[26] Fearing that the moral condemnations of Hiroshima and Nagasaki might lead the United States into a new isolationism, Conant had wanted to get straight the immediate past, establishing for the record that it had not been wrong to use the atomic bombs on Japan. The recent controversy over the *Enola Gay* exhibit at the Smithsonian notwithstanding, the end of the Cold War has exempted analysts of the current transition from any comparably charged exploitation of the past; but the current uncertainty about science and government in the United States invites a look at history, particularly the history of previous transitions in federal science.

The post–World War II transformation rewards scrutiny, if only because it has achieved the status of a creation myth: Vannevar Bush said, "Let there be federal support of basic research and training," and, lo, the postwar system of federal research and development was born, ushering in a golden age of basic research.[27] In truth, the creation of the system was embattled, and a good deal of contemporary relevance is to be gleaned from revisiting both some of the key issues that were fought and the way they were contested. Another revealing transition occurred during the 1890s. No myth surrounds that episode; it is hardly known to most analysts of federal science policy. Yet it merits attention because it eerily adumbrates several of the issues that now confront the science-government relationship in the United States.

The 1890s

General understanding has it that federal support of science before World War II was insignificant and that before the 1930s, little, if any, science of consequence was done in the United States. That view comes from the physicists of the Los Alamos generation. It is their story of science in America, and it is mistaken, not least because, beginning in the post–Civil War years, the earth sciences and certain branches of the life sciences were pursued in the United States with considerable distinction and no small degree of government patronage.

The expansion in federal patronage bespoke a willingness to support research in disciplines relevant to one of major national missions of the era: the exploration, settlement, and economic development of the land, especially in the Far West. In 1878, the venerable Coast Survey, established in the administration of Thomas Jefferson, was renamed the Coast and Geodetic Survey, signifying the enlargment of its duties beyond mapping the shoreline to determining the intensity and inclination of the earth's magnetic field throughout the continental United States. In 1870, the United States Army Signal Corps established the country's first federal weather service. In the early 1880s, a center in Washington, D.C., was gathering reports of local weather that were telegraphed from across the country, collating them into predictions, and supporting research into meteorology by a small staff of physicists.

By then, the U.S. Geological Survey, created in 1879, led all other federal scientific agencies in the scope and prominence of its work, thanks to the energy, imagination, and political skills of its director after 1881, John Wesley Powell. Authorized to construct a geological map of the country, Powell employed topographers, geologists, and paleontologists, farmed out work to university consultants, and published the results of much of the resulting research in bulletins from the Government Printing Office. The Survey's work in pure and applied geology rapidly achieved world-class distinction. Between 1881 and 1884, Powell's budget jumped fivefold, reaching $500,000 a year. The sum was considerable—a sixfold greater fraction of the federal budget than the Geological Survey commands today—and made a significant difference in the science of the time. Between them, the several federal scientific agencies of the era made Washington the home of much of American science. The Government Printing Office was the nation's principal publisher of research. Relative to population, more scientists worked in the capital than in any other city in the country, including Cambridge, Massachusetts.

The expansion of federal science was an integral part of the program of capital investment for economic development that the federal government enthusiastically fostered during the post–Civil War years. This same program also yielded a number of other developmental incentives, including the land-grant colleges, the Homestead Act, and the transcontinental railroads. It was dominantly a Republican program. It exploited public resources, including tax revenues but particularly land. Parts of it were stained with corruption, and all of it was vulnerable to the charge that it expressed an inappropriate enlargement of federal power and authority. It was also plagued by tensions between its practitioners and the political system that were by no means transient. Critics contended that its scope was too broad, that it was engaging in abstract work of no utility—for example, meteorological studies that would not lead to more reliable weather prediction or paleontological investigations that satisfied no public want—and that much of it could better be left to private enterprise. To these critics, federal science needed to be brought under closer control.

Federal scientists retorted that, in the phrase of one, the surveys were "not fomenting science"; they were doing practical work for practical purposes. Powell asserted that scientists would grow "restive and rebellious when their judgments are coerced by superior authority" and that the control of science had to be kept out of the hands of "officers or functionaries" whose principal interest was "official position or dignity." Powell added hotly that not even "a hundred millionaires" could support the research of the federal agencies and that the progress of American civilization should not have to wait on the philanthropic inspiration of a hundred rich men. The national government should support and publish whatever science advanced the people's welfare.[28]

The tensions in federal science played a major role in precipitating the first transition, which began in 1892. A two-thirds majority of

Democrats, many of them economy-minded conservatives, the product of the 1890 elections, now dominated the House. Congress also
contained agrarians of both parties, who, sensitive to the mounting
populist revolt on the cotton fields, plains, and prairies, wondered
why the government should allocate funds for research on the slimy
things of the earth when human beings were earning too little to keep
their farms. The agrarians and the pro-economy Democrats, each for
their own reasons, formed a coalition that threatened expenditures for
superfluous science. The House applied the ax to both the Geological
Survey and the Coast and Geodetic Survey. Congressman William S.
Holman of Indiana, the wry chairman of the appropriations committee, liked to poke at the House for overtaxing poor people; he told the
spenders that the practical value of geodesy was "very remote" and
that the government could not indulge in purely scientific work when
the Treasury was "cramped." Hilary Abner Herbert, a conservative
Democrat from Alabama, hauled out prior charges of extravagance,
insisting that the Geological Survey was going far beyond the proper
bounds of a frugal government and successfully demanding cancella-
tion of funding for paleontology.[29]

In the Senate, where Republicans still held a slim majority, Powell's
friends did their best to restore most of the cuts. However, responding to the political forces that had transformed the House in 1890, the
Senate resounded with testimonials to economy from the Republican
side of the aisle, too. Moreover, Powell had alienated Republicans
from the Far West several years earlier by advancing a proposal—a
conservation measure generated by his agency's survey of irrigation
prospects in the region—to withdraw irrecoverably arid lands from
traditional homestead settlement. "We in the West want more of substantial benefit and less of ornament," a western Republican de-
claimed, arguing in favor of cuts of almost 50% in the survey's activities in general geology and paleontology.[30] Despite the efforts of
Powell's friends, the cuts for his agency went through the Senate on a
close vote and were ratified in the House, which also refused to con-
cur in the partial restoration of funds even for the Coast Survey. In
1892, every major scientific bureau emerged from the congressional
session with a significantly reduced appropriation. Not even John
Wesley Powell could beat back a coaliton of economy-minded conservatives and midwestern agrarians, joined now to cut the fat out of
federal science.

In 1893, Grover Cleveland, a Democrat, was inaugurated president
and, because of the depression, the order of the day in the White
House and on Capitol Hill was retrenchment. The secretary of agriculture announced that he would drop all "useless scientists" from

the Weather Bureau (it had been transferred from the Army to the Department of Agriculture), explaining, "What the people most want is knowledge beforehand of what is to happen . . . rather than a scientific diagnosis . . . after it is all over."[31] Hilary Herbert, now the secretary of the Navy, tried to engineer the abolition of the Coast and Geodetic Survey and, though unsuccessful in that venture, did manage to reduce its staff. Powell left federal service, as did scores of lower-ranking scientists, many of whom were fired. The great expansion in federal patronage of the earth sciences seemed not only to have ended but to have been reversed. The halcyon days of the surveys appeared over.

As a matter of fact, when prosperity returned to the country, in 1897, appropriations for the surveys swung upward once again, more than doubling by 1914.[32] Yet the fiscal turnabout did not yield just more of the same. The forces of political economy that had produced the cutbacks in federal science during the 1890s masked a fundamental change in the national agenda. The frontier was closed, and the country was swiftly urbanizing. After the Spanish-American War (1898), the nation also began to flex its muscles as a world power, self-consciously engaged in international economic competition. The new agenda was concerned much less with the acquisition of new land and resources and much more with the conservation of the land and resources already in the nation's possession and with the exploitation of nature to produce new goods for domestic and foreign markets.

After the turn of the century, in keeping with the new agenda the purposes of federal science were reconfigured. Federal emphases in the earth and life sciences turned partly to conservation, responding to the environmental movement of the day. The United States Geological Survey's major duties now included mapping of the national forests and—in pursuit of policies that vindicated Powell—the drawing of topographical maps that would assist the new Reclamation Service in fostering irrigation. Similarly, federal biological surveys were strengthened to track and study wildlife. And new stress was placed on federally supported agricultural research in the belief that it would boost productivity and prosperity on the farm. The federal government provided important opportunities for such research both in its own bureaus and at the agricultural experiment stations that the Hatch Act of 1887 had established at land-grant colleges and universities and that was enriched by the passage of the Adams Act, in 1906. That act, which provided grant funds for agricultural research projects evaluated for their merit, made the federal agricultural research program into a distributional hybrid, a merger of allocations to the states and to projects of merit.

The experiment stations, jointly supported by the federal and state governments, were key sites for research in the new science of genetics. Since the late nineteenth century, agricultural policymakers had argued that if American agriculture was to be competitive on the world market, improved varieties of plants and animals would have to be devised. After 1900, farmers and breeders began taking an interest in Mendel's newly rediscovered theory of heredity as a means of achieving that end. Adams Act funds permitted the young geneticist Raymond Pearl to join the staff of the Maine Experiment Station and pursue investigations of inheritance in poultry. He wrote to a friend in England, "I am under no restrictions as to giving the work a practical turn. On the contrary, I am expected to work exactly as if I were taking up the study of heredity for my own purely scientific ends."[33] Even experiment station scientists who had to concern themselves with practicality more than Pearl did contributed significantly to genetics. By World War I, the United States was a major world power in genetics, both pure and practical, partly because of the brilliant work of Thomas Hunt Morgan and his colleagues at Columbia University but also because of the work that his fellow biologists were able to conduct in schools of agriculture around the country, particularly at the experiment stations.

Yet perhaps the most salient feature of the new agenda was its attentiveness to assisting what is known as the "second industrial revolution," the revolution that depended on the exploitation of the laboratory sciences of physics and chemistry to produce new products. By the turn of the century, that revolution was already well under way and had yielded such marvels as electric light and power, telephones and moving pictures, and the petroleum products that fueled and lubricated the horseless carriage. Manufacturing was already generating some 30% more of the national income than mining and agriculture combined. Since the 1880s, American physicists and chemists had advocated greater federal investment in laboratories devoted to their disciplines. Now they pointed out that the governments of Germany and England had recently established handsomely equipped laboratories for the determination of standard physical and chemical units. The lack of such a laboratory in the United States was said to be both humiliating and commercially costly. The increasing technical complexity of industry made more pressing the need for uniform standards not only of weight but also of chemical and electrical quantities. Most measuring devices were imported, and domestic manufacturers were disinclined to use the products of American's nascent instrument industry unless they bore the seal of a European testing laboratory. In 1899, a drive was mounted to satisfy the need for such a laboratory. In response, Congress in 1901 created the National Bureau of Standards, enabling the agency not only to establish and maintain standards of measure but also to engage in whatever research might be necessary to do so.

During congressional hearings on the matter, Secretary of the Treasury Lyman Gage had declared, expressing a salient feature of the new national agenda, in applied science and trade, "in all the great things of life," the United States was in competition with the older and more thoroughly established nations of the world.[34] By the end of World War I, the great things had come to include military competition. The Army and Navy established new agencies devoted to research in particular areas of the the physical sciences, notably the Chemical Warfare Service and the Naval Research Laboratory; and the National Advisory Committee for Aeronautics was created for investigations into the sciences that undergirded the newest machines of transport and war. Although these agency initiatives did not generally extend federal support to the physical sciences and engineering in colleges and universities, they were harbingers of the transformation that the new national agenda would work in the relationship of the federal government to the physical sciences with the coming of World War II.

Post–World War II

The dramatic transition in federal science that occurred in the 1940s was not crafted out of whole cloth. On the contrary, it was strongly shaped by, so to speak, the scientific economy that had been constructed in the United States since the turn of the century. That economy was strongly connected to its European counterpart and, in the physical sciences, relied heavily on the European enterprise for intellectual capital in the form of basic scientific knowledge and human capital in the form of scientific training. But from the turn of the century, the American scientific economy was marked by heavy private investment designed to build an indigenous scientific capability in the physical sciences and strengthen the one that already existed in the earth and life sciences. The goad was the spreading recognition, particularly in the high-technology-related parts of the private sector, of what Secretary Gage had testified to but also of the fact that the country's domestic prosperity and health depended increasingly on the enlargement of technical knowledge. The scientific frontier, as Vannevar Bush would say in his celebrated report, had become a new frontier for national development.

Before World War II, part of the investment in technical and human capital came from the public sector. At the federal level, the ongoing support of agricultural research in the land-grant colleges and universities was supplemented in new areas by the general-welfare initiatives of the New Deal including support for research in forestry, soil conservation, and health, notably with the creation of the National Cancer Institute in 1937. Before the war, the more important public-sector support comprised the appropriations that state governments made to public universities for education and research. Some private investment in intellectual capital was provided by the industrial research laboratories, several of which—for example, the General Electric Research Laboratory and the Bell Telephone Laboratories—operated at a high level of scientific quality. Although industrial corporations did not supply much support to academia for basic research and training, industrially generated wealth provided a great deal. Individual philanthropists paid for laboratories and fellowships. Andrew Carnegie, concerned for "our national poverty in science" and eager to "change our position among the nations," endowed an entire institution devoted to scientific research.[35] But the greatest and most influential private support came from the philanthropic foundations that after the turn of the century increasingly populated the American eleemosynary landscape. The greatest of these was the Rockefeller Foundation, which between the world wars decisively encouraged the physical and life sciences in the United States by concentrating its programmatic largesse in the best institutions and supporting a system of national postdoctoral fellowships that concentrated talent in the same places.

As a result, on the eve of World War II, the American scientific economy was flourishing. Extending a trend that had started in the 1890s, it was producing its own doctorates at an exponentially increasing annual rate. It was generating distinguished research in virtually every field of basic science. It was pluralist, spread across the continent, yet it was also hierarchical, dominated by the better public and private universities. And it prospered from multiple sources of public and private patronage. Many of its characteristics were exemplified by the cyclotron laboratory that Ernest O. Lawrence had built at the University of California, Berkeley, which obtained roughly 40% of its operating dollars from the state of California and another 20% of the same costs plus an equal fraction of the capital expenditures from the federal government. All the rest—roughly 40% of the operating costs and 80% of the capital costs—came from private sources comprising individuals, corporations, and foundations.

This scientific economy was mobilized for the war by the Office of Scientific Research and Development (OSRD) and under its auspices worked military miracles. The most salient of them, the product of physicists, were microwave radar, proximity fuzes, solid-fuel rockets, and the atomic bomb, but members of the OSRD Committee on Medical Research had several miracles to their credit, including the development of penicillin. To many scientists and policymakers at the end of the war, it seemed evident that in the interests of the nation's military security, public health, and economic welfare, the federal government had to support programs of basic and applied scientific research and training. But the question of how that goal should be accomplished ignited major battles over the structure and control of postwar science.

One point of conflict was whether defense-related research should come under the principal control of military or civilian authority. The first proposal to establish the Atomic Energy Commission (AEC), advanced by the Truman administration in 1945, struck many scientists as likely to give the military undue influence over the nation's postwar nuclear program and subject its operations to excessive security restrictions. Although the measure was supported by key leaders of wartime science, the scientific rank and file mounted a campaign to beat it back, buttonholing members of Congress and educating the public on the matter. Out of the effort, they gained the creation, in 1946, of a civilian-controlled AEC that was, among other things, to foster the civilian as well as the military uses of nuclear energy and that was enabled to ensure the widespread dissemination of nuclear information consistent with the requirements of national security.

Outside the nuclear area, the Navy stepped in to sponsor a broad range of work in basic scientific research and training under its new Office of Naval Research (ONR). In 1946, ONR was supporting some six hundred academic research projects that involved roughly two thousand scientists and an equal number of graduate students in fields ranging from betatron physics to botany and plant cells. Yet Harlow Shapley, the Harvard astronomer and political activist, expressed a widely shared worry that the government's "intercession in American science . . . has altered and perhaps become ominous . . . because of the Navy's great move in supporting science on a wide basis," adding, "Those who were worried about domination of freedom in American science by the great industries, can now worry about domination by the military."[36]

Indeed, the Cold War increasingly made national security the predominant focus of federal policy for research and development. Some 90% of federal R&D funding came from various bureaus of the armed services, which were consolidated in the Department of Defense (DOD) by the National Security Act in 1947, and from the Atomic

Energy Commission, which, under the pressures of the Cold War, devoted its research efforts overwhelmingly to the uses of atomic energy in national security, especially the development of nuclear and then thermonuclear weapons. In 1949, Lee DuBridge, the head of the wartime Radiation Laboratory at MIT and now president of the California Institute of Technology, warned, "When science is allowed to exist merely from the crumbs that fall from the table of a weapons development program, then science is headed into the stifling atmosphere of 'mobilized secrecy' and it is surely doomed—even though the crumbs themselves should provide more than adequate nourishment."[37]

Scientists like DuBridge had no quarrel with reasonable secrecy, and high-quality research did indeed flourish in classified environments, several of which were connected with distinguished universities.[38] But security restrictions were being imposed that struck most scientists as unreasonable. The restrictions were perhaps tightest in the nation's atomic energy program, the source of the weapons that many policymakers expected would keep the Soviet Union indefinitely at bay. In 1950, the Joint Congressional Committee on Atomic Energy decided to require security clearances for all recipients of fellowships from the Atomic Energy Commission, whether they were engaged in classified research or not. Senator William Knowland, a conservative Republican from California, declared, "There is always the chance that some student, even if pursuing nonsecret studies, might "hit upon a 'superduper' atom bomb and be off to Russia."[39] The State Department refused to grant various foreign scientists, including the Nobel laureate physicist Paul A. M. Dirac, visas to attend scientific congresses in the United States, and it denied Linus Pauling one to travel abroad for scientific purposes. Meanwhile, McCarthyite intimidation drove talented scientists like David Bohm to leave the United States.

The Truman administration had actually approved the Navy's entrance into large-scale support of fundamental research only as an interim arrangement, pending the establishment of a suitable civilian structure for federal support of basic research and training. However, the building of the structure was significantly slowed by a second line of dispute over how to achieve the goals of postwar science—that between the heirs of the practically oriented critics of late-nineteenth-century science and the heirs of John Wesley Powell, with his strong conviction that unfettered science best served the general welfare.

The latter-day enthusiasts of practicality found an exponent in Senator Harley M. Kilgore, a New Deal Democrat from West Virginia. A small-town lawyer, Kilgore was devoted to the cause of organized labor and quick to admit "utter, absolute ignorance" of science and technology. However, during the course of wartime hearings on the better mobilization of the nation's technological resources, he had learned a good deal about the importance of science to the national interest. He began to develop legislation for postwar science that called for the establishment of a national science foundation that would advance science and technology and help plan federal research activities to accommodate liberal social purposes—for example, aiding small business or fostering pollution control or low-cost rural electrification—goals that the market economy by itself would not likely attend to. Kilgore insisted that lay interest groups, like labor and consumers, should have a role in shaping federal science policy and that at least part of the money in all fields should be distributed on a geographic basis. He also urged federal support of the social sciences, which were then widely identified as tools for distributing the benefits of science and technology more equitably among the population.[40]

Vannevar Bush had a sharply different answer to the question of postwar science, and he prepared *Science—the Endless Frontier* not only to advance it but also to head off Kilgore. Bush, the son of a Protestant minister in Boston, was a no-nonsense electrical engineer with a strong sense of duty to public service. He had spent most of his prewar career on the MIT faculty, where the electrical engineering curriculum emphasized training in the basic sciences and the department stressed research. He played an influential role in transforming MIT into a research-oriented institution not only of high-tech engineering but also of basic science. Bush recognized the powerful inclination in America's practical culture to foster the applications of knowledge rather than the advancement of knowledge as such. From the war effort, he also knew full well that advances in seemingly impractical, esoteric fields such as nuclear physics or microbiology could lead to the creation of radically new weapons or powerful medical agents.

In Bush's view, the wartime production of technological miracles such as the atomic bomb and penicillin had drawn heavily on the capital account of basic science, depleting the reservoir of fundamental knowledge and the supply of newly trained men and women technically capable of generating it. The national welfare thus demanded not just replenishment but ongoing enlargement of the account—in accord with conditions that Bush regarded as essential to the health of science, which were contrary to Kilgore's. Bush aimed to superimpose federal support of research and training on the economy of basic research and training that had been built up before the war in ways that maintained the vitality of the system and respected its pluralism, diversity, and autonomy.

Thus *Science — the Endless Frontier* omitted consideration of the social sciences; Bush did not respect them intellectually and regarded them for the most part as political propaganda masquerading as science. The report made no mention of the geographic distribution of research funds; like the managers of the prewar Rockefeller Foundation, Bush judged that such monies should be distributed to the best investigators, wherever they were located (in recognition, undoubtedly, that most of the significant progress in a field of science is generated by its small fraction of most capable practitioners). And it rejected targeting research to particular social or economic purposes and including lay interest groups in the shaping of federal science policy. Bush held, above all, that the social and economic benefits of basic scientific research and training were best realized by the mechanisms of the free market, by private initiative. *Science — the Endless Frontier* stressed that federal science policy should be insulated from political control since, in Bush's view, such control would permit the political system—by which he meant politics influenced by a Kilgore-like socioeconomic program—to determine the kind of research to be encouraged.

Bush proposed to institutionalize his program in a different National Science Foundation (NSF) that would be the flagship agency of basic research and training in all the major areas of science, including those related to medicine and the military. Although he had supported the military-oriented version of the Atomic Energy Commission, he staunchly opposed general military dominance of science in peacetime, partly on the principle that military power in American life ought to be kept limited, partly because he counted civilian scientists who were autonomous, as they had been under OSRD, better able to innovate even for military purposes than those who were subordinate to the military itself. Bush's vision for the NSF did not prevail, either immediately or entirely. Dispute over the purposes and control of the NSF, particularly its responsiveness to the political system, delayed its establishment until 1950, by which time it had been prempted in the medical as well as in the military areas.

Federal sponsorship of medical research was increasingly dominated by the National Institutes of Health, which was established in 1948 as an umbrella to cover the National Cancer Institute and the new National Heart Institute and which now comprised five more research institutes, making a total of seven. The creation and expansion of NIH expressed the New Deal–Fair Deal commitment to using the powers of the federal government to advance the general welfare.

Neither had much, if anything, to do with the Cold War. Indeed, their budgets reflected the fact, accounting in 1951 for less than 5% of federal expenditures for research and development. Still, while the quality of much of the in-house research conducted at the Cancer Institute, which dominated the NIH budget, left a good deal to be desired, its programs of grants for basic research and training in universities generally conformed to Bush's principles of scientific patronage.

By 1950, scientists like DuBridge had no hope of reversing the military's dominant role in basic research. Nor did they want to. DuBridge himself took arms against a proposal to transfer ONR's support to the National Science Foundation, stressing to a high official in the Eisenhower administration that the poor-relation NSF would have to be granted appropriations "ten times their present level" to do the job properly, an amount of money that Congress would surely decline to provide. The NSF, DuBridge added, was "wholly unsuitable for the support of large research projects at large research centers. The California Institute of Technology, for example, would go broke very promptly if all of its basic research support were suddenly transferred to the National Science Foundation."[41] What DuBridge omitted to say was that he and most other scientific policymakers regarded military agencies like ONR as highly suitable as sponsors of academic research, and for reasons that went beyond their relative munificence.

ONR exempted its basic research programs from irritating red tape, avoided the imposition of crippling security restrictions, and went out of its way to allow the scientists it supported enormous leeway in deciding what research topics to pursue. ONR operated in such an enlightened manner because scientists like DuBridge, Bush, and Conant had worked hard to educate the naval officers who controlled it about the autonomy and freedom that are necessary to the flourishing of first-rate science. The leaders of the Los Alamos generation similarly spent a good deal of time and effort teaching the same lesson to other military officials and key members of Congress, with the result that they managed eventually to fend off excessive secrecy in basic research even in areas like nuclear physics. In all, the kind of open, self-regulated system of basic research and training laid out in *Science — The Endless Frontier* was achieved less by broad legislative or administrative enactment of Bush's vision than by education, negotiation, and lobbying in its favor, almost month to month, agency by agency.

The leadership of the Los Alamos generation succeeded in realizing the fundamentals of Bush's vision for several reasons. They enjoyed enormous prestige as the miracle makers of World War II, the magicians who had won the war with radar and ended it with the atomic bomb. Now they were regarded as an expert cadre indispensable to national defense. What they declared as required for science to flourish carried considerable weight. Yet they also commanded high respect because they manifestly cared about more than just scientific fellowships, jobs, and research grants. They were outspoken enthusiasts of science as such. They unabashedly extolled what they believed about it—that it fostered impartiality, challenged and dissolved prejudice, and carried forward the task of enlightenment. They proudly celebrated the triumphs of science, contending, for example, that investment in high-energy accelerators not only protected the United States against Russian surprises but also advanced the glorious march toward understanding the structure of matter and energy.

At the same time, they recognized that more was at stake in the postwar world than the advancement of science. To them, science was an integral instrument of the new national agenda that World War II had defined for the United States, particularly the maintenance of freedom in hazardous circumstances. A number of them held that scientists had a "social responsibility," to use the phrase current in the period, to participate in the great issues of the day. Many of them were, in fact, passionately engaged in issues of nuclear weapons, a highly classified technology under ongoing development in a nation that felt itself threatened by the Soviets not only from without but also from within. They disagreed with each other, often profoundly, over the particulars of national security policy, but they appeared sensitive to the larger public interest that at once embraced yet transcended science.

To the minds of many scientists, mobilization for the Cold War jeopardized both individual freedom and national safety. In the postwar decade, some people in and out of science clamored for a preventive war against the prenuclear Soviet Union and for open-ended technological superiority after it got the bomb. A secret National Security Council directive disapproved public debate on the moral issue of when to use nuclear weapons; factions called for the virtual militarization of American society, including its universities; and right-wing politicos campaigned to suppress dissent, especially dissent from a hard-line anti-Soviet policy. Bush, Oppenheimer, DuBridge, and others like them contested such moves in the counsels of government and in the public forum, making themselves prominent figures in the shaping of policy and opinion on the charged issues of the postwar transition.

Perhaps the most prolifically outspoken of them was James B. Conant. Through the most frigid period of McCarthyism and the Cold War, Conant resisted secrecy in atomic policymaking, refused to allow classified research on the Harvard campus, opposed loyalty oaths for teachers, and defended politically controversial Harvard faculty against demands for their dismissal. He called passionately, if fruitlessly, for a universal military service with no deferments for anyone, including college students, insisting that national policy express a dedication to "equality of sacrifice as well as equality of opportunity."[42] He held repeatedly that the United States had to intensify the battle against poverty and racism at home, employing especially the weapon of education, if it was to convince the Soviet Union that it meant to win the Cold War and people in the undeveloped world that an American victory was desirable.

To be sure, Conant often undermined his principles with expediency, tolerating a variety of national security incursions and restrictions on Harvard life. Nevertheless, in the judgment of his recent biographer, James G. Hershberg, he was on balance "a brave, calm, cool, rational far-sighted voice in an age of anxiety and hysteria."[43] In January 1949, Conant published a widely applauded moral attack on preventive war, and he tried to halt the technological juggernaut by spearheading the atomic advisory opposition to the construction of a hydrogen bomb, marching ahead of J. Robert Oppenheimer in the matter. In 1954, when Oppenheimer was accused of being a security risk, not least because he had been an insufficient enthusiast of the H-bomb, Conant insisted on coming to his defense, even though Secretary of State John Foster Dulles told him, as he recorded in his diary, that "I should know this might destroy my usefulness to govt." (To which Conant replied, "I said I quite realized this and he only had to give the word and I was through!")[44] Conant justified every one of his actions and moral compromises on grounds that it would promote a tense stalemate with the Soviet Union, a long, uneasy period of "no war"[45]—he hesitated to call it peace—that would give the democratic system a chance to triumph. He believed it would, and it would seem from the events since 1989 that it generally has in Eastern Europe and the former Soviet Union, bringing the Cold War to an end.

Beyond the Cold War

The mythical standing of Vannevar Bush's report is so powerful that it has tended to obscure the realities of federal R&D policy during the half century after 1945. To be sure, the government embraced programs of basic research and training to an unprecedented degree and empowered university scientists to shape them. Yet even during the golden age after 1945, just as in the late nineteenth century, federal patronage of science was characterized by considerable concern for utilitarian policy goals that expressed the evolving national agenda of the era. A significant fraction of the NIH budget has always been devoted to research, much of it clinical, in the causes and treatment of particular diseases, notably cancer. A sizable part of the budget of the Department of Energy (and of its predecessor agencies going back to the Atomic Energy Commission) was given to research in pursuit of the policy goals of national defense (nuclear weapons) and nuclear power. Similarly, the NASA research budget has been overwhelmingly committed to the achievement of national goals—at first, those of the Apollo Program and, in recent years, the shuttle flights and the space station. If academic scientists participated in the shaping of federal research policy, they had to compete with scientists and engineers from many other constituencies, and they were not always successful. It is probably not an exaggeration to say that during the past fifty years, a great deal of federally supported research, not only applied but basic, has in fact been mission-oriented—tied directly or indirectly to the goals of combating particular diseases, providing for defense, and exploiting space for a variety of purposes.[46]

Congressman Brown's report to the contrary notwithstanding, the federal R&D system yielded rich practical payoffs. The dividends from defense and space R&D included microelectronics, computers, lasers, jumbo jets, communication satellites, metals, and plastics, to mention some of the most notable. The payoff from biomedical research comprises an enormous variety of clinical and diagnostic methods and technologies as well as the biotechnology industry. One of the most important and influential dividends of the basic research enterprise has been the production of trained scientists and engineers. Even research not directly related to utilitarian goals created human capital in the form of highly knowledgeable and skilled scientists and engineers, many of whom went into the private sector and contributed enormously to national health, defense, and economic vitality. A striking case in point is the doctorates in molecular biology who have been indispensable to the growth of the biotechnology industry.

Seen against the past, both distant and recent, the post–Cold War shift in federal R&D policy to targeted civilian research does not constitute a new departure but a redirection of emphasis in what is targeted, much like the redirections that occurred after the turn of the century and after World War II. The post–Cold War redirection— away from defense and toward social and economic exigencies—was actually adumbrated during the era of Vietnam and its aftermath. The national defense fraction of the federal R&D dollar dropped below 50% and the fraction devoted to research in socially relevant areas such as environment and alternative energy sources was correspond-ingly enlarged. At the time, historically minded observers noted that a revival of Kilgore's program was under way. The revival lost energy in the late 1970s as the Carter administration renewed attention to national defense, and it was rendered moribund by both the enor-mous defense buildup and conservatism of the Reagan years. How-ever, the end of the Cold War called forth something akin to it—a reorientation of research policy to foster the socioeconomic aims that occupy centrists in the post–Cold War era.

The highest item on the centrist agenda has been research to bolster international economic competitiveness. The prominence of that goal had been building since the mid-1970s, when analysts had begun pointing to the increasingly vigorous foreign competition that the United States faced, especially from Japan. The challenge reflected the flourishing recovery of Japan as well as Europe from World War II. Japan had become a robust competitor of the United States even in our own technological markets. The trend was taken to be worrisome, since the country had been depending on a strongly positive balance of trade in R&D-intensive goods to offset a negative one in non-R&D-intensive goods. The R&D-intensive balance had actually risen during the first half of the 1970s, yet industrial spokesmen argued that the rate of technical innovation was slipping. By the mid-1990s, anxiety about competitiveness was even more acute. The United States was estimated to lead the world in twenty-seven areas of technology criti-cal for the economy and national security, but Europe was deter-mined to be dead even or only slightly behind in twenty-five of those areas, while Japan was found to be tied or slightly behind in seven-teen of them and closing in fast in five others.[47]

Tying research to post–Cold War national goals, especially the goal of competitiveness, was made policy by the administration of George Bush. When Allan Bromley, the science adviser in the Bush White House, took up his post, he deliberately reduced the fraction of time that the office devoted to national defense and increased the amount it gave to industrial technology. He renamed his Office of Science Pol-icy the Office of Science and Technology Policy, taking care to assure fellow White House officials that the administration could take the lead in technological development without compromising conserva-tive principles. Given all the changes that were occurring in the world, Bromley later told a reporter, it was not at all obvious that "Vannevar Bush's blueprint is as appropriate for the first half of the 21st century as it was for the last half of the 20th century."[48] It was not all that obvious either to Walter Massey, director of the National Sci-ence Foundation, who in 1992 began reconfiguring the agency's program to include more research of industrial relevance.[49] Nor was it obvious to Bernadine Healy, director of the National Institutes of Health, who on taking office in 1991 promptly initiated a $500 million study of women's health. She drew up a goal-directed strategic plan for her agency, enlarging its purpose to include the fostering of health-related research "that contributes to the nation's economic well-being and ensures a continued high return on the public investment in research." Pointing out that "1992 is not 1952," she admonished critics that NIH could not expect to succeed with Congress by simply continuing to sell undirected basic research grants as "its *numero uno* strategic priority."[50]

Soon after assuming office in 1993, President Bill Clinton made good on what candidate Bill Clinton had promised—that his administration would push civilian technological development even more pointedly, cooperating with industry but relying less on the free market. In a briefing to reporters after the president's first State of the Union address, his science adviser, Jack Gibbons, announced that the federal government would no longer rely on the kind of "serendipity" that had characterized the spin-off of commercial technologies from defense research. The Clinton administration aimed to bring about parity between civilian and military R&D, partly by pursuing so-called dual-use technologies in its defense program, technologies that would serve both military and civilian purposes. It proposed high investment in research in areas that would directly foster economic growth and competitiveness, notably high-performance networks, computing, and the information superhighway, high-speed railways, improved aircraft, and smart cars. It would also stimulate research into technologies that would strengthen environmental protection and into global change to assist in environmental management.[51] Although the Clinton administration made no extraordinary commitment to biomedical research, it did favor the Human Genome Project, which promised to yield powerful biotechnologies. It established as the flagship of its technological initiatives a new Advanced Technology Program in the National Institute of Standards and Technology (NIST), which was the reconstituted National Bureau of Standards. The NIST budget skyrocketed from $10 million in 1990 to a proposed $750 million for fiscal 1996.

Clinton's technological initiatives were welcomed in many quarters of high-tech industry, and enthusiasm for research linked to centrist goals of socioeconomic utility was widespread. The idea was endorsed by numerous commentators and by nonprofit think groups such as the Carnegie Commission on Science, Technology and Government.[52] On Capitol Hill, support for such initiatives came not only from Congressman Brown but also, insistently, from Senator Barbara Mikulski, a liberal Democrat from Maryland, who chaired the appropriations subcommitee in charge of the National Science Foundation. Mikulski badgered the NSF to fund more strategic research of benefit to American industry, threatening to shift funds into more amenable agencies if the foundation refused. Allan Bromley recalled Mikulski's telling him when he was in the White House, "'Bromley, we need to have trophies to take home to our voters,' and by that she meant parking garages, sewer systems, and deeper harbors."[53]

In fact, neither NSF nor any other major research agency had to devote itself to anything resembling sewer systems. For all their respective technological emphases, Bush and Clinton did not slight basic research. On the contrary, both held such research to be a wise investment for the long-term future. Both steadily increased the fraction of the total federal R&D budget that went to research, as distinct from development, and both enlarged the fraction that went to basic research correspondingly (see Table 4). Budget is policy, it is said. As of 1995, the numbers characteristic of post–Cold War federal R&D expressed a mixed design, a coupling of long-term investment in basic research and short-term investment in technological research. George Brown eloquently articulated the meaning of the numbers for the new national agenda as he and the Clinton White House saw it:

> Over the last half century, we have achieved spectacular scientific and engineering accomplishments in the service of a Vigilant Society. We now need to enlist our science and technology in the service of a Humane Society where work is meaningful, families are secure, children are well fed and well educated, where prevention is the first line of defense in health care, where the environment is respected and protected for future generations, and where sustainable development becomes the conscience of our progress.[54]

But what gratified Clinton, Brown, and Mikulski did not please many of the Republicans whom the elections of 1994 brought to power. Ferociously determined to slash the federal budget, they found R&D fat prey because, at $73 billion, it accounted for almost 15% of the domestic discretionary budget uncommitted to entitlements. They lambasted research targeted at strategic technologies, calling it a form of industrial policy. They deemed such a policy unwarranted because it chose technological winners and losers and unacceptable because it interfered with the free market. They attacked the dual-use technology program as draining resources needed for military readiness. (Allan Bromley had earlier criticized the Clinton administration's plans to vest control over dual-use contracts in the

TABLE 4

Federal Obligations for R&D, Basic Research, and Applied Research, 1975–1995 (in millions of constant 1987 dollars, for fiscal years ending in year indicated)

	1980	1985	1988	1989	1990	1991	1992	1993	1994	1995
Total federal R&D	42,253	51,283	54,796	56,753	56,846	52,524	54,615	54,727	55,498	53,856
Total research	16,427	17,109	19,192	19,192	19,403	20,538	20,392	21,862	22,356	21,864
Percentage of total R&D	39%	33%	33%	34%	34%	39%	37%	40%	40%	41%
Basic research	6,621	8,291	9,799	9,799	10,077	10,429	10,400	10,893	11,199	11,026
Percentage of total R&D	16%	16%	17%	17%	18%	20%	19%	20%	20%	20%
Applied research	9,806	8,817	9,394	9,394	9,327	10,110	9,993	10,968	11,156	10,839
Percentage of total R&D	23%	17%	16%	17%	16%	19%	19%	20%	20%	20%

Sources: U.S. Bureau of the Census, *Statistical Abstract of the United States, 1994,* 114th edition (Washington, D.C.: U.S. Government Printing Office, 1994), p. 613; U.S. Bureau of the Census, *Statistical Abstract of the United States, 1996,* 116th edition (Washington, D.C.: U.S. Government Printing Office, 1996), p. 603.

Advanced Research Projects Agency in the Defense Department as "an irresistible temptation to create the Mother of All Pork.") The Republican majority intended to kill off the Advanced Technology Program and to increase defense research, with the requirement that the defense agencies stick to research for the development of weapons. Many went after environmental research as a way of undermining environmental regulation, proposing to cut into it more than twice as deeply for 1996 as into overall nondefense research.[55]

The 104th Congress was not antiscience as such. In the House, know-nothingism was far less influential in shaping federal R&D programs than disputes over policy. The assault against targeted research was led by Congressman Robert Walker, who had represented his district for twenty years and was, in the description of a staff member, "intellectual," "quirky," "not a fire-breathing legislator." Now chairman of what had been George Brown's committee, renamed the House Committee on Science, he insisted that the slashes in targeted research were designed to "get back to doing good basic science and get rid of the phony science done in the name of corporate welfare."[56] Walker actually fought to protect basic research against the budget-cutting zealots in the House.

However successful he might prove to be, it was clear that in its particulars R&D policy had become an arena of contest energized by differences between the post–Cold War visions of the new Republicans, on the one side, and the Clinton White House and its congressional allies, on the other. Much federal support of science was an instrument of national programs for economic development, environmental protection, and health care as well as defense. Battles over these programs inevitably rippled into the disposition of R&D, and to the extent that R&D was tied to the nation's missions, it was a political creature of the reemergent, overarching dispute about the role of the federal government in American life. Indeed, R&D was by no means singled out for niggardly treatment in the 104th Congress. The new Republican majority applied its machete to a broad range of programs for investment in human and material capital, including aid to education, scholarships and loans, job training, Head Start, highways, housing, and libraries.

Whether the new Republican majority was a momentary phenomenon or the harbinger of a sea change in American politics was anyone's guess, but its penny-pinching was in a sense a radical version of cutbacks in long-term capital investment that had marked public activities in the United States since the Reagan years. For some while, observers had been pointing to the country's deterioration of infrastructure, to inadequacies that ranged from its schools to its bridges and even to the computers that controlled the flow of its air traffic. The turn away from long-term investment in human and intellectual capital marked the private sector, too. Downsizing companies cast off employees who were fixtures of their workforces, shattering confidence that hard work, loyalty, and the accumulation of know-how and skill would make people valued and secure. Industrial expenditures for research had been flat in constant dollars since the mid-1980s. More of it was devoted to projects with short-term production payoffs, less of it to obtain a purchase on the long-term future. In December 1993, Edward David remarked that central corporate research laboratories were increasingly viewed "as anachronisms, isolated from the critical activities of the corporation. They are seen as expensive and unresponsive. Downsizing has been progressing for some time. Corporations are increasingly lean, mean, and *stupid*."[57]

In the face of these broader trends, scientists are actually advantaged in the federal budgetary wars because they continue to possess considerable power—far more than, say, welfare mothers or the homeless. They remain an elite in modern society, made indispensable by their Baconian role in it. The Cold War is over, but the war against disease is not, as Harold Varmus, director of NIH and a Nobel laureate biologist, pointed out in 1994, noting that the ongoing desire to combat disease protected NIH scientists from excessive demands for strategic research. Lobbying from the biotechnology industry helped significantly to prompt the Republican congressional majority to grant NIH a sizable increase in its 1996 budget, $175 million more than the Clinton administration's request.[58] In the physical sciences and engineering, the basic research community enjoys the support of powerful allies, notably in the industrial sector. Despite—or perhaps because of—the shortsightedness of industry's investment policies, a number of chief corporate executives—from TRW, General Electric, Du Pont, Motorola, and other comparable firms—warned Congress in a letter published in newspapers across the country in the spring of 1995 against cutbacks in academic science.[59]

Scientists are often reluctant to flex their muscles in the political system, particularly on their own behalf, but the book of the post–World War II generation supplies ample precedent for doing so. Just as Bush, Conant, Oppenheimer, and myriad others educated the lay public in and out of Congress about the importance of basic research and training, so does the post–Cold War leadership need to inculcate the same lesson to the new generation of policymakers and legislators. From the vantage point of his political hot seat, Jack Gibbons has declared, "The science community must not sit back and think that we enjoy a permanent state of grace. We've got to earn our keep,

and we've got to let the rest of society know why we think it's important to do certain things and why we think our work is a sound
investment."[60]

A growing number of scientists have been driven, perhaps by des-
peration, into the political fray. In 1992, a flood of letters from scientists and their friends helped turn the National Science Foundation
from rushing headlong into strategic research. In September 1995,
twenty-five American Nobel laureates in physics went on record with
a statement that the National Institute of Standards and Technology—
"this national treasure"—should not be abolished, calling it, in echo
of their turn-of-the-century predecessors, "unthinkable that a modern
nation could expect to remain competitive without these services."[61]
Midway through the 104th Congress, it seemed likely that NIST
would survive, though likely without its Advanced Technology Program, and that similar lobbying would save the United States Geological Survey from extinction. In April 1996, Robert L. Park wrote in his
biting weekly report, *What's New*: "Scientists who would have choked
on the word 'lobby' just a few years ago are fast becoming effective
grass-roots lobbyists."[62]

However, in its political engagement, the American scientific community has not been immune to self-centered parochialism, venturing
into the public square only to address primarily the issues of research
budgets, scientific job prospects, and local institutional health. Many
of its members, deploring the bleak prospects of graduate students
and postdoctoral fellows, neglect to consider that a good deal of the
responsibility for the current difficulty belongs to the past dynamic of
academic science itself. In the decade ending in 1987, scientists and
engineers entered the workforce at four times the rate of people in
other fields. The exponential trend was especially acute in the biomedical sciences, which during the same period awarded some 48,000
Ph.D.'s, twice the total added to the life sciences in the 1960s. In 1987,
more than 107,000 life science doctorates were employed, a rise of
more than 50%. (Between 1981 and 1990, in constant dollars, the NIH
budget also rose about 50%—two thirds more than the constant-dol-
lar increase in total federal outlays.)[63] Funds for biomedical research
(or any other field) will not, because they cannot, increase indefinitely
to accommodate the production of Ph.D.'s at an exponentially increasing rate.[64]

In 1991, Frank Press, who had been President Carter's science adviser and was president of the National Academy of Sciences, reminded his fellow scientists that "no nation can write a blank check
for science" and that, if the number of scientists had doubled in
twenty years, there was no reason why taxpayers should come to the

rescue or why science should take precedence over other meritorious demands on the federal treasury."[65] People in all walks of life are being forced to find new kinds of work, and it is nowhere written that scientists, more than other groups, should be guaranteed precisely the job for which they trained.

Recently, several thoughtful assessments by the National Academy of Sciences have argued against both parochialism and panic and for wise adjustment to the changed circumstances of American science— and of the United States—in the world.[66] Unemployment rates among recent science Ph.D.'s are remarkably low compared with the overall national rate, and the flood of foreign-born students, which has swelled graduate ranks since the 1970s, has been tapering off. Frustration and disappointment among recent scientific Ph.D.'s centers on the difficulty of finding jobs in academic research. One of the assessments urged academic scientists to quit attempting to replicate themselves in their students and to begin equiping their doctoral children for careers outside of basic research by diversifying their graduate training. Another, recognizing the revived and growing vitality of science abroad and the limitation on resources at home, recommended that the United States should not expect to be preeminent in every scientific field. It must pick and choose the fields in which it will shine most brightly, using criteria that include importance to the national welfare. If a big-science project—the Supercollider, for example—fails to meet that criterion, it should not be pursued without the support of other countries.

Such departures from parochialism are salutary, and they could well go further. The more the scientific community behaves merely like an interest group, the more will it be treated merely like an interest group. It may be that contemporary scientists, having grown up under a system of federal largesse, tend inevitably to be overwhelmed by questions of federal dollars and cents. In 1993, the physicist Walter E. Massey, director of the National Science Foundation, observed that people drew selectively on the past of the science to predict its future, that they started "with World War II as if there was no science in the world or in America" before then, and that they held that "the only standards" available for "quality of life" are those that prevailed during "the last forty years."[67] In this connection, it is worth remembering that in the half century before 1940, most science in the United States progressed in dependence on money provided for basic research by state legislatures, industrial corporations, individual donors, and philanthropic foundations, especially the Rockefeller Foundation. In a sense, the current reduction in federal research dollars has been forcing science in the United States to cope with pre-1940-

like circumstances, at least to a limited degree; in recent years, a similar mixture of nonfederal public patrons and private ones has been providing an increasing fraction of support for science in universities.

The philanthropic fortunes that aided science through midcentury came from the pioneers of the extractive industries, like oil, and from the heavy manufacturing ones, like steel and automobiles. During the Cold War, they derived from the makers of the more high-technology defense industries like aircraft, electronics, and instruments. In recent years, new fortunes have been accumulating in the newer regions of high technology, notably computers and biotechnology, and they may well turn into philanthropies tappable for investment in the kind of research that made them possible. Private support alone is inadequate to the scale and scope of the contemporary scientific enterprise, but it can make a difference—and does, as the impact in the biomedical sciences of the Howard Hughes Medical Institute attests—in fostering high-risk, innovative science that is at a disadvantage in competing for scarce federal research dollars.

Even so, the principal key to the scientific future is the federal government, which remains the most generous single patron of American science. In contending for their share of the public purse, American scientists might serve their cause and their country better if they were to emulate the scientific leaders of both Powell's day and of the post–World War II transformation, particularly their propensity to tie the fortunes of science to the larger purposes of their era's national agenda. What is often missing in the debates over the post–Cold War transition is a vision of the larger purposes that science can and should serve, of the kind of good society that it can and could help create both at home and abroad. Not all scientists think mainly about the self-interested issue of how much money science needs; some remain concerned with the public-interest matter of the larger aims that their enterprise might serve. They need to raise their voices.

Competitiveness, economic growth, environment, health—these and much more are matters in which scientists as citizens and as residents of the planet have as much a stake as anyone else. The time is propitious for a renewal of the social responsibility of science that the post–World War II generation was unashamed to embrace. Since the late 1960s, a variety of public-interest groups in science—for example, the Union of Concerned Scientists and the National Resources Defense Council—have injected scientific knowledge and perspective into policy debates, much to the advantage of the public interest. Studies by the National Academy of Sciences have contributed to the same end. The national leadership of American science—individual scientists who have won renown and the presidents of science-related institutions, particularly universities—could well follow suit. They might emulate the Oppenheimers and Conants better than they do, dwelling less, perhaps, on budgets and resources and more, certainly, on the relationship of scientific learning to the great issues that confront their country and the world, and recognizing that science is not alone in the jeopardy it faces.

Scientists and their allies have a good deal to contribute to the resolution of questions in government and society that prompt widespread worry and a sense of beleaguerment: How to reconcile environmental preservation and economic growth? How to maintain privacy and civil liberties in the information age? How to harness the marvels of technology to the creation of a more equitable (and well-employed) society? How to make the scientific enterprise work better for a multicultural society? How best to mobilize basic biomedical knowledge to combat the onset of epidemic diseases? How to shape the ethical controls over science and technology that society increasingly expects so that they serve both socially sensible and scientifically realistic purposes? And how to accommodate the needs and ambitions of basic science itself to the ongoing demand for useful knowledge?

The shift in federal science that began in the early 1990s was precipitated, like the shift in the 1890s, by economic recession, and it was pressed forward by a coalition of political forces resembling those of a century ago—conservatives insisting on budget cutting and liberals demanding more socially purposeful research. An upturn in the economy may ease the overall constraints on federal science, but the demand for social relevance is not likely to disappear once the new century turns, just as it did not after the turn of the last century. The problems that plague us—including environmental degradation, resource loss, and public health—are so suffused with science and technology as to command major ongoing attention from government.

We need not worry about the advancement of science. History suggests that the quest for basic knowledge can flourish amid ultimate utilitarian commitments. The geological work of Powell's survey, the fundamental genetics pursued in the experiment stations, the advances in myriad fields accomplished under the mission-oriented programs of national defense all argue that a great deal of basic science is to be done in the so-called targeted programs of post–Cold War federal R&D. Environmental management, for example, poses significant issues in ecology, field biology, and atmospheric physics and chemistry. Instead of resisting socially purposeful scientific programs, the scientific community might better come to grips with the fact that lay participation in the allocation of resources for research is now an irreversible fact of American scientific life. They might also seek to shape federal R&D programs so that these serve both the scientific and the public interest.

Yet it would be disappointing if, in helping to articulate a vision for science, its practitioners omitted what presumably concerns them most—the gloriously tonic intellectual enterprise of which they are a part. They write popular books on the marvels of the contemporary laboratory—molecular biology, neurobiology, complex systems, nanotechnologies, and astrophysics, to name a few—but the books give scant attention to the system of public and private support that makes the marvels possible.[68] In the public policy arena, they tend to confine themselves to the language of profit and loss—capital investment, dividends and returns, indicators of national technological prowess. If all are essential considerations on Wall Street, they do not necessarily move many hearts and spirits on Main Street. Advocates of the Superconducting Supercollider were unembarrassed to tell congressional committees that the accelerator was imperative to probe to the next level of understanding in the relationship of matter and energy and to learn more about the origins of the universe. The advocates lost, of course, for compelling reasons of political economy; investment in science that serves the human spirit must compete more than ever with other demands for scarce resources. Still, their failure does not delegitimize the merits of having stressed the scientific reasons for the machine or, in general, of investment to satisfy the sheer human hunger to know.

In the public arena, American scientists behave as though they have lost their nerve. Instead of evangelizing for what they care about most, their science, they try to sell—and usually end up overselling— the public on what science will do practically. Even the advocates of the Supercollider claimed that it "might eventually cure everything from cancer to dandruff," Allan Bromley noted even before the project was finally killed off, adding that they thereby undermined their case and credibility.[69] History makes indelibly clear that science will, in fact, do a lot, most certainly over the long term. By and large, the short-term payoffs will be limited with regard to the knowledge derived from basic research. However, history, especially since 1945, also reveals that what basic research can be relied on to produce in the short term—trained scientists and engineers—can yield rich utilitarian results. Acknowledgment of the realities of the scientific enterprise, including how it actually serves society in both the long and short term, might go some distance toward the restoration of credibility.

What American scientists may need most is a restoration of nerve—

a willingness both to engage in the major issues of the post–Cold War era and to extoll the value of the larger intellectual purposes of science. Just as scientists in Powell's day and after World War II unabashedly celebrated not only the utility but also the adventure of the science that federal support made possible, scientists in the post–Cold War era would do well to consider injecting the intrinsic intellectual merits and excitement of science back into the arguments for science policy. It may not be possible to reconfigure the terms of debate in federal R&D. Still, the scientific community has little to lose in the public arena by contending for science as such with verve and audacity.

Notes

1. U.S. Congress, Senate, *Congressional Record*, 102nd Cong., August 3, 1992, p. S11165.
2. Eliot Marshall, "Military Labs Hit by Funding Retreat," *Science*, July 12, 1991, p. 131; Billy Goodman, "Uncertainty Marks DOE Scientists Efforts to Adapt As Their Labs Take on New Missions, New Objectives," *Scientist*, July 25, 1994, p.1.
3. Ralph Vartabedian, "Colleges Fear Research Cuts by Pentagon," *Los Angeles Times*, July 22, 1994, p. 1; "Always Let a Thousand Scientific Flowers Bloom," *Los Angeles Times*, (editorial), August 1, 1994, p. B6; Eric Schmitt, "House Battle Threatens Big Research Universities with Loss of Millions," *New York Times*, August 17, 1994, p. B7.
4. J. Michael Bishop, Marc Kirschner, and Harold Varmus, "Science and the New Administration," *Science*, January 22, 1993, p. 444.
5. Colin MacIlwain, "Cost-Cutting and Downsizing Take Their Toll on U.S. R&D," *Nature*, November 2, 1995, p. 3.
6. Susan U. Raymond (ed.), *Science, Technology, and the 104th Congress: Perspectives on New Choices* (New York: New York Academy of Science, 1995), p. 2.
7. J. Michael Bishop, "Paradoxical Stress: Science and Society in 1993," adapted from the John P. McGovern Lecture on Science and Society, delivered at the February 1993 Annual Meeting of Sigma Xi, p. 31; Leon Jaroff, "Crisis in the Labs," *Newsweek*, August 21, 1991, pp. 45–51.
8. Bishop, "Paradoxical Stress," p. 14; Stephen Burd, "Clinton's Budget Increase for Breast Cancer Research Divides Scientists and Activists and Satisfies No One," *Chronicle of Higher Education*, June 9, 1993, p. A22.
9. Burd, "Clinton's Budget Increase," p. A22.
10. Paul Selvin, "Alaskan Pork: Aurora Fantasia," *Science*, November 23, 1990, p. 1073.
11. "Conversations with Allan Bromley: Reflections on Exiting Center Stage," *Physics Today*, January 1993, p. 56.
12. U.S. Congress, House, Chairman's Report to the Committee on Science,

Space, and Technology, *Report of the Task Force on the Health of Research*, 102nd Cong., 2nd Sess., July 1992, p. 6.

13. Ibid., pp. 10–11.

14. George E. Brown Jr., "It's Down to the Last Blank Check," *Los Angeles Times*, September 8, 1992, p. B5.

15. *Report of the Task Force on the Health of Research*, p. 2; Brown, "It's Down to the Last Blank Check."

16. Burd, "Clinton's Budget Increase," p. A22; Christopher Anderson, "Brown Starts Debate with His Report Asking Science to Improve Economy," *Nature*, September 17, 1992, p. 175.

17. *Science & Government Report*, December 15, 1993, p. 3.

18. Colin MacIlwain, "SSC Decision Ends Post-War Era of Science-Government Partnership," *Nature*, October 28, 1993, p. 773.

19. *Science & Government Report*, December 15, 1993, p. 4; Graeme Browning, "The Endless Frontier's Fall from Grace," *National Journal*, June 18, 1994. See also John Maddox, "Can the Research University Survive?" *Nature*, June 30, 1994, p. 703. The Nobel laureate physicist Leon Lederman, the former director of Fermilab, declared that "something very dark and dramatic is taking place in our universities, a deep sense of discouragement, despair, frustration, resignation, a quenching of the traditional optimism of research scientists." Quoted in J. Michael Bishop, "Paradoxical Stress," pp. 16–17.

20. *Report of the Task Force on the Health of Research*, p. 6; David L. Goodstein, "The Coming Dark Age of U.S. Research," *Los Angeles Times*, August 31, 1994, p. B7.

21. U.S. Council of Economic Advisers, *Supporting Research and Development to Promote Economic Growth: The Federal Government's Role* (Washington, D.C.: U.S. Government Printing Office, October 1995), p. 13; William J. Broad, "GOP Budget Cuts Would Fall Hard on Civilian Science," *New York Times*, May 22, 1995, p. 12; "Crippling American Science," editorial, *New York Times*, May 23, 1995, p. 16; John H. Gibbons, "Choices amidst Change: S&T Resource Priorities for U.S. Global Leadership," in Raymond, *Science, Technology, and the 104th Congress*, p. 28.

22. Kenneth Reich, "Geological Survey to Fire 500 Workers," *Los Angeles Times*, August 15, 1995, p. 3; *Science and Government Report*, December 15, 1995, p. 1.

23. "Crippling American Science," p. 16; Broad, "GOP Budget Cuts," p. 1.

24. *What's New*, September 22, 1995; Marlene Cimons, "CDC Lab Sees Budget Cuts As Deadly Threat," *Los Angeles Times*, May 19, 1995, p. 4.

25. See, for example, National Academy of Sciences, Committee on Science, Engineering, and Public Policy, Study on Graduate Education, *Reshaping the Graduate Education of Scientists and Engineers* (1995), available on the Web at *http://www.nas.edu/nap/online/grad/committee.html*; National Academy of Sciences, Committee on Science, Engineering, and Public Policy, *Science, Technology, and the Federal Government: National Goals for a New Era* (Washington, D.C.: National Academy Press, 1993); and *Vannevar Bush II: Science for the 21st Century, 1995 Forum Proceedings, March 2–3, 1995* (Research Triangle Park, N.C.: Sigma Xi, 1995).

26. James G. Hershberg, *James B. Conant: From Harvard to Hiroshima* (New York: Knopf, 1993), p. 287.

27. For a view that the golden age was far more alloyed than is commonly believed, see Nathan Reingold, "Science and Government in the United States since 1945," History of Science, vol. 32, 1994, pp. 361–385.

28. "Report of the National Academy of Sciences . . ." and Powell to Allison, February 2, 1886, in "U.S. Congress, Joint Commission to Consider the Present Organization of the Signal Service, Geological Survey, Coast and Geodetic Survey, and the Hydrographic Office of the Navy Department with a View to Secure Greater Efficiency and Economy of Administration of the Public Service . . . ," *Testimony*, 49th Cong., 1 Sess., Sen. Misc. Doc. 82, Series 2345 (hereafter, Allison Commission, *Testimony*), pp. *1–*10, 54, 178, 381, 1075, 1078.

29. U.S. Congress, House, *Congressional Record*, 52nd Cong., 1st Sess., May 10, 12, and 24, 1892, XXIII, pt. 5, 4238, 4283–84, 4389–96, 4632, 4634.

30. Ibid., July 14, 1892, pt. 6, 6155.

31. *New York Times*, July 13, 1893, p. 10.

32. Between 1897 and 1914, the Coast Survey's appropriation rose from $501,070 to $1,039,720; the Geological Survey's, from $489,000 to $1,305,520. Figures taken from the Sundry Civil Expenses bills for the respective years.

33. Raymond Pearl to Karl Pearson, December 9, 1906, Karl Pearson Papers, University College London, Pearl file.

34. U.S. Congress, Senate, Subcommittee of the Committee on Commerce, *Hearings upon the Bill to Establish a National Standardizing Bureau*, Sen. Doc. 70, 56th Cong., 2nd Sess., December 28, 1900, pp. 1–2, 9.

35. Daniel J. Kevles, *The Physicists: The History of a Scientific Community in Modern America* (Cambridge, Mass.: Harvard University Press, 1995), p. 69.

36. Harlow Shapley to Isaiah Bowman, November 6, 1946, copy in Vannevar Bush Papers, Library of Congress, box 13.

37. Paul Forman, "Behind Quantum Electronics: National Security As a Basis for Physical Research in the United States, 1940–1960," *HSPS: Historical Studies in the Physical and Biological Sciences*, vol. 18, no. 1, 1987, p. 185.

38. Michael Aaron Dennis, "'Our First Line of Defense': Two University Laboratories in the Postwar American State," *Isis*, September 1994, pp. 427–455.

39. J. Stefan Dupré and Sanford A. Lakoff, *Science and the Nation: Policy and Politics* (Englewood Cliffs, N.J.: Prentice-Hall, 1962), p. 128.

40. Daniel J. Kevles, "The National Science Foundation and the Debate over Postwar Research Policy, 1942–1945: A Political Interpretation of *Science—the Endless Frontier*," *Isis*, March 1977, pp. 5–27.

41. DuBridge to Arthur Flemming, August 12, 1953, Karl T. Compton/ James R. Killian MSS, Archives, Massachusetts Institute of Technology, Cambridge, Mass., box 257, folder 1.

42. Hershberg, *Conant*, pp. 548–549.

43. Ibid., p. 9.

44. Ibid., p. 691.

45. Ibid., pp. 542–543.

46. Even the NSF's programs were shaped or justified in relation to the practical needs of the Cold War. See Daniel Lee Kleinman and Mark Solovey, "Hot Science / Cold War: The National Science after World War II, *Radical History Review*, vol. 63, 1995, pp. 110–139.

47. David Dickson, *The New Politics of Science* (New York: Pantheon, 1984), pp. 32, 39, 131, 166, 277; Gibbons, "Choices amidst Change," p. 29.

48. "Conversations with Allan Bromley," pp. 53, 55, 58.

49. Joseph Palca, *Science*, August 21, 1992, 1035.

50. Joseph Palca, "Scientists Take One Last Swing," *Science*, July 3, 1992, p. 20; Janny Scott, "Bernardine Healy," *Los Angeles Times*, July 26, 1992, p. M3; Eliot Marshall, "NSF, NIH under the Microscope," *Science*, February 14, 1992, p. 789.

51. "Science Policy: The Candidates' Responses," *Science*, October 16, 1992, p. 385; Eliot Marshall, "R&D Policy That Emphasizes the 'D,'" *Science*, March 26, 1993, pp. 1816–1817; Eliot Marshall and Christopher Anderson, "Clinton's Mixed Broth for R&D," *Science*, April 16, 1993, p. 284. See also *Technology for Economic Growth: President's Progress Report*, November 1993.

52. Commission on Science, Technology, and Government, *Enabling the Future: Linking Science and Technology to Societal Goals* (Washington, D.C.: U.S. Government Printing Office, September 1992), p. 58.

53. Eliot Marshall, "Senate Turns Up the Heat on NSF," *Science*, September 17, 1993, pp. 1512–1513; D. Allan Bromley, *The President's Scientists: Reminiscences of a White House Science Advisor* (New Haven, Conn.: Yale University Press, 1994), p. 238.

54. George E. Brown Jr., quoted in William J. Clinton and Albert Gore Jr., *Science in the National Interest* (Washington, D.C.: Executive Office of the President, Office of Science and Technology Policy, August 1994), p. 17.

55. "Scientific Community Warily Looks at Incoming Congress," editorial, *Los Angeles Times*, November 25, 1994, p. B4; David E. Sanger, "Clinton's Aid to Industry Is GOP Target," *New York Times*, May 23, 1995, p. C1; Ted Johnson, "Prime Target," *Los Angeles Times*, March 26, 1995, p. D3; "Conversations with Allan Bromley," p. 56; *Science & Government Report*, December 15, 1995; NDRC Online, "Everyone Loses: An Issue Summary on Science Funding Cuts," December 23, 1995.

56. Andrew Lawler, "Science Chair Walker Calls It Quits," *Science*, December 22, 1995, p. 1917; Andrew Lawler, "Robert Walker: The Speaker's Right Hand on Science," *Science*, August 11, 1995, pp. 749–751; Robert L. Park, *What's New*, November 17, 1995.

57. *Science & Government Report*, December 15, 1993, p. 3; "Conversations with Allan Bromley," p. 55.

58. Jeffrey Mervis, "U.S. Research Forum Fails to Find a Common Front," *Science*, February 11, 1994, p. 752; "Key Funding Issues for Research Universities in the Fiscal Year 1996," AAU Summary, *www.tulane.edu:80/~aau/KeyFundingIssues.html*; Robert Pear, "Health Research Gets a Raise Instead of Threatened Trims," *New York Times*, January 16, 1996, p. 10.

59. Ralph Vartabedian, "Research Cuts Decried as Detrimental to U.S.," *Los Angeles Times*, May 18, 1995, p. D2.

60. "Conversation with Jack Gibbons on Coordinating Science Policy," *Physics Today*, August 1994, p. 51.

61. Eliot Marshall, "NSF: Being Blown Off Course?" *Science*, November 6, 1992, pp. 880–881; Malcolm W. Browne, "25 American Nobel Laureates Join to Save Technical Institute," *New York Times*, September 12, 1995, p. B9.

62. Robert L. Park, *What's New*, April 26, 1996.

63. Browning, "The Endless Frontier's Fall from Grace"; Daniel J. Kevles and Leroy Hood (eds.), *The Code of Codes: Scientific and Social Issues in the Human Genome Project* (Cambridge, Mass.: Harvard University Press, 1992), p. 303.

64. "Nothing can go on increasing exponentially forever," David Goodstein reminds us in "The Coming Dark Age," p. B7. See also David L. Goodstein, "After the Big Crunch," *Wilson Quarterly*, Summer 1995, pp. 53–60.

65. Irwin Goodwin, "Funding Gloom: Mood of Foreboding Pervades Forum at Science Academy," *Physics Today*, February 1991, p. 76; Irwin Goodwin, "Distress Call from Three Physicists: Is the Image of Science out of Sync?" *Physics Today*, June 1991, p. 94.

66. National Academy of Sciences, *Reshaping*; National Academy of Sciences, *Science, Technology, and the Federal Government*. See the related series of articles published in the section titled "Science: Careers '95: The Future of the Ph.D.," *Science*, October 6, 1995, pp. 121–146, and the accompanying editorial, Floyd E. Bloom, "Launching *Science*'s Next Wave," p. 11.

67. "Roundtable: Physics in Transition," *Physics Today*, February 1993, p. 39.

68. Two notable exceptions are Leon Lederman with Dick Teresi, *The God Particle: If the Universe Is the Answer, What Is the Question?* (New York: Delta, 1993); and Steven Weinberg, *Dreams of a Final Theory: The Search for the Fundamental Laws of Nature* (New York: Pantheon, 1992). Though different in their emphases, both stress the need for federal support of the Supercollider in connection with the historical development of high-energy physics.

69. "Conversations with Allan Bromley," p. 56.

New Policies for New Times

FRANK PRESS

IN HIS ESSAY, Daniel Kevles has traced the course of American science policy from its beginnings in the nineteenth century to the present, drawing lessons from history to help in designing policies appropriate for the times. He represents the current decade by the phrase "beyond the Cold War," and he characterizes it as a time in which Cold War confrontation is replaced by social and economic exigencies as major drivers of federal science budgets and constrained resources as a new reality. Thus concerns such as international competitiveness, environment, health, economic growth, jobs, and training may be dominant influences of the allocation of R&D funds, as well as a new imperative of both parties—balanced budgets in seven years. Kevles points out that redirection of emphasis to civilian national needs has historic roots, having occurred around the turn of the twentieth century and after World War II.

I would like to add some variations to several of his themes and propose new policies for the allocation of resources, appropriate for the times that he describes so well. I will conclude with a discussion of the underappreciated contribution of the Internet and the information revolution in making research more egalitarian and increasing the productivity of scientists—both important at a time of fiscal constraint.

Ideology and Science Policy

An ideological divide between the two political parties has developed since 1994 about utilitarianism as a factor in defining federal science and technology policy. Although it is not unprecedented in history, the sides of the issue taken by the two parties show reversals from past policies, and the degree to which it dominates debates in Congress, even involving the president and vice president, is surprising.[1] Briefly stated, the Republicans want to constrain federal R&D spending to R, arguing that this is the most appropriate role of government and that technological applications are the purview of industry. Cutting D also contributes to deficit reduction. Thus the Republican majority in Congress would eliminate programs such as the Advanced Technology Program (ATP) of the Department of Commerce and reduce the Technology Reinvestment Program (TRP) of the Defense Department. Both are partnership programs in which the government subsidizes private companies for up to 50% of the development cost of an important new technology that would otherwise have been delayed or ignored for foreign competitors to exploit. The Internet is an example of a successful government-subsidized program. It would have been delayed for many years, if started at all, since the private sector expressed little interest before government intervention. By contrast, about half of government subsidies under ATP have gone to private firms that would have developed a technology even without a government subsidy, though perhaps more slowly.[2]

The sides taken by the two parties in 1996 budget debates are contrary to previous positions: the partnership programs were initiated in the previous Republican administration; utilitarian research was pushed by the Nixon administration (for example, the ill-fated Research Associated with National Needs, or RANN, a technology program in the National Science Foundation), and President Carter wanted to be known as the "basic research president." One way or another, the outcome of the budget debates will set a course. The decisions will be of particular importance to university engineering and computer science departments and federal laboratories that receive major support from Defense Department and NSF technology programs. The debates reflect the new reality mentioned earlier: science policy is now caught up in a defining moment of American political history when the government is being restructured in size and scope, federal departments and agencies are considered for merging or elimination, entitlement programs are being reduced, and the discretionary budget is shrinking.

The Brilliant Strategies of Pluralism and Merit Review

Vannevar Bush's role in creating the National Science Foundation has been duly acclaimed. However, the initiation and growth of science and technology programs in the mission agencies may have been the primary factor in the ascendancy of the United States to a world leadership position in the decades following World War II. The historic precedent of science capacity in a few federal departments goes back to the nineteenth century, as Kevles documents. However, it remained for influential scientists like Jerome Wiesner, who served as President Kennedy's science adviser, to promote the growth of technical capacity in almost all mission departments, even State and Foreign Assistance.[3] The strategy was brilliant in many ways: it contributed to improved performance of government departments, thus providing a politically defensible rationale for the expenditure of public funds; it met the needs of mission agencies and therefore national needs in health, resources, energy, environment, economic growth and competitiveness, defense, agriculture and food, and other social, economic, and security issues the public cares about. In aggregate, pluralism and the general license for the National Science Foundation to support science as a mission in itself built an infrastructure of research universities and federal laboratories that was productive on a scale not duplicated in any other country. The totality of all of the separate agency programs provided the nation with a well-supported, diversified portfolio of science and technology programs, covering almost every field in depth. Just as important, it underwrote a program of training large numbers of highly qualified scientists and engineers. Pluralism and decentralization also protected the enterprise against the occasional foolish leader who with too much power could inflict great damage that would take years to recover from.

Merit review needs little discussion. Despite some flaws, it is singularly appropriate for the allocation of research funds because of the way science progresses. Across the four centuries that make up the history of modern science, advances were remarkably fast because of the combined contributions of the gifted individuals who made the revolutionary discoveries and the talented followers who filled the gaps and gathered the data that made the next paradigm change possible. Merit review works to identify and support both. It is telling that countries with failed systems of centralized, politically controlled distribution of research funds are now trying to re-create the American system of merit review.

Allocation of R&D Funds in the Period beyond the Cold War

The end of the Cold War does not mean that the political consensus for government support of science and technology will fall apart. Earlier, I listed the social and economic exigencies described by Kevles as factors that will influence the allocation of R&D funds: international competitiveness, environment, health, economic growth and jobs, and others.

However, the defense science and technology base will hold a high position on this list. The Cold War may be behind us, but military threats remain, their sources uncertain. They may not involve super-power confrontation, but they certainly include terrorism and the increased access of rogue nations to missiles and weapons of mass destruction. Under these circumstances of uncertainty, a strong national S&T base provides a relatively low-cost insurance policy against unforeseen crises and security hazards. This is the view of the civilian leadership in the Defense Department,[4] but apparently not the military chiefs.

The lead of the United States in the computer-electronics-information revolution opens up an array of sophisticated surveillance and smart weapons technologies of singular importance, highly visible to the world in the 1991 war with Iraq. Computers, telecommunications, sensors, smart weapons, and other sophisticated concepts that flow from science and technology will be the determinants of military power and defense security in future confrontations, and the United States leads in these areas and will work hard to stay ahead. Some Russian observers symbolically attribute the downfall of the former Soviet Union as a military power to its inability to manufacture a reliable personal computer.[5] Knowledgeable and willing Defense Department officials will find in this a modern rationale to award grants and contracts for work in the physical sciences and engineering in the universities and federal laboratories in the years ahead. The accompanying spillover of benefits to the "social and economic exigencies" of the future will not be lost on those who remember their history.

Kevles documents the rich utilitarian results that can be expected to flow from science and technology. His historic overview of such benefits is the same as that used to justify a new approach to allocating federal funds for science and technology by a committee that I chaired under the auspices of the National Academy of Sciences and its sister organizations the National Academy of Engineering and the Institute of Medicine. The committee's report, released at the end of 1995, was commissioned in bipartisan legislation introduced by the Senate Appropriations Committee.[6]

The committee sought the advice of its sponsors in the Senate, the leading figures on science policy in the House, the president's science adviser and his Council of Advisers on Science and Technology, and heads of government science agencies in framing the study. We were advised to recognize the end of the Cold War and changing national priorities, to expect austere budgets in the years ahead, to identify the most successful science policies of the past, and not to make politically unfeasible proposals to reorganize the executive branch or Congress. With this advice and drawing on considerations of our own, we arrived at a framework for the study that can be summarized succinctly by the following syllogism: *If it is in the national interest that U.S. fundamental science and technology occupy a world leadership role and if the nation is in a period of severe budget stringency, the overall R&D budget allocations must be optimal as measured by quality, productive use of funds, and responsiveness to national needs.*

I will now discuss the committee's recommendation's by first enlarging on the two premises and then explaining what is meant by optimal allocations.

The Minor Premise: Severe Budget Austerity

Out-year projections of budgets have been notoriously inaccurate, so why should we use them as a basis for formulating a new science and technology policy? The seven-year goal for balancing the budget is an affirmed policy of both political parties. Never before have we witnessed paralysis of the government to the extent seen in 1996 over debates on how to achieve a balanced budget. Professional organizations, government officials, and experienced observers generally agree that although the prospects of individual agencies are difficult to foretell, overall science and technology funding will be constrained under any realistic forecast.[7]

The Major Premise: A World Leadership Role in Fundamental Science and Technology

The committee describes fundamental science and technology (FS&T) as typical of the activities carried out in the science, social science, and engineering departments of our research universities. It is a portfolio that is well known and is generally viewed as appropriate for government support. Here are some of the examples provided in the report:

Basic: Exploring the chemistry of photosynthesis at many university and federal laboratories with support from the National Science Foundation and the Department of Agriculture. Characterizing the mechanism of Alzheimer's disease at many universities and NIH, supported by NIH.

Applied: Discovering flexible, manufacturable, high-temperature superconducting wire at Los Alamos National Laboratory with support from the departments of Energy and Defense.

Fundamental Technology: Building a prototype gene-sequencing machine at Caltech, supported by the National Science Foundation.

In doing this, the committee hopes to sidestep the ideological debate about whether the government role should include applied research and technology. It reflects our view that the boundaries between basic and applied research and between science and engineering are eroding. FS&T also encompasses the work in many federal laboratories.

Scientists may find it discomfiting to speak of world leadership when the ethic of international cooperation and free exchange of information is so important to their practice. Nevertheless, the United States has invested large sums to build its capacity in science and technology. It has shared the results of its research and its training facilities freely with other countries. It may be the nation's primary comparative advantage as it faces the economic exigencies of the future. And it is the only remaining superpower to which the democratic world turns at times of economic, medical, and security crises. There is much to justify a leadership role for the United States.

The panel adopted a definition of world leadership proposed in an earlier recommendation of the National Academies of Sciences and Engineering's Committee on Science, Engineering, and Public Policy (COSEPUP):[8]

> The United States should perform at the world level in the major fields of S&T, so that it is positioned to seize opportunities that arise from new discoveries wherever they may occur. Performance at the world level implies a capacity equivalent to the top few nations and not necessarily the best among them. This is a "poised to pounce" strategy. It keeps in place the ability to respond rapidly to important future discoveries wherever they may occur.
>
> The United States should strive for preeminence in a smaller number of fields selected on the basis of well-defined criteria. Such criteria might include economic importance, national security, unusual opportunity in a field, global resource or environmental issues, control of disease, mitigation of natural disaster, food production, opportunity for international cooperation and cost-sharing, a presidential initiative such as human space flight, or an unanticipated crisis.

Optimal Allocations

We propose to optimize the allocation of federal science and technology expenditures by defining a new budget concept, the federal science and technology budget. It is both a pool of funds and a disciplined process of trade-offs within the pool. It avoids creating a centralized department of science and does not jeopardize the pluralism that has been so effective in the past. However, it recognizes that the aggregate effect of separate budget decisions of each of the federal departments and agencies is what determines the overall competence of the United States in fundamental science and technology. For this reason, it proposes a mechanism to coordinate such decisions.

Federally, R&D spending totals are conventionally given as around $70 billion. However, this is a fiction because about half of that is mostly in the budget categories 6.3B–6.6, which involve such things as product engineering and manufacturing setup of large-scale weapons and space systems in the Defense Department and NASA. Although clearly of importance to the national interest, these activities do not represent long-term investments in obtaining new knowledge or investments in creating substantially new applications—that is, they do not fit conventional definitions of R&D in this country and abroad.[9] If they were excluded, the real government investment in R&D becomes about $35 to $40 billion. The FS&T pool is what supports fundamental science and technology in the universities and most federal laboratories.

Defense and space industrial contractors are the largest recipients (45%) of the conventional R&D budget, another indication that much of it is not true R&D. Under the FS&T budget, federal laboratories and universities become the largest recipients of R&D funds (70%), as would be expected for fundamental science and technology.

However, the FS&T concept makes sense at a time of austerity only if it embodies more than numbers and definitions. It is a disciplined process for upgrading the science and technology portfolios of agencies by forcing trade-offs, transfers of funds from poorly evaluated or obsolete programs to those of higher quality or more responsive to social and economic exigencies. In this way, if austere budgets are to come, government agencies could still improve the performance of their intramural and extramural programs. It would still be possible to "support more people and more programs than would be necessary if there were a sure way of predicting the winners."[10] This means that the broad support of merit-selected scientists and engineers in universities and federal laboratories, so important to maintaining the standing of American science and technology, could continue. The FS&T budget is an instrument that looks at the real R&D pool, moves funds around within it, and keeps a running score on what is happening. Without something like it, the budget debates will see worthy programs picked off, mindless decisions will be made without coordination and awareness that everything connects, and great damage will be done to the S&T enterprise. How the process might work is illustrated in an extract from a hypothetical budget message from a president to Congress:

The federal science and technology budget is $42 billion. Although it represents an increase over last year for inflation only, international comparisons show that it will enable us to maintain a world-class position in fundamental science and technology and a leadership position in the select fields of A, B, and C. The budget is adequate because we have terminated a number of projects and laboratories no longer necessary or of poor quality. Within this budget I am recommending increases in funding for the physical sciences at the National Science Foundation; material sciences in federal laboratories and university materials research centers; research on the causes of violence at the National Institutes of Mental Health; research on genetic origins of disease at the National Institutes of Health; and microelectronics and sensor development in Department of Defense programs. These initiatives will meet mission needs and contribute to the nation's overall strength in science and technology. . . .

The report was written in the form of a practical manual, describing how an FS&T budget would be developed in the executive branch and how agency science managers would be involved. It describes a process for Congress to consider the overall FS&T budget before it is disaggregated and sent with guidance to the twenty-five or so separate committees that consider it.

The FS&T concept has been criticized on several grounds:[11] it provides Congress with a visible target to shoot at in its war against the deficit, and the conventional $70 billion budget is a larger pool within which money may be found for transfer to fundamental science and technology. The report has also been characterized as biased in favor of universities and against federal laboratories. Briefly, the committee would respond that it is better to fully inform Congress than to present it with a fictitious and even more visible $70 billion figure. Within this figure, transfers of funds from fundamental science and technology accounts into weapons and space systems projects occur more frequently than flows in the other direction. The committee favored universities because of their combined role as centers of training and merit-reviewed research, but it argued that well-evaluated federal laboratories that fulfill the needs of their sponsors and provide unique resources should not be diminished.

The Internet: An Instrument for Enhanced Accessibility and Productivity

In discussions of science policy, a new instrument that costs little, transforms big science into "small science," and magnifies the productivity of scientists enormously deserves recognition. Although all working scientists know it and use it, the Internet is generally underappreciated for making an enormous contribution to the research enterprise. I will describe how it has affected my own research. I have two partners working with me on a problem in geophysics. One is in Palo Alto; the other, in Pasadena. We communicate by e-mail—not just memos but data files, graphs, news, and other discourse typical of research collaborators. Our data are contained in huge and current archives located in Boulder, Seattle, Berkeley, and Palo Alto. We use software made available freely by colleagues elsewhere, often downloaded from the Internet. A new advance reported in a seminar almost anywhere reaches us by e-mail within a day. Our paper will be sent for publication to a journal by e-mail, forwarded to reviewers by e-mail, and eventually submitted preformatted for printing. It will also be archived electronically so that it can be found and recovered by search words almost instantaneously. Unlike my earlier papers, it will never be lost!

If you visit my laboratory, you will find scientists at workstations accessing the data archives of the Hubble Space Telescope, even remotely steering it in space or doing the same with obervatories on other continents. Some of my colleagues will be reviewing data gathered on oceanographic cruises, running supercomputers elsewhere, and even drawing new information from previously classified archives with data from military and intelligence satellites. Similar stories can be told by biologists searching remote archives for gene sequences or protein structures or physicists examining trajectories of colliding particles obtained at remote accelerators. The data gathered in big science experiments and formerly limited to analysis by a few investigators are now accessible to thousands of scientists, thus transforming big science into small science with a large number of investigators involved. We are moving toward a situation where all scientists supported by public funds would archive their original data a year or so after they have obtained them for easy remote access by others. A scientist and his or her students at a small teaching college, provided with a workstation and funds for travel to meetings, can compete with or collaborate with colleagues at big national laboratories or elite university laboratories. Much of this is already happening. This is another instance of technology providing benefits for science and partially compensating for diminished resources.

Notes

1. "Clinton's R&D Policy Tilt Towards Technology," *Science*, February 23, 1996, pp. 1049–1050; "Gore's Scientific Approach to GOP Cuts," *Washington Post*, February 28, 1996.

2. General Accounting Office, *Measuring Performance: The Advanced Technology Program and Private-Sector Funding*, Report RCED-96-47 (Washington, D.C.: U.S. Government Printing Office, 1996).

3. Wiesner also enhanced the visibility and added to the prestige of the chief science officers of the agencies and the president of the National Academy of Sciences by bringing them to the White House as ex-officio members of the president's Science Advisory Committee, giving them the opportunity to meet frequently with the president and his assistants.

4. "Deputy Secretary of Defense Announces Science and Technology Strategy," Department of Defense News Release No. 569-94, October 5, 1994.

5. Joseph S. Nye Jr. and William A. Owens, "America's Information Edge," *Foreign Affairs*, March-April 1996, pp. 20–36. See also Eliot A. Cohen, "A Revolution in Warfare," *Foreign Affairs*, March-April 1996, pp. 37–54.

6. Committee on Criteria for Federal Support of Research and Development, *Allocating Federal Funds for Science and Technology*, (Washington, D.C.: National Academy Press, 1995).

7. "In essence this nation is getting ready to run an experiment it has never done before—to see if we can reduce the federal investment in non-defense R&D by one-third and still be a world leader in the 21st century." NSF Director Neal Lane, American Association for the Advancement of Science annual meeting, February 9, 1996. Robert Walker (R-Pa.), chairman of the House Science Committee, supports the recommendation that the United States "achieve preeminence in a select number of fields and . . . perform at a world-class level in the other major fields," but he added that "there will be no more blank checks. . . . It is time for the science community to provide us with guidance and priorities." Statement at March 4, 1996, hearing.

8. National Academy of Sciences, Committee on Science, Engineering, and Public Policy, *Science, Technology, and the Federal Government: National Goals for a New Era* (Washington, D.C.: National Academy Press, 1993).

9. "R&D comprises creative work undertaken on a systematic basis in order to increase the stock of knowledge, including knowledge of man, culture and society, and the use of this stock of knowledge to devise new applications." R&D itself includes three activities: basic research, applied research, and experimental development. Organization for Economic Cooperation and Development, "Proposed Standard Practice for Surveys for Research and Experimental Development," *Frascati Manual*, 1993 (Paris: Organization for Economic Cooperation and Development, 1994).

10. Since it is difficult to predict achievements of projects, it may be wise policy to follow the advice of Sir Rudolph Peirls: "Support more people and more institutions than would be necessary if there were a sure way of predicting the winners. By all means, study the form of your horses and back the ones that seem promising, but keep your stable broad." *London Times*, June 6, 1985.

11. See for example: *FYI*, no. 37, March 5, 1996.

On the Future of America's Scientific Enterprise

MAXINE SINGER

DAN KEVLES gives us a historical perspective on U.S. science from which we can view the present and consider the future. He reminds us of the central influence of the Cold War on the context and funding of science over most of the past half century and of social, political, and economic elements that contributed to the shaping of the American scientific enterprise. Importantly, he points out that regardless of the spin put on it by scientists, Americans have supported science in the past, with both public and private funds, mainly because they expected practical benefits. His story also describes a fickle political process. Apparent trends in funding and support for science were often short-lived. Although dramatic changes occurred from one Congress to another, over the decades, science flourished. Will this overall support of science continue, in spite of ups and downs? Or have we really come to a change in the basic character of our nation and of science?

Two general matters are of some interest here. In each instance, the relevant context is the extraordinary scope of the scientific opportunities that have emerged from the scientific successes of the past decades. The first matter has to do with how scientists communicate those opportunities to the public. The second relates to the global nature of the research enterprise.

Scientific research matches well the historically adventurous and independent spirit of the United States, a spirit that flourished because of its marriage to a fundamental pragmatism. Kevles urges us to evangelize in that spirit, to eschew the hard sell for a statement of vision. But is there an audience receptive to the spirit driving science? Kevles brands science with a "loss of nerve," but there is also a broader national loss of nerve. Today, few people in the federal government or in private industry seem enthusiastic about the adventure of science. The same is true of several of the largest foundations, although their resources have expanded substantially, thanks to the markets. With several notable exceptions, the agenda of the increasingly bureaucratized foundations is more and more determined in-house, rather than by the innovative ideas brought to the foundations by thoughtful, creative individuals. Frequently, foundation programs are motivated by a dedicated interest in solving national problems: the welfare of children or improvement of the environment, for example. But often they are flawed by an assumption that we know what to do to ameliorate these sad and threatening current situations and by a tendency to avoid risks. Rigorous research into the scientific basis of the problems is too often off the table for support.

In part, the foundation problem reflects a widening gulf between scientists' views of the natural world and those of the general population—a gulf that exacerbates the general national withdrawal from adventure. Even many senior citizens, people well and broadly educated in their own times, have given up trying to keep pace with the speed of scientific change. Many younger people never even began; "not on my screen," they would say, ignoring the fact that their everyday world is virtually defined by the science of the past century. Scientists themselves rarely understand even the outlines of fields other than their own. This growing gulf now motivates many scientists to devote attention to science teaching in the schools; improving the general understanding of science and how it works is surely an important task.

A few examples will illustrate the problem of communicating science to the public. The first is from high-energy physics. As Kevles points out, part of the strategy on behalf of the Superconducting Supercollider was a hard sell. But part of it was evangelical. Consider Steven Weinberg's book, *Dreams of a Final Theory*, probably the best available description for the lay public of what twentieth-century physics is all about.[1] But as an argument for the expenditure of billions of public funds, it fails. There is, for one thing, a dissonant resonance in the term *Final Theory*; physicists should have recognized that "Final" enterprises, with a capital *F*, have had a bad ring since World War II. For another, there is an arrogance of tone that could hardly appeal to the public or even scientists in other fields who generally ascribe to the notion that scientific theories are provisional. Then there is a problem with words, as in this sentence: "Any symmetry principle is at the same time a principle of simplicity."[2] This occurs shortly after Weinberg introduces the idea of the symmetry of the laws of nature, as opposed to the symmetry of things. Careful reading of Weinberg's explanation indeed clarifies why he considers this simplicity. But anyone reading casually or without a scientific perspective to begin with will surely have been sweating through the preceding pages; simplicity is the last thing they will have in mind. According to Weinberg, "simplicity" is an attribute of "beauty," and the beauty of a physical theory is, for him, a major criterion for its evaluation. For instance, Einstein's theory of gravitation is judged more beautiful than Newton's, because of its simplicities. As a scientist, I understand this argument. But I am not the point; how will it play with my tax-paying neighbors? And how can the Congress deal with "beauty" in apportioning those taxes?

In contrast, the very successful efforts of the biomedical community in congressional budget debates has had very little to do with the beauty of modern biology, of which there is plenty, and everything to do with a well-organized lobbying effort and the public's interest in health problems. Scientists worked in many congressional districts to be sure that members of Congress knew about the biomedical research in local institutions and the jobs and money that federal grants provide. One can argue, as I do, that concentrating the lobbying effort on one field of science to the exclusion of others was not ideal, but as an example of what works, the results speak for themselves.

Astronomy provides quite a different example of what succeeds in capturing support. This is surely a science with a minimum of obvious practical application. But it is one that captures people's imagination. There is an object lesson in the cosmologists' ability to explain their science in an inspiring way, a lesson that has eluded high-energy physicists. Discoveries in astronomy, particularly when coupled with an adventure in space, as provided by the Hubble Space Telescope, are avidly reported and followed. Moreover, almost uniquely in the scientific communities, astronomers have been willing to debate and then state their priorities. Remarkably, both public and private monies have continued to flow. Few people realize that the funds are secure for the Gemini Project: two national 8-meter telescopes, one each in the northern and southern hemispheres. It is true that this is at the expense of several smaller, older national telescopes, but it is probable that these will be purchased by private and state institutions—at bargain prices—and continue to operate. At the same time, privately funded new telescopes are going up at an exciting pace: the two 10-meter telescopes funded largely by the Keck Foundation for CalTech and the University of California have a public component in the investment by NASA on behalf of astronomers nationwide; the Magellan Project for two 6.5-meter telescopes at the Carnegie Institution's Las Campanas Observatory in Chile is proceeding as a consortium of private and state institutions; the Sloan Foundation has provided the wherewithal for a consortium (including Princeton) to build a special galaxy survey telescope. The cost of all of these together is small in comparison to that of the now defunct Superconducting Supercollider, but the difference in public interest has to be a component in the very different endings to the stories.

Recent designated increases in funds for research on breast cancer (which Kevles describes) provide yet another distinctive case. Negative reactions to the proposed set-aside by basic scientists overlooked the stimulus and support that a real human need can give to fundamental research. In the past year, two genes that, when mutated, are associated with breast cancer have been identified. One of them, BRCA-1, has a role in both inherited and acquired breast and ovarian cancer. It has turned out to be a new kind of oncogene, and it provides an important tool for determining risk and perhaps even a direction for therapeutic approaches. We can expect similar results from the ongoing pressures for biomedical research to be more attentive to women's health problems.

In fact, many scientists often fail to confront the obvious fact that the amazing national support for biomedical research embodied in the history of the NIH has its roots in a national desire to improve health care. Nevertheless, the NIH has been the greatest supporter of fundamental research in history. Congress went along with the NIH program even in this troubled year and gave the NIH a 5.7% increase in its appropriation. The essential point, which seems to have been successfully conveyed to lawmakers, is that to improve the treatment of disease, one must increase understanding of biological phenomena. The NIH's investment in basic research on even bacteria, yeast, flies, and worms is directly applicable to current understandings of cancer, nervous system disease, and human behavior.

There is now a movement to convince Congress to establish a National Institute for the Environment, organized somewhat like the National Institutes of Health. The proposal recognizes that if we are to deal with the environmental challenges to the long-term viability of our species, then one component of the NIE must be support for increasing knowledge. This can be an important stimulus for basic research in many fields.

Kevles tells us that in the decades after the Civil War, tensions over federal investments in science waxed and waned, just as they have a century later. We learn from him that only in the last decade of the nineteenth century, when national economic problems were seen as overwhelming, were serious cutbacks made. After five years, the support of science again turned upward, but with a new agenda determined by a perception of economic hard times, as well as new national goals and scientific opportunities. It is a familiar story.

Scientists' perceptions of the present situation are those of any group facing major change; the status quo is perceived as preferable to any possible but unknown future. Such perceptions are exacerbated by the large size of the scientifically trained population and fears of unemployment and lack of opportunity, especially for young people. They are exacerbated too by a sense of not being heard or understood by the current Congress. Most scientists recognize what George Brown has said: science has not resulted in solutions to contemporary social problems. But they also recognize that in a substantial number of instances, it was the political establishment that failed by standing in the way of scientifically sound policies. Moreover, science is not, of course, the issue in some social problems. But science can take credit for major contributions to human concerns—for example, a level of food production that could, if permitted, sustain the 5.7 billion members of our species now on the planet. No wonder scientists thought that particular Brown barb unfair. And although scientists are constantly urged to express their priorities in a world of shrinking support, they see the emptiness of that exhortation when faced with continued public support for the space station or the success of pork-barrel funding of questionable scientific projects.

Kevles makes a good point when he says that scientists too often fail to make the case for science. Public information about science is now, to a large extent, in the hands of institutional public relations departments, the science policy establishment, and the media. If scientists are to act on Kevles's wise advice, they will need to recapture access to the public. They must also put brakes on their own tendency toward hype. When and if they do so, much can be gained by recognizing that progress in fundamental science and national goals can be mutually sustaining.

The Cold War has ended and with it a substantial part of what some people saw as a major national goal for scientific research. For some, the new perspective is an invitation to isolationist tendencies in science and other affairs. But it would be a terrible error to believe that the end of the Cold War means that we can consider science from a narrowly national perspective. Science itself is more an international enterprise than ever before. I know of no more cogent words than those of Lewis Thomas at the dedication of the Whitehead Institute for Biomedical Research at the end of 1984. Speaking of the establishment of the institute, he remarked:

Science is indeed the only form of organized human behavior that I can think of that simply *must* be carried on as an international, transnational activity, and it can work in no other way. . . . For it is the style and essence of modern science that it makes its way without respect for national borders. . . . The work has reached its present state of high promise as the result of the most intricate system of communication ever devised on an international scale, and it will have to progress in the same way if it is to be successful. . . . The mechanism for the international exchange of scientific information is informal and seemingly casual. . . . Subversive is exactly the right word . . . I am not surprised that governments are edgy about the scientific communities under their governance; I am surprised that they are not more worried. . . . If things like [revolutionizing the ideas of people under their rule] are to take place, the statesmen would prefer to arrange them in advance.[3]

And Thomas spoke before the advent of faxes and the Internet.

I did an informal survey of a couple of recent issues of *Nature*, a British publication, and *Science*, an American one. In two issues of *Nature*, there were eighteen papers from U.S. institutions, nine from institutions in other countries, and eight from combinations of American and foreign institutions. Similarly, in two issues of *Science*, there were twenty-one from U.S. labs, seven from foreign labs, and seven with international origins. Some of these papers represent long-distance collaborations, made easier by electronic communications. In biology, large genome databases are shared around the world, and they are crucial to much more than genetics; they are essential for clinical investigations, drug development, and developmental and evolutionary biology, for example.

International collaborations are also a major factor in astronomy. At the Carnegie Institution's observatory in Chile, besides the Magellan telescopes being built by American institutions, the University of Warsaw, in partnership with Princeton, has just completed a telescope, and the University of Nagoya is constructing one. At Mauna Kea in Hawaii, a new large Japanese telescope is being built, and a consortium of European countries is building four 8-meter telescopes at another site in Chile.

When projects get even bigger than these, as they do, for example, in physics, international efforts become even more critical. Regardless of how one feels about the wisdom of the Superconducting Supercollider project in Texas, there is no question that its demise has seriously compromised U.S. credibility in the international scientific community. As reported in *Science*, the situation in Japan is quite different, and the number of major projects now being built or planned is impressive.[4] Currently, scientists from the United States and other nations are going to Japan in record numbers, in spite of the well-known difficulties of living and working in that country. Anyone who appreciates the extraordinary benefits the United States has obtained over the past six decades from the influx of foreign scientists has to be worried about our ability to compete over the long term.

According to Joseph E. Stiglitz, chairman of the President's Council of Economic Advisers, U.S. spending on nondefense R&D as a percentage of the gross domestic product lags behind that of Japan, Germany, and France, and the gap with Japan and Germany has been growing for more than twenty years. Even when total R&D is considered—including defense—we lag behind Japan. Actual dollars spent by the U.S. government are expected to fall behind those of Japan by 1997 according to some figures discussed by Stiglitz.[5]

The international language of science has changed in the course of history. Latin was replaced by French and German. Ever since World War II, English has been the medium of scientific discourse. It has been a tremendous advantage to American scientists especially as the U.S. education system is notably poor at teaching foreign languages. With scientific leadership comes the ability to set the language of discourse. What has changed before can change again. If we could listen to a scientific meeting in 2050 or 2096, would it be in Japanese or Chinese or some quite unexpected language? And how would the world differ now if it had been Russian that became the language of science during the years when the USSR was believed to be a power equal in influence and potential to the United States?

I came of age in the era when statesmen like Senator William Fulbright and General George Marshall were heroes with international vision and American business was provincial and inner-directed. Now the situation seems reversed. We hear a great deal from politicians about international economic competitiveness, but it is not at all clear that they understand what this entails. Meanwhile, U.S. corporations are now global in outlook and ambition, as is the scientific community. Increasingly, English is the language of the international global economy. The common international outlooks of science and business recognize that ideas and markets, as different as ideas and markets are in these two fields, depend ultimately on smart and well-trained people, on vision, and on resources. Any national debate about the support of science then has very broad implications. Reference to national issues alone cannot suffice. Will we be among the world's leaders or followers? It seems unlikely that we can retain the broad leadership in science that emerged here in the decades following World War II. Other nations will excel in some areas, in proportion to the individual talents they nurture and train and the investment they make. Are we ready to give up even the potential for substantial leadership in many scientific areas? Without such leadership, it is unlikely that we can fulfill our national goals.

Notes

1. Steven Weinberg, *Dreams of a Final Theory* (New York: Pantheon Books, 1993).

2. Ibid., p. 138.

3. Text provided by the Whitehead Institute.

4. Dennis Normile, "Big Science Is Booming in Japan," *Science*, February 23, 1996, pp. 1046–1048.

5. Joseph E. Stiglitz, personal communication.

Index

Kennedy, Donald, 131, 138–39, 140
Keohane, Nannerl O., 69
Kerr, Clark, 12, 176
Kilgore, Harley M., 217–18
Killing the Spirit (Smith), 5
King, William, 132, 134
Kingston, Joyce, 144, 145
Knowland, William, 217
Kopp, Wendy, 4
Kramer, Larry, 201, 204

Land-grant colleges, 6, 212, 215
Lawrence, Ernest O., 215
Legal accountability, 20
Legislative committees, accountability and, 29, 34
Lieberman, Gerald, 141
Light, Donald, 127, 175, 176, 178, 194
Local regulatory bodies, accountability and, 28–29, 32–33
Lorenzo's Oil, 200–201
Lougee, Carolyn, 131, 140
Lowell, A. Lawrence, 81, 101
Lyman, Richard, 15

Madison, James, 3
Magellan Project, 253
Malkiel, Nancy Weiss, 11
Management, professional conduct and poor, 125
Market mechanisms, as an alternative to accountability, 26–28
Massey, Walter E., 224–25, 231
Massification, 173, 174, 180
May, William F., 129
McCosh, James, 10, 104
Mentoring, decline in, 121–22

Messor, Asa, 81
Metzger, Walter, 127
Mikulski, Barbara, 226
Minority students at Princeton, increase in, 6
Moral training, responsibility of university presidents, 78–80
Morgan, Thomas Hunt, 213
Morrison, Toni, 3
Murtha, John, 200

Nader, Ralph, 4
NASA, 223
National Academy of Engineering, 244
National Academy of Sciences, 30, 35, 38, 231, 232, 244
  Committee on Science, Engineering, and Public Policy, 246
National Advisory Committee for Aeronautics, 214
National Bureau of Standards, 214, 225
National Cancer Institute, 215, 219–20
National Heart Institute, 219
National Institute for the Environment, 254
National Institute of Standards and Technology (NIST), 225, 230
National Institutes of Health (NIH), 200, 201, 204, 219–20, 223, 225, 229, 254
National Science Foundation (NSF), 200, 207, 219, 220, 224–25, 226, 230
  Research Associated with National Needs (RANN) of, 242

William G. Bowen is president of The Andrew W. Mellon Foundation and former president of Princeton University. **Harold T. Shapiro** is president of Princeton University.